International
Library of the
Philosophy of
Education

**Concepts of
indoctrination**

International
Library of the
Philosophy of
Education

General Editor

R. S. Peters

Professor of Philosophy of Education
Institute of Education
University of London

# Concepts of indoctrination:
## Philosophical essays

Edited by

# I. A. Snook

Department of Education
University of Canterbury, New Zealand

## Routledge & Kegan Paul

London and Boston

*First published 1972*
*by Routledge & Kegan Paul Ltd*
*Broadway House, 68–74 Carter Lane,*
*London EC4V 5EL and*
*9 Park Street,*
*Boston, Mass. 02108, U.S.A.*
*Printed in Great Britain by*
*C. Tinling & Co Ltd,*
*Warrington Road, Prescot, Lancashire*
*© Routledge & Kegan Paul 1972*
*No part of this book may be reproduced in*
*any form without permission from the*
*publisher, except for the quotation of brief*
*passages in criticism*

*ISBN 0 7100 7279 1*

# Contents

Baker & Taylor

3 $\frac{80}{1}$

30 $\frac{72}{1}$

45793

# General editor's note

There is a growing interest in philosophy of education amongst students of philosophy as well as amongst those who are more specifically and practically concerned with educational problems. Philosophers, of course, from the time of Plato onwards, have taken an interest in education and have dealt with education in the context of wider concerns about knowledge and the good life. But it is only quite recently in this country that philosophy of education has come to be conceived of as a specific branch of philosophy like the philosophy of science or political philosophy.

To call philosophy of education a specific branch of philosophy is not, however, to suggest that it is a distinct branch in the sense that it could exist apart from established branches of philosophy such as epistemology, ethics, and philosophy of mind. It would be more appropriate to conceive of it as drawing on established branches of philosophy and bringing them together in ways which are relevant to educational issues. In this respect the analogy with political philosophy would be a good one. Thus use can often be made of work that already exists in philosophy. In tackling, for instance, issues such as the rights of parents and children, punishment in schools, and the authority of the teacher, it is possible to draw on and develop work already done by philosophers on 'rights', 'punishment', and 'authority'. In other cases, however, no systematic work exists in the relevant branches of philosophy—e.g. on concepts such as 'education', 'teaching', 'learning', 'indoctrination'. So philosophers of education have had to break new ground—in these cases in the philosophy of mind. Work on educational issues can also bring to life and throw new light on long-standing problems in philosophy. Concentration, for instance, on the particular predicament of children can throw new light on problems of punishment and responsibility. G. E. Moore's old worries about what sorts of things are good in themselves can be brought to life by urgent questions about the justification of the curriculum in schools.

There is a danger in philosophy of education, as in any other applied field, of polarization to one of two extremes. The work could be practically relevant but philosophically feeble; or it could be philosophically sophisticated but remote from practical problems. The aim of the new International Library of the Philosophy of Education is to build up a body of fundamental work in this area which is both practically relevant and philosophically competent. For unless it achieves both types of objective it will fail to satisfy those for whom it is intended and fall short of the conception of philosophy of education which the International Library is meant to embody.

R. S. P.

# General editor's preface

If anyone talks to teachers nowadays about moral or religious education he will become very quickly aware of a wide-spread suspicion that some kind of indoctrination is being advocated. And nowadays that is enough to condemn it. Yet not very long ago indoctrination was thought of more calmly as a necessary, even as a desirable type of process. Has the concept of 'indoctrination' changed? Or have our moral attitudes changed? What is indoctrination? How does it differ from instruction? Must it involve the inculcation of doctrines? And, if it *is* morally undesirable, what makes it so?

In the past ten years philosophers of education have become very interested in the various issues clustering around this concept and a considerable body of literature has developed as a result. In this volume Dr Snook has collected most of this literature together and has attempted to set it out in a way which clearly indicates the main points of disagreement. His collection illustrates well the main objective of the new International Library of Philosophy of Education, the application of philosophical thinking to important educational issues.

R. S. P.

# Notes on contributors

**R. F. Atkinson** is Professor of Philosophy at the University of York. He is the author of *Sexual Morality*, and *Conduct: An Introduction to Moral Philosophy*. His articles have appeared in *Mind, Analysis, Philosophical Quarterly, Philosophical Review*.

**Brian Crittenden** is an Associate Professor at the Ontario Institute for Studies in Education, and the University of Toronto. He edited the proceedings of two seminars at the Institute, *Philosophy and Education* and *Means and Ends in Education*. He is the author of a chapter in *Aesthetic Concepts and Education* and has contributed articles to several journals, including *Studies in Philosophy and Education, The Journal of Value Enquiry*, and *Educational Theory*.

**Antony Flew** has been Professor of Philosophy at the University of Keele since 1954. His publications include *A New Approach to Psychical Research, Hume's Philosophy of Belief, God and Philosophy, Evolutionary Ethics*, and *An Introduction to Western Philosophy*. He has published numerous articles in philosophical journals.

**Richard H. Gatchel** is Director of Studies and an Assistant Professor at San Francisco Theological Seminary. He has directed a project on 'Freedom in Higher Education'.

**Thomas Green** is a Professor of Education at Syracuse University. He is the author of *Work, Leisure and the American School* and *The Activities of Teaching*. His articles 'A Topology of the Teaching Concept' and 'Teaching, Acting, and Behaving' have been influential and he has published several other papers on educational topics. In 1970 he was a consultant to the OECD, Paris, and is currently Co-Director, Educational Policy Research Center, Syracuse.

**I. M. M. Gregory** is a Lecturer in Philosophy at the University of York.

**William Heard Kilpatrick,** who died in 1965, was a Professor of

Education at Columbia Teachers' College from 1913 until his retirement in 1938. Among his fourteen books are *The Project Method, Foundations of Method, The Educational Frontier*, and *Philosophy of Education*. During his active academic life he published some four hundred articles.

**Willis Moore** is Chairman of the Department of Philosophy at Southern Illinois University. He contributed chapters to *Education and the Social Order, The Language of Value, Introduction to Home Economics*, and *Essays on Wittgenstein's Tractatus*. He has published articles in various philosophical and educational journals.

**I. A. Snook** (the editor of the present volume) is a Lecturer in Education at the University of Canterbury, New Zealand. He is the author of *Indoctrination and Education* and co-author of *Philosophy of Education*. He co-authored 'Contemporary Models of Teaching' in the *Handbook of Research on Teaching* and has published in *The Australasian Journal of Philosophy, Studies in Philosophy and Education, Educational Theory*, and the *New Zealand Journal of Educational Studies*.

**J. P. White** is a Lecturer in Philosophy of Education at the University of London Institute of Education. He contributed to *The Concept of Education* (ed. R. S. Peters).

**John Wilson** is Director, Farmington Trust Research Unit, Oxford. He is the author of *Thinking with Concepts, Language and the Pursuit of Truth, Equality, Education and the Concept of Mental Health*, and *Education in Religion and the Emotions*. He co-authored *An Introduction to Moral Education* and has published articles in *Mind, Philosophy, Analysis*, and the *British Journal of Educational Studies*.

**R. G. Woods** is a Lecturer in Education in the School of Education, University of Leicester.

# Acknowledgments

The editor and publishers wish to thank the following for their kind permission to reproduce extracts from the works cited:

'Evolution of Concepts of Indoctrination in American Education' by R. H. Gatchel in *Educational Forum* 23, March 1959, reprinted by permission of Kappa Delta Pi, an Honor Society in Education, owners of the copyright.

*Introduction to Moral Education* by J. Wilson, N. Williams and B. Sugarman, reprinted by permission of Penguin Books Ltd.

*Philosophy of Education* by W. H. Kilpatrick, reprinted by permission of the Macmillan Company, copyright 1951.

'Instruction and Indoctrination' by R. F. Atkinson from *Philosophical Analysis and Education*, ed. R. D. Archambault, reprinted by permission of Routledge & Kegan Paul Ltd. and Humanities Press Inc., New York.

'Indoctrination' by J. P. White from *The Concept of Education*, ed. R. S. Peters, reprinted by permission of Routledge & Kegan Paul Ltd. and Humanities Press Inc., New York.

'Teaching, Educating and Indoctrinating' by B. Crittenden in *Educational Theory* 18, Summer 1968.

'Indoctrination' by I. M. M. Gregory and R. G. Woods from *Proceedings of the Philosophy of Education Society of Great Britain* iv, January 1970, Basil Blackwell and Mott Ltd., Oxford.

'Indoctrination—A Reply' by J. P. White from *Proceedings of the Philosophy of Education Society of Great Britain* iv, January 1970, Basil Blackwell and Mott Ltd., Oxford.

*Studies in Philosophy and Education*, Southern Illinois University, Edwardsville, Illinois, for the following articles:

'A Topology of the Teaching Concept' by T. F. Green, iii, Winter 1964–5, pp. 284–319.

*Acknowledgments*

'What is Indoctrination?' by A. Flew, iv, Spring 1966, pp. 281–306. 'Indoctrination as a Normative Conception' by Willis Moore, iv, Summer 1966, pp. 396–403.

'Comment on Flew's "What is Indoctrination?" ' by J. Wilson, iv, Summer 1966, pp. 390–5.

' "What is Indoctrination?" Comments on Moore and Wilson' by A. Flew, v, Spring 1967, pp. 273–83.

'The Concept of Indoctrination' by I. A. Snook, vii, Fall 1970, pp. 67–108.

# Introduction

A few years ago a leading philosopher described philosophy of education as 'a subject struggling to be born'. It is now a healthy infant, still very dependent on its parents (the traditional philosophical disciplines), but rapidly acquiring a personality of its own. That this has occurred is due in large part to the interest that 'analytic' philosophers have shown in concepts of educational importance. It is not that there is anything sacrosanct about analysis as a philosophical method but the fact is that when applied to educational concepts, this method has opened up a new and stimulating route into the perennial problems of education.

For if there has been a birth, it is a re-birth. Thinkers since Plato have wrestled with problems of education in relation to a theory of society, an epistemology, and an ethical system. Analytic philosophy of education has provided another way into these issues, and by establishing methodological links with contemporary philosophy, has re-established the connections which must exist between the basic issues of education and the subject-matter of philosophy.

As a result, students of education are finding renewed interest in the philosophical problems which face educators, and philosophy students are seeing in education a field worthy of their talents and skills.

'Indoctrination' is one of the topics which has captured the imagination of these students and their lecturers. And this is not surprising. Philosophically, it leads us quickly into questions about how we ought to treat people (ethics) and the status of knowledge claims (epistemology). It also spills over into areas such as philosophy of science, philosophy of religion, and even metaphysics. Educationally, it opens up discussion of the rights of children and parents, the possibility of 'natural' education, and the part that society is entitled to play in determining the curriculum of the school. More specifically, it bears directly on the problems associated with moral, religious, and political education.

Some of the papers presented in this volume are already widely used in courses in philosophy of education. Lecturers who already deal with this topic will find it convenient to have the papers available in one volume. Those who do not may gain from these papers an insight into how worthwhile this topic can be. No further justification of this anthology is necessary.

The sophisticated reader will notice with some dismay two omissions. These are John Wilson's 'Education and Indoctrination', and R. M. Hare's 'Adolescents into Adults', both of which appeared in T. H. B. Hollins (ed.), *Aims in Education: The Philosophic Approach* (Manchester University Press, 1964). These are significant not only for their quality, but also because they served as the spark to re-ignite interest in the concept of 'indoctrination'. Most of the recent work on this concept stems from these two papers and a familiarity with their content is essential for a full understanding of the subsequent writings. In the organization of the present volume, these papers should have preceded paper 6 by Antony Flew. Unfortunately, for reasons of copyright, it was not possible to include them.

The papers in this volume are concerned primarily with the meaning of the term 'indoctrination'. The writers are interested in becoming clearer about what we mean when we say that someone is indoctrinating. In order to do this, the contributors adopt various strategies. Some of them attempt to provide an account of how we in fact use the term in everyday life; others define it as a quasi-technical concept in educational theory or make prescriptions as to how it might best be used to make distinctions of educational importance; others try to bring out its meaning by a comparison with other concepts such as 'conditioning' and 'propaganda'.

Whatever the approach, the conflict concerning this term centres on *method, content* and *intentions*. That is to say, some (although not many) think of indoctrination as a particular method of teaching and they attempt to spell out what sort of a method it is. Most of the contributors, however, deny that there is any method which is distinctive of indoctrination or at least require that the method be viewed in relation to the particular subject being taught.

The majority of the writers argue either for a content criterion or for an intention criterion. Most place at least one restriction on the content: indoctrination must involve the handing on of beliefs as distinct from skills, attitudes or ways of behaving. Whether there are any further content restrictions is one of the principal points on which there is substantial disagreement. Some hold that any beliefs can be indoctrinated; others argue that 'indoctrination' can be used only of doubtful or false beliefs; a third group argue that only doctrinal beliefs are subject to indoctrination.

Those who hold that there are no limits to the sorts of beliefs tend to distinguish indoctrination from other forms of teaching in terms of the intentions of the teacher. Two teachers may deal with identical content but because they intend different outcomes, one may be an indoctrinator while the other is not. Supporters of the other positions argue that the presentation of contentious beliefs constitutes indoctrination regardless of what the teacher intends.

This, then, is the basic dispute in terms of which the argument proceeds as the reader moves from paper to paper. Underlying it all, however, is another dispute, which ultimately is perhaps of greater significance for the theory and practice of education. It is whether 'indoctrination' is necessarily pejorative, or to put it another way, whether indoctrination is necessarily a bad thing or might sometimes be ethically or educationally justifiable. Decisions on this, of course, are intimately connected with what the writer takes 'indoctrination' to mean.

Dr Gatchel's paper serves as an introduction by reminding us that the concept of 'indoctrination' has evolved over the years and that only comparatively recently has it acquired the pejorative connotation which most of the contributors assume it now has. Gatchel himself is ambivalent towards the question whether indoctrination is always indefensible. He regards it as 'a controversial method which . . . is either desirable or not' depending on which concept of indoctrination we have in mind and on our general philosophy of education. He regards it as a *method of teaching*, a view which most of the other authors are at pains to deny, with the exception of Willis Moore (7) who asserts that in the United States this is still the predominant usage.

John Wilson (2) distinguishes 'indoctrination' from 'conditioning' by arguing that 'indoctrination' has an intimate connection with *beliefs* as distinct from *behaviour*. We condition people to do something; we indoctrinate them to believe something. The other contributors tend to accept this distinction with the possible exception of Atkinson (5) who raises the possibility of indoctrination in moral behaviour. Wilson deals with the issue of whether indoctrination is always wrong by arguing that what we *call* a process is not important. What is important is whether the process interferes with the child's rationality. Kilpatrick (4) makes a similar point and basically the concern of all the authors is with the fostering of the child's rationality.

Professor Green (3) elaborates the distinction between behaviour and belief and between conditioning and indoctrinating. Unlike most of the other contributors, however, Green does not hold that belief systems are always logically organized. The intensity with which beliefs are held is more a matter of psychology than of logic.

He suggests, however, that beliefs can be held 'evidentially' or 'non-evidentially' and that the *manner* in which the person holds his beliefs is the distinguishing feature of indoctrination. He therefore, rejects the views of Flew (9), for example, that religious teaching *must* be indoctrination. Green argues that religious beliefs can be held evidentially although he admits that often they are not. For Green, then 'indoctrination' is not restricted to the imparting of any special types of beliefs: 'The only beliefs . . . which must be rejected are those which prevent us from being open to reasons and evidence on all subsequent matters'.

William Heard Kilpatrick (4) argues that indoctrination means the implanting of *doctrines* which are to be held uncritically Flew (6 and 9) and Gregory and Woods (13) also assume an intimate connection between doctrines and indoctrination. Kilpatrick is opposed to this uncritical teaching of doctrines on the grounds that it violates the child's right to be treated as a person: an end in himself, not a means. Relating his discussion to the moral training of the young child, Kilpatrick argues that it is the parent's *intention* which determines whether or not he is indoctrinating. If he intends to make the child critical of moral standards as soon as possible, he cannot be accused of indoctrinating. White (10 and 14) and Snook (12) also regard the educator's intentions as central to the issue of indoctrination.

Professor Atkinson (5) also deals with indoctrination in relation to morals. He argues that any distinction between indoctrinating and instructing rests on the assumption that in the field in question there are clear criteria of truth, cogency, or correctness. After summarizing some of the recent work in moral philosophy, Atkinson concludes that since it is impossible to establish ultimate moral criteria, attempts at moral education are almost certainly to be indoctrination. He does, however, suggest that there might be a form of moral education which consists in teaching people *how* to go about the task of making moral decisions. Such a training, since it deals with the *style* rather than the *content* or moral decisions, need not be a form of indoctrination.

The paper by Professor Flew (6) is a reply to, and a 'synthesis' of, the papers by Wilson and Hare in the Hollins volume already re-ferred to. Mr Wilson had argued that the issue of indoctrination arises only in those domains where there is uncertainty: indoctrina-tion is distinguished from other forms of teaching by reference to the *content* being taught. He was more optimistic than Atkinson (5) about the possibility of moral education. Even if there are no established facts or principles, there can still be 'rational communication' between individuals on moral matters and this does not constitute

4

indoctrination. Professor Hare had argued against Wilson that content will not serve as the criterion of indoctrination since it is open to any indoctrinator to insist that his content (moral principles or religious doctrines, for example) is quite rational and he is therefore justified in teaching it. Hare located the criterion of indoctrination in the *aims* of the teacher. Parents and teachers will, of course, influence their children morally, but 'indoctrination only begins when we are trying to stop the growth in our children of the capacity to think for themselves' (Hare, op. cit., p. 52). In his paper, Flew critically examines the positions of Wilson and Hare, and finds them both deficient. 1 He believes first of all that their preoccupation with morals is misguided. Morality, he argues, is concerned not with what *is* but with what *ought to be* and so morals 'provide a possible content for indoctrination only to the extent that they are, wrongly, thought to be and presented as a kind of fact'. Flew believes that it is the teaching of religion which provides the paradigm case of indoctrination. 2 Secondly, he believes that both *aim* and *content* have to be accounted for in any adequate analysis of 'indoctrination'. Indoctrination consists in the aim of implanting doctrines. Flew makes some attempt to spell out what he means by a doctrine and this task is taken up more wholeheartedly by Gregory and Woods (13).

Dr Willis Moore (7) reminds the English contributors that the topic of indoctrination has been hotly debated in the United States for some time and he asserts that in that country at least, indoctrination is still regarded as a *method* of teaching, and the intentions of the teacher are an unimportant consideration. He follows this view to its logical conclusion by insisting that indoctrination is not always ethically unjustifiable and that with young children it is absolutely necessary. Moore, then, is at variance with most of the other contributors in his denial that 'indoctrination' is necessarily pejorative. As he himself concludes, he has removed 'the topic from the black versus white type of thinking, which is rarely, if ever, appropriate in a value situation'.

Mr Wilson (8), replying to Flew (6), elaborates his distinction between indoctrination and conditioning, and agrees that in any full account of indoctrination, *aim, method* and *intention*, must play a part. He counter-attacks on the issue of religion by suggesting that dubious empirical beliefs or authoritarian moral values may not be the central core of religion at all. Religions may be 'ways of seeing the world' and before we insist that the presentation of these must be indoctrination we would have to examine the structure of such systems and how they function 'psychologically and socially'. It is interesting to note the similarity with the position of Green (3).

5

Flew (9) is disturbed by Moore's suggestion (7) that indoctrination is a particular method of teaching since this renders indoctrination inevitable. Flew asserts again that *whatever the method* there is a vast difference between teaching the multiplication tables and teaching highly debatable political and religious ideologies: distinctions of *content* are essential. He is very critical of Wilson's attempt to place religion in a separate category. Some religions may be merely 'ways of seeing the world' but it is clear, argues Flew, that Christianity (and especially Roman Catholicism) puts forward 'would-be-factual' statements which the adherent is meant to believe. If indoctrination is concerned with beliefs, Christian beliefs certainly qualify. Therefore, in England at least, the paradigm case of indoctrination is the enormous effort made by the Christian Church 'to fix in the minds of children an unshakable conviction of the truth of its specific distinctive doctrines'.

Mr White (10) broadens the discussion from the moral and religious areas in which it has become imbedded in the previous papers. By means of a conceptual analysis he concludes that when educators are worried about indoctrination, the concept they have in mind is one which intimately involves the *intentions* of the teacher. He argues that the intention which is the criterion of *this* concept of indoctrination is that 'the child should believe that "p" is true, in such a way that nothing will shake this belief'. He explicitly attacks the suggestion that doctrines are a necessary feature of the concept, and he produces counter-examples in which, he argues, we would describe the teacher as indoctrinating although no doctrines or ideologies are involved. Ideologies are useful *methods* of indoctrinating but there are other methods and so any connection between indoctrination and doctrines is merely contingent. At the conclusion of his article he relates his analysis to the teaching of political history, religion, and morality and implicitly criticizes some of the early papers in this volume.

Dr Crittenden (11) argues that an analysis of the concept as it is used in ordinary language is not the most fruitful method of dealing with the problem of indoctrination. He attempts to approach the topic through the concepts of 'teaching' and 'education'. He argues that there are no procedural or ethical restrictions on what can count as teaching, but there are restrictions on what can be termed 'education'. Thus, teaching can be educative or mis-educative; mis-educative teaching is indoctrination. Indoctrination occurs when, in the interest of some 'world-view or comprehensive "philosophy" of life', violence is done to the criteria of inquiry in a particular subject. Such mis-education is not affected by whether or not the teacher is in good faith: the criteria are objective. Consistently with this account, Crittenden rejects aims or intentions as crucial factors since a teacher or parent can be mis-educating regardless of his aims. He also implicitly rejects the analysis given by Flew (6 and 9) for whereas Flew regards any teaching of ideologies as indoctrination, Crittenden reserves the term for teaching of ideologies where there is a violation of 'the criteria of inquiry'. For similar reasons, he is not satisfied with Wilson's criterion of dubious content since again it depends on how this is presented. In fact, although he does not state it, Crittenden comes close to Moore (7), in seeming to favour a *method* criterion, although the appropriate method will vary according to the content in question.

Snook (12) follows White (10) in arguing that the intention of the teacher is the important factor. More explicitly than the other contributors, he holds indoctrination to be ethically indefensible and hence discusses 'indoctrination' in terms of moral responsibility. He, therefore, construes 'intention' more broadly and allows it to encompass both what is actively desired and what is foreseen. He allows no conceptual limit on what can be indoctrinated and hence is quite at variance with most of the other writers, with the exception of White (10 and 14). Snook claims that in his critique of intentions, Crittenden confuses criteria for the use of a term with the procedures for ascertaining whether it is applicable.

Messrs Gregory and Woods (13) base their paper on a careful critique of White (10) and by implication criticize the account given by Snook (12). They argue that when White refuses to place restrictions on the content of indoctrination, he defies ordinary usage. 'Indoctrination', they argue, is intimately bound up with doctrines and the authors (unlike other supporters of this view) attempt a lengthy analysis of the term 'doctrine.' However, for them indoctrination is the *inculcation* of doctrines and the notion of 'intention' is logically connected with 'inculcation'. Similarly, since doctrines are the sorts of things to which allegiance *cannot* be secured purely by rational persuasion, non-rational methods must (logically) be employed at some stage. According to Gregory and Woods, therefore, *content*, *aim*, and *method* are all conceptually connected with the concept of 'indoctrination'.

White (14) replies by arguing that the concept of a 'doctrine' is not at all clear and that the analysis made by Gregory and Woods cannot altogether be sustained. He goes further to argue that even if 'doctrine' is understood in a minimal sense as 'an inter-connected set of beliefs' it is not a necessary feature of indoctrination. He produces a series of cases aimed at showing that where the intention is the same, the presence or absence of a set of doctrines is irrelevant to what is really going on: intentions, not doctrines, are the essential characteristic of indoctrination. The notion of 'unintentional in-doctrination' makes sense only because *in some way* the teachers can be held *responsible* for the beliefs which the pupils come to accept. White here moves towards the view held by Snook (12) that there is a connection between intention and responsibility. Finally, White is not quite as confident as he was in his early paper that *any* proposition can be indoctrinated. He cites as a possible counter-example the proposition 'You ought to critically examine all your beliefs'. Perhaps this could not (logically) be indoctrinated since it would apply to itself: but White isn't sure of this and is inclined to stand by his original view that any proposition can be indoctrinated.

# The evolution
# of the concept

## Richard H. Gatchel

I

'To brand any act of teaching as propaganda or indoctrination is to
damn it in the eyes of the educational world.'[1] So wrote Ernest Horn,
Professor of Education at the State University of Iowa, 1937.
Although Professor Horn did not fully agree with such a derogatory
concept of indoctrination, he nonetheless indicated the low estate of
the term among many American educators and educationists. If
anything, indoctrination is in even greater disrepute today. But
such a concept of the term is of rather recent vintage. It may be
surprising to many that little over half a century ago the employment of 'indoctrination' was no more offensive in educational circles
than the use of 'education'. Indeed, the two terms were practically
synonymous. The interaction of socio-political and educational
forces in relation to indoctrination during the past fifty years provides a basic framework for the study of significant developments in
concepts of education in a democratic society.

For more than three years, I was a student of W. H. Cowley,
David Jacks Professor of Higher Education at Stanford University.
During those years it became increasingly evident to me that Professor Cowley both needed and desired someone to do extensive
research for the purpose of fitting together the factual and conceptual components of an epochal change in concepts of indoctrination. The research appeared to be especially relevant to concepts
of indoctrination in relation to the process of cultural transmission
in a pluralistic society, that is, in a society which, like that of
the United States, allows diverse social institutions to control
educational philosophy and procedure.

Professor Cowley has called the pluralism which exists in the
United States 'limited', because this variety of pluralism 'accepts
the premise that the civil government is paramount but stresses the
premise that it should not be permitted to be omnipotent'.[2] The
civil government, while paramount, allows other social institutions
to perform important social functions.

Pursuit of the suggested study brought an increasing awareness
of changing concepts of and attitudes toward indoctrination which
are possible under limited pluralism. The investigation revealed

*Richard H. Gatchel*

also a close connection between these concepts and attitudes and an increasing understanding of social democracy. Finally, the conceptual fruits of the factual research resulted in a dissertation, entitled as this article. It might well have been called 'The Road to "Enculturation" ' in that this term, denoting the whole process of cultural transmission, subsumes indoctrination under American limited pluralism.

In brief, the dissertation analyzes the evolution of concepts of indoctrination through distinct historical periods from the 1890s to the present. The first of these, 1894–1919, explores the developments in education, philosophy, psychology, and sociology and also the socio-political changes which underlay the ensuing controversy over indoctrination. Here appear the various roots, historical and contemporary, which made indoctrination a controversial issue during this period. In the ensuing period, 1919–1932, indoctrination faced more definite concepts of social democracy and became a focal problem for many American educators. The writings of Dewey, Kilpatrick, Bode, Childs, and other Progressive educators together with the American reaction against German authoritarianism made this period one of increasing objection to the term indoctrination. The publication in 1932 of George S. Count's *Dare the School Build a New Social Order?* brought the conflict to a head. The debates which resulted centered about (1) the diverse value judgments concerning indoctrination even as biased instruction and (2) the effort by some educators to check the tendency toward an exclusively derogatory definition of indoctrination. The debate ended in the widespread derogation of the term.

The final chapter of the study, which concerns the period since the close of the Second World War, relates indoctrination to concepts of socio-political control in American democracy. The author describes how current discussions of indoctrination fall short of the central issue and concludes that the discussion must focus on its place in a pluralistic society. An analysis of Professor Cowley's point of view that limited pluralism constitutes the core of American democratic socio-political control shows the inevitability of indoctrination in a free society. Finally, the study of Melville J. Herskovits' and Professor Cowley's use of 'enculturation' presents this term as descriptive of cultural transmission, indoctrination being a kind of enculturation. The following pages represent a more protracted summary analysis of this study of evolving concepts of indoctrination in American education.

10

## II

First, an etymological investigation of 'indoctrination' and related words discloses the following developments:

1. The word indoctrination meant in its incipient phase the implanting of doctrines. In the Middle Ages under the autonomous control of the Roman Catholic Church, medieval European education became synonymous with the implanting of Christian doctrine. Even the word *doctrina*, or teaching, came to be associated almost exclusively with Christian doctrine. Hence indoctrination came to designate the total educational process. In view of this constricted, authoritarian character of medieval education the evolution of concepts of indoctrination at this point can be viewed in either of two ways: (1) the term 'indoctrination' broadened to indicate the whole process of education or (2) education became so restricted as to be little more than doctrinal implantation and hence became synonymous with 'indoctrination'.

2. Although indoctrination originally indicated a liberal concept of implantation, it gradually assumed the connotations of a coercive type of education. The concept of education was universally accepted at the time and continued to hold sway even through the liberalizing periods of the Renaissance and Enlightenment. These periods produced profound conceptual developments in both democracy and education, but the generally accepted ideas of the educational process retained their connotations of coercion. 'Indoctrination' continued its long association with this accepted concept of education.

3. Since about the seventeenth century, increasing expression of and experimentation with concepts of democracy have brought with them considerably different ideas about education. Development of these concepts has been particularly notable in the United States, especially in the present century, but for the most part their advocates have dissociated the term indoctrination from emerging concepts of democratic education. 'Education' has been permitted its natural evolution, but the growth of 'indoctrination' has been stunted by continued association with authoritarian education.

4. The present truncated definitions of indoctrination make it inadequate to describe the highly developed processes of democratic education. Another word—enculturation—shows promise of filling this need. But even 'enculturation' carries some implications of 'indoctrination's' limitations. Its sponsors associate the term with 'conditioning' which, at least among members of the Progressive education group, denotes but a part of the educational process.

The foregoing analysis indicates the need for much closer scrutiny of the evolution of concepts of indoctrination, especially as they have developed in association with concepts of democratic education among twentieth century American educators. The continued growth of science in general with its attendant social repercussions, the early development of a science of education in particular, outstanding and influential progressive educational leadership in the United States, social action and reaction through participation in a global war—these constituted mainline influences upon concepts of American education from 1894 to 1919. But the entrenchment of conservative, traditional control of educational practice made it unnecessary for the 'old' education to take the 'new' educational theory too seriously. Hence the 'progressives' attack upon external imposition—ultimately upon the principle of indoctrination—remained an 'academic question'.

This question concerned the doubt in the minds of such Progressive educators as Francis Wayland Parker and John Dewey as to whether or not education could be both constructive, in relation to individual growth, and coercive, in the sense of uncritical implantation of beliefs. It seems improbable that Parker's use of the term indoctrination in its present restricted sense of imposition of class bias was particularly startling in the 1890s. The absence of reaction against his attack upon such educational procedure indicated a general lack of distinction between indoctrination and sound educational practice. Since 'education' was the popular word and 'indoctrination' its synonym, the latter word found relatively little use. As Parker, Dewey, and other voices of the 'new' education began to differentiate more and more clearly between democratic and absolutistic concepts of education, such terms as 'imposition', 'inculcation', and 'inculation' became antonyms of the 'new' education. Since the etymology of its restricted meaning goes back to 1832, it is probable that educationists of the 'new' school counted 'indoctrination' among these antonyms. But the term found little written expression during this period.

The advent of the United States' participation in the First World War and the people's subjection to 'thought control' acted as a catalyst in precipitating American consciousness of a difference between democratic and absolutistic processes. The demand for nationalistic ardor prevented popular reaction to intolerance and external imposition during the war years. But upon conclusion of the armed conflict, the very defeat of a totalitarian power awakened many in the United States to the futility of efficiency through absolutism. Also, there can be little doubt that great numbers of Americans were beginning to resent the wartime restrictions upon constitutional rights and welcomed the opportunity to rebel without threat of social and economic ruin. Hence the social setting was primed for accession to the progressive voice. And, for the most part, the progressives did not miss their cue.

It was the increasing practical involvement of American education in anti-authoritarianism or, as it were, anti-indoctrination which constituted the focus of the period from 1919 to 1932. In this period of little more than a decade, concepts of indoctrination among American educators metamorphosed from interesting bits of academic table talk into branding irons for educational policy and practice. Before this period such men as Parker and Dewey certainly did much to deepen America's understanding of social democracy and of the sort of education such a society must foster. But only with the coming of the First World War, its regimentation, propaganda, authoritarianism, etc., was there provided the contrast necessary to awaken American education to its responsibility—indeed, destiny—in a free society. It was in June, 1919, that William H. Kilpatrick asserted:

> Indoctrination, however, is fundamentally and essentially un-
> democratic. It intends to anticipate choice. It inherently
> uses the individual as a means to an end, and this danger is
> present wherever any type of authoritarianism prevails.[3]

The Twenties witnessed a general re-evaluation of the educational process in the United States and of democratic education in particular. Eminently creative leadership in the education departments of colleges and universities gave impetus to the movement. By and large the development of experimentalism and the organization of progressive educational thought in the Progressive Education Association served first to challenge and then to disrupt traditional educational philosophy and practice. In that indoctrination was practically synonymous with coercive, habituating traditional education, it too suffered at the hands of the newcomers, and it soon found itself in the dusty tracks of the anti-indoctrination 'bandwagon'.

### III

But the forces for indoctrination, though literarily rather mum, were not inactive. Finally George S. Counts of Teachers College, Columbia University, vocalized their position, asserting that indoctrination for liberal-mindedness was just as progressive as the Progressives and much more stable.[4] Up to the time of Counts' reaction—especially his 1930 *The American Road to Culture*—the actual use of the word indoctrination was sparse indeed, but he merely fired a pistol that was already loaded and cocked.

In a post-war era, then, American educators, almost of necessity, came to grips with the meaning of social democracy and the educational philosophy which emanated from it. Increasingly educational leadership came to view indoctrination as the antithesis of education for life in a democracy. But the period which followed found American educators facing the problems of economic depression and its effect upon the social order. The focus shifted from the individual, even as a responsible citizen, to the social order and to the hand which education might offer in planning its improvement.

Writing in 1932 for an American audience which was grasping for a socio-economic panacea, Counts gained much support for his positive answer to the question: 'Dare the school build a new social order?' He contended that although there must be no deliberate distortion or suppression of facts to support any theory or point of view 'all education contains a large element of imposition, that in the very nature of the case this is inevitable, that the existence and evolution of society depend upon it, that it is consequently eminently desirable, and that the frank acceptance of this fact by the educator is a major professional obligation.'[5] Even the Progressive Education Association became absorbed in the Thirties with what was to become a permanent preoccupation with planning for a more constructive social order.

Experimentalists such as Kilpatrick, Dewey, and Bode feared the danger of a 'planned' rather than a 'planning' society, asserting that indoctrination, as uncritical imposition, could lead only to the former type of society. Nonetheless B. F. Pittenger, Dean of the University of Texas School of Education, in his 1941 book *Indoctrination for American Democracy* acknowledged the Countsian position, asserting the necessity of indoctrination in American education.[6]

The war years witnessed a rather cool attitude toward indoctrination for emotional, nationalistic loyalty; but they also showed the constructive effect of an unconscious assimilation of those democratic values which Pittenger enumerated, many of which had no doubt come through indoctrination. Hence the term remained ambiguous.

Certainly the comparative measurement of American behavior in two world wars indicated a momentous growth in both the scholarly and popular concepts of social democracy. This growth was especially evident in educational circles where attention focused on the problems of a philosophically consistent perpetuation and improvement of such a social democracy's core values. Counts and Pittenger had termed this process 'indoctrination,' but they had lost out to the experimentalists' derogation of the word. While a variety of concepts continued to surround the term, 'indoctrination in the bad sense' gained increasing conceptual support, especially among educators and educationists.

In the years since the close of the Second World War the struggle between the world's two major political philosophies has revived the indoctrination issue in relation to the methods which nations use to assure the continuity of their political and social philosophies. Many leading educators and educationists today maintain that the primary function of education is to transmit a society's cultural values so as to maintain their continuity and that all other educational functions are supplementary. Education in this context, then, must be considered as essentially prescriptive rather than permissive. Since conflicts over indoctrination have centered in its association with prescriptive education, the current discussion of education in terms of cultural transmission is highly significant for the present study.

Integrally related to the kind of cultural transmission that a society sanctions is the nature of that society's socio-political control or authority. As noted earlier, Professor Cowley has asserted limited pluralism to be the nature of this control in American democracy. With the legitimate control of education by diverse social institutions indoctrination naturally takes its place as one of the many facets of the enculturative process in the United States. In present discussions of indoctrination in the context of enculturation, however, the term appears as a controversial educational method which, depending upon the definition of the word and the educational philosophy of the educators, is either desirable or not. Contemporary discussions of indoctrination in terms of its desirability or undesirability seem to fall short of the central issue, which, to the mind of the present writer, concerns the rightful place—let alone particular value orientations—of indoctrination as part of the enculturative process in a pluralistic society.

If limited pluralism be accepted as the basic tenet of American democracy, then such proposals as R. Bruce Raup's 'community of persuasion' and Theodore Brameld's 'defensible partiality', when considered as the sole basis of educational and social control, circumvent the heart of the indoctrination issue. That is to say, the heart of the issue is the fact that the school as the main agency of formal education interacts with other institutions. Considered in this light, education for the attitudes and beliefs of future generations in a pluralistic society must be the joint responsibility of all interested social groups. If indoctrination be considered merely as pedagogical partiality in the enculturative process, then it pervades the process. If, however, the term is defined in the sense which predominates today, namely, the uncritical implantation of beliefs, then it constitutes but one permissible part of the process. Let it be emphasized that the function it performs despite—or, better, because of—its association with derogatory concepts of educational purposes and method is *essential* to the continuation of limited pluralism so long as institutions exist which desire to indoctrinate.

But one more significant development in the evolution of concepts of indoctrination remains. With the derogation of the term American educators and educationists have been obliged to devise a word to describe the process of cultural transmission in a pluralistic society. 'Socialization' was and might have continued to be the answer to this need except for (1) its association by some educators with 'socialism' and (2) its truncation by Melville J. Herskovits in his 1948 book *Man and His Works*. There he distinguished between the simpler process, which he termed socialization, whereby animals learn to become members of their respective societies and the more complex process whereby a human society transmits its culture to its own members.[7] While retaining 'socialization' to describe the simpler learning experiences of man Herskovits introduced the term enculturation to denote the process of cultural transmission. Professor Cowley, however, has made the concept of enculturation even more inclusive. Convinced that the socialization of man influences and is influenced by culture he includes this process in his concept of enculturation.[8]

'Enculturation', then, as coined and defined by Herskovits and Cowley, meets the qualifications of the needed term. It is at once relatively free from 'indoctrination's' association with particular normative positions and conceptually broad enough to subsume indoctrination, the relative significance of which depends upon the nature of control in the enculturating society.

1 Ernest Horn, *Methods of Instruction in the Social Studies*, New York: Charles Scribner's Sons, 1937, p. 81.

2 W. H. Cowley, 'An Appraisal of American Higher Education', unpublished lectures, Stanford University, Fall 1956, p. 310.

3 William H. Kilpatrick, 'Education of Adolescents for Democracy', *Religious Education*, Vol. 14, No. 3, June 1919, p. 130.

4 George S. Counts, *The American Road to Culture*, New York: The John Day Co., 1930, p. 193.

5 George S. Counts, *Dare the School Build a New Social Order?* New York: The John Day Co., 1932, p. 12.

6 B. F. Pittenger, *Indoctrination for American Democracy*, New York: The Macmillan Co., 1941, p. 1.

7 Melville J. Herskovits, *Man and His Works*, New York: Alfred A. Knopf, 1948, p. 38.

8 W. H. Cowley, 'Introduction to American Higher Education', unpublished lecture, Stanford University, Fall 1955, p. 233.

# Indoctrination and rationality

## John Wilson

One way of expressing our general thesis is to say that we do not have absolute moral rights over children (including the right to make them accept our moral values), but only a *mandate* over them. We protect and educate them so that they may grow up into free adults. Questions may be raised about what gives us the right to assume this role: but to some extent it appears that we cannot avoid doing so. Newly-born infants are not rational people: to make them so, we have to teach them to think and talk, to formulate their wants and purposes, and in general to acquire the equipment of a fully adult person who has rights of his own. Questions may also be raised about how long this mandate should last: what do we do about a boy of fourteen who wants to run away to sea, for instance, or a girl of fifteen who wants to get married? These questions are partly conceptual, but I cannot deal with them here. It is the way in which the mandate should be used that we shall consider.

It is clear enough, as we have shown earlier, that this mandate includes the right to use *force* or *compulsion* on the children, and the right to *condition* their behaviour to some extent. I am thinking here of such things as making a child go to bed, inducing feelings of fear or guilt about touching dangerous electrical equipment, and so forth. These methods are necessary partly in order to establish the preconditions for moral education. But it may help to clarify our thesis if we consider the question of *indoctrination*. Are we entitled to indoctrinate? Can we help indoctrinating? And, first of all, exactly what is meant by indoctrination?

### Indoctrination as opposed to conditioning and force

We must distinguish indoctrination from conditioning[1] and both these must be distinguished from straight-forward force. Roughly, if I illegitimately (whatever this may mean) persuade a child to think that God will punish him for masturbating, this is indoctrination: if I simply give him a feeling of fear and repulsion about it, this is conditioning: if I tie his hands behind his back, this is force. It is peculiar to indoctrination that the will of the person is not *directly* overridden. Someone conditioned may say: 'I have an irresistible feeling of repulsion about doing X, though I know it is perfectly all right to do it.' Someone physically forced, or commanded under the threat of force, may similarly remain free in his beliefs, and even in his feelings. But the indoctrinated person subscribes to a belief. For the concept of belief, more is required than that a person should utter certain words and behave in a certain way. It is required that he should be able to offer some sort of reason, however bad, for his belief: and that the belief should be intelligible.

One might now feel inclined to ask 'How is indoctrination logically possible?' For a moral belief, or any belief for which the believer has reasons (not just causes), is something which you can (logically) only accept for yourself. The notion of 'making someone agree to something' or 'making someone accept something' may seem logically incoherent. The rough answer to this is that in-doctrinated beliefs are those which a person may think that he has accepted freely, for good reasons, but which in fact he has accepted when his will and reason have been put to sleep or by-passed by some other person, who has some sort of moral (as we significantly say) hold over him, by virtue of his authority or some other power-bestowing psychological factor. The indoctrinated person, as Sartre would say, is in a state of self-deception: he is sleep-walking, or (in extreme cases) double-thinking. His belief cannot be totally ir-rational, i.e. non-free and non-reasoned, otherwise it would not be a belief—and perhaps some utterances which we take to be beliefs are not really so; but it is irrational to the extent that it is indoc-trinated. (Of course it may also be irrational for other reasons: be-cause he is stupid or misinformed or neurotic, for instance: what characterizes indoctrination is that another person is responsible for implanting the belief.)

## Aim, method and content

Indoctrination is an intentional activity: you cannot indoctrinate by accident, and it would be odd to say that physical objects, or a particular kind of environment, or even robots could indoctrinate people (unless the robots had been specially programmed by men, in which case it is really the men behind the machines who are indoctrinating). But indoctrination is not wholly to be defined by the conscious aims of the indoctrinator; we should call some of the things that Roman Catholics or Communists (justly or unjustly) are supposed to do 'indoctrination', whatever description they gave, however sincerely, of their *aims*. They might say, and believe, that they were helping people to form their own beliefs rationally and freely; but this might not be what they were in fact doing. To be an indoctrinator, a person must certainly intend his pupil to arrive at a certain belief, but he need not specifically intend that the pupil should always maintain the belief in the face of reason, or that he should reach it as a result of bowing down to the indoctrinator's authority, or anything else of that kind.

This is simply to point out that what a person says to himself that he is doing is not the same as what he actually *is* doing. If I thought that some food was common property when in fact it was private, and with this belief took it away and ate it, I should have stolen it. Although I am acting intentionally, neither my aims nor my intentions can be correctly described by the word 'steal'; but my actions can be so described. So too with 'indoctrinate' and many other words. It is thus possible to indoctrinate without knowing that you are indoctrinating: and it is also possible to try to indoctrinate but fail, without knowing that you are failing. Many (perhaps most) people, indeed, might have no very clear idea of the method or process they were using when they taught their pupils to hold certain beliefs. We might often be able to guess that their aims and intentions were indoctrinatory, if their actual behaviour suggested it: but a person's aims and intentions (except perhaps for his unconscious intentions) are not wholly to be verified by observing his actions.

Besides this (non-specific) intention, it is also logically necessary to the concept of indoctrination that the indoctrinated person arrives at the belief by non-rational methods. The indoctrinator must (consciously or unconsciously) be using such a method, thereby implanting a belief which is causally motivated (by a desire to obey authority for instance) rather than rationally motivated. Any such belief will necessarily be (so to speak) dogmatic: that is, either the believer will not be able to give relevant reasons for it at all, or else the reasons he gives will not in fact be the true motivators of his belief—they will be rationalizations. This might apply, for instance, to a person who had been taught by a very sophisticated indoctrinator to parrot what were in fact good reasons for a belief, but who, nevertheless, did not really *found* his belief on those reasons. It is not surprising that the word 'indoctrination' implies that the beliefs are usually of a certain kind, namely, those that might properly be called *doctrines*: for these are the kinds of beliefs to induce which, because of our ignorance of how to use rational methods of teaching, non-rational methods have commonly been used instead—par excellence in the case of political, moral and religious beliefs.

There is, in this way, a logical as well as a practical connexion between the methods of acquiring a belief and the rationality with which it is held. Somebody who has never faced the facts or thought for himself cannot, I think, be said to hold a belief rationally: the belief may be (accidentally, as it were) true, but part of what we

C                                                                                          19 mean by a rationally-held belief is that it is causally based on the real world, and will change only if the world changes (as opposed to if some authority changes its mind, or if the believer's inner feelings change). For much the same reasons only a certain type of process— namely, a process which brings the pupil up against the real world, and helps him to control it by the use of language, perceptions, and logic—can teach the pupil to behave rationally; that is, to follow rules in virtue of which his behaviour will be more than that of an automaton, and his beliefs more than parroted words. There is a concealed contradiction in supposing that you could condition or 'programme' somebody to carry out any rational activity: I take this to be a truth of logic that remains true however clever your conditioning or 'programming' might be.[2]

Indoctrination occupies a kind of half-way house between conditioning and rationality. As we have seen, a completely conditioned person could not strictly be said to have beliefs since he could not *mean* the words he was conditioned to utter. Indoctrinated beliefs, if they really are beliefs, must be meant: what distinguishes them is that they are irrational. We have also seen that the content of such beliefs may in reality be very different from what the words of the belief suggest: that is, the person may mean something different by them from what he appears to mean. Often he may not be at all clear what he *does* mean: and sometimes, no doubt, he may not be using the words to state a *belief* at all—it may rather be (for instance) an expression which merely signifies a willingness to obey authority.

### Is indoctrination always wrong?

If we say that indoctrination implies that a person is implanting certain types of beliefs by non-rational or illegitimate methods, we intend some criticism by the word 'illegitimate'. Suppose, however, that it is sometimes right to make children believe certain myths in order to give them more security—even, perhaps, to fulfil the ultimate objective of bringing them up to be free and independent adults. Thus we might persuade a child to believe that 'Daddy will stop anything nasty happening to you', 'Mummy will always be there,' or 'Jesus will always protect you': and suppose that we do not give the child any real evidence for these beliefs, but just encourage his wishful thinking.[3] This process is illegitimate, not in the sense that it is a morally wrong thing to do, but rather in the sense that the methods used in relation to these beliefs are non-rational, or logically inappropriate. If it is sometimes morally right to use such a process as this, we have two options: either we continue to call it 'indoctrination', remembering that 'illegitimate' does

not here imply 'morally wrong': or else, if we feel that 'indoctrination' has always to be a word of moral dispraise, we can refuse to call
it 'indoctrination'.

The normally pejorative element in 'indoctrination' might also
make us want to withdraw the term from some such case as this:
Suppose a child believes something for very bad reasons indeed, e.g.
that he ought to steal something because his gang-leader says so.
Now suppose I persuade him to believe that he ought not to steal
something by saying things like 'Doesn't your conscience prick you?'
or 'Don't you feel guilty about it?' Assuming the second reason to be
a slight improvement on the first, we should certainly have helped
the child in the direction of rationality: but at the same time our
methods would have been far from ideally rational. Here too, if we
wish to approve of such cases, we might not want to call them
'indoctrination'.

The important point here, in my view, is not so much whether we
call something 'indoctrination' or not, but whether a particular
process increases or diminishes rationality. What we need is a good
phenomenological account of indoctrination, or (more widely) of
rational or sane thinking in general as opposed to rationalized or
compulsive thinking. One reason why the borderline between indoctrination and other kinds of compulsive thinking is so hard to
demarcate is that there are all sorts of ways in which we can compulsively direct another person's thinking. Granted, inculcation of
feeling is conditioning; and of beliefs, indoctrination: but what are
we to say, for instance, of the sets of verbal descriptions which we
make available to children, and the built-in implications of value
that parts of our language inevitably contain? Suppose we describe
certain behaviour as 'dirty,' 'uncivilized', or 'inhuman', or say of
some misfortune that 'these things are sent to try us'? It is we, or our
neighbours, who teach children to *see things in a certain way* via the
descriptions and language we offer them. Is this indoctrination or
not? Whatever the linguistic issue, I should be inclined to say that the
substantive question has partly to be settled, in any particular case,
by empirical psychology, and that the test is 'Does this way of seeing
things, this sort of language, increase or diminish the child's rationality, in the sense of his appreciation of and control over reality?' This
question is extremely vague but I do not see how we can avoid it.

No doubt the linguistic issue in such cases depends on whether
we can be said to be giving the children a *belief* of a certain kind (as
opposed, perhaps, to particular feelings or particular concepts). If
we take our stand here, as we must if we are to retain any clarity for
the concept of indoctrination, then we shall be prepared to admit in
principle that there can be justifiable cases of indoctrination. The

word will still carry pejorative implications, since we shall probably think that a diminution of rationality in beliefs is for the most part to be deplored: but as with other pejorative words ('stealing', 'lying', etc.), we shall be prepared to make exceptions. If we take this line, however, we must take care to be aware of the particular dangers of indoctrination, which are worth a brief mention here.

If I force or condition a child, by making him go to bed or giving him guilt-feelings about dirt, at least I have not tampered with his *intelligence*. He is still able to say 'Well, I've got to go to bed' or 'Well, I just feel I must clear up this mess', and add 'but I think it's jolly silly, and when I'm grown up I shan't bring up my children like that'. But if you deliberately indoctrinate somebody, knowing what you are doing, you are *pretending* that certain reasons, which are in fact bad reasons, are good ones which the child ought to accept. Even if you indoctrinate without meaning to, which I have claimed to be a possible situation[4] you still act as if this were true: you convey to the child the impression that a certain type of (invalid) reason is valid. This may be because you yourself are muddled about what types of reason are valid; or it may be because your technique in communicating with the child is so inefficient that you fail to make clear what these valid types are, so that the child (for instance) believes something just because you say so rather than because he sees the merit of the reasons you advance. In all these cases you have (to put it rather baldly) given the child a false impression of how to think morally.[5]

Now it may be true, as we imagined earlier, that there are cases in which we would be prepared to give the child this sort of false impression in order to save it from a worse fate; and from these cases I would not want to withdraw the word 'indoctrination'. But to allow the child to remain under this false impression, or to create or sustain it except when absolutely necessary, seems to me dangerous in a way in which force or conditioning are not. For here we have taken over, or put to sleep, a central part of the child's personality—his ability to think rationally in a certain area. To put it dramatically: there is always hope so long as the mind remains free, however much our behaviour may be forced or our feelings conditioned. But if we occupy the inner citadel of thought and language, then it is difficult to see how a person can develop or regain rationality except by a very lengthy and arduous course of treatment. To indoctrinate is to take over his personality in a much more radical way than anything we do by way of force or conditioning: it is, in effect, to take over his consciousness.

I hope that this very brief analysis will at least lessen the temptation to claim that all ways of bringing up children are equally impositions—that 'you can't help indoctrinating'. Of course in practice our education will not be 100% free from unjustified imposition: but the reasons for this will lie either in our own incompetence or in hard facts about the world which may make it desirable, and not in any logical inevitability. Briefly, if you bring children up to think for themselves, it is not intelligible to say, in general, that you have indoctrinated them: because 'indoctrination' is opposed to 'thinking for oneself'—it is not a word which we apply to *any* context or system of education. If I use my commanding presence, an admixture of fear, and constant parrot-like repetitions to make a child believe that stealing is wrong, then I have indoctrinated him: but if as a result of unprejudiced discussion and his own personal experience he comes to believe, for good reasons, that it is wrong, the word 'indoctrination' is out of place—if one called *that* 'indoctrination', the word would have lost its meaning.

But we must be careful to remember that our mandate over children in this respect is not adequately fulfilled merely by *avoiding* such things as indoctrination. Indoctrination and the imposition of our own values is only one of many possible enemies to rationality. Another enemy is within the child himself, and consists of his own (largely unconscious) fears, desires and other feelings which may dominate his conscious mind in just as tyrannical a way as any external indoctrinator: indeed, it is roughly true to say that external indoctrinators could hardly succeed if they did not play on these inner fears and desires for their own advantage. The external enemy is no doubt easier to identify and easier to shoot at: but the inner is probably the more important. Indoctrination should be regarded not so much as a wicked attempt to interfere with the child's 'natural' development, but as a boring failure to tackle the problem at all.

Finally, a word of caution. In this part of the book we have been concerned only with the drawing of certain very basic conceptual distinctions. We opposed rational to non-rational methods of education, and of the non-rational methods we have tried to distinguish indoctrination from conditioning and force. Some of these terms, e.g. 'conditioning', are used by psychologists to refer to certain specific mechanisms: I have used them rather to make distinctions which may or may not correspond to differences in psychological mechanism by which these phenomena are produced. I think that the connexion between certain mechanisms and certain types of phenomena is not purely contingent: for instance, that rational thinking can only be generated by particular kinds of methods. But there is still a great gulf between the technical terms used by empirical scientists for a particular purpose, and general terms (sometimes

John Wilson

signified by the same words) in common use which nevertheless
need a more precise definition.

There is a great deal of work that needs to be done here by way
of bridging that gulf. Thus one would want to distinguish between
the sense of 'action' in which psychologists sometimes talk of a
'reflex action' (as in the behaviour of Pavlov's dogs), and the fuller
(intentional) sense in which a person will go off to a restaurant if he
is hungry. It would be interesting to see how far one particular type
of learning-mechanism correlated with one particular type of
phenomenon as described in more general terms. Again, our very
brief discussion of 'indoctrination' is only a nibble at one of the concepts in this area. We would need to consider a whole range of non-
rational processes, including overt force, threats, different kinds of
'influence' or 'persuasion', 'propaganda', 'hypnotism', 'suggestion',
'brain-washing' and many other such. But this is beyond our present
scope.

## Notes

1 It will be seen that I am not using the word 'condition' in any of the
  specialized senses familiar to psychologists, but in a looser and more
  general way.
2 *Pace* A. Flew's attack on A. C. MacIntyre in *Brain and Mind*, ed.
  J. R. Smythies, Routledge & Kegan Paul, 1965.
3 I don't myself think this supposition is necessary in practical education,
  but it is logically possible. Another case might be this: in the jungle it
  might be best to indoctrinate soldiers to believe that their officers
  always knew the way, were sure about where the enemy were, etc.:
  otherwise they lose confidence and cohesion, and everybody gets
  killed.
4 [In an earlier section of the book—ed.]
5 Of course there are many different types of case. One thing the indoctrinator does very often is, not so much to offer invalid reasons as
  valid, but rather to inhibit the child from reasoning at all: so that
  the child becomes as it were more subject to causal compulsion in his
  thinking, and less guided by reasons in general.

# Indoctrination and beliefs 3

## Thomas F. Green

The point is not, therefore, that instructing necessarily requires communication. The point is rather that it requires a certain *kind* of communication, and that kind is the kind which includes giving reasons, evidence, argument, etc., in order to approach the truth. The importance of this fact can be seen if we consider what happens when the conversation of instruction is centered less and less upon this kind of communication. It takes no great powers of insight to see that in proportion as the conversation of instruction is less and less characterized by argument, reasons, objections, explanations, and so forth, in proportion as it is less and less directed toward an apprehension of truth, it more and more closely resembles what we call indoctrination. Indoctrination is frequently viewed as a method of instruction. Indeed, we sometimes use the word 'instruction' to include what we quite openly confess is, in fact, indoctrination. Nonetheless, indoctrination is a substantially different thing from instruction, and what is central to this difference is precisely that it involves a different kind of conversation and therefore is differently related to matters of truth.

We can summarize the essential characteristics of these differences by saying that indoctrination is to conditioning as beliefs are to habits. That is to say, we may indoctrinate people to *believe* certain things, but we condition them always to *do* certain things. We do not indoctrinate persons to certain modes of behavior any more than we condition them to certain kinds of beliefs. But the important thing is to observe that *insofar as* conditioning does not aim at an expression of intelligent doing, neither does indoctrination aim at an expression of intelligent believing. Conditioning is an activity which can be used to establish certain modes of behavior quite apart from their desirability. It aims simply to establish them. If a response to a certain stimulus is trained or conditioned, or has become a fixed habit, it will be displayed in the fact that the same stimulus will produce the same response even when the person admits it would be better if he responded otherwise. This is an unintelligent way of behaving. In an analogous way, indoctrination is aimed at an unintelligent way of holding beliefs. Indoctrination aims simply at establishing certain beliefs so that they will be held quite apart from their truth, their explanation, or their foundation in evidence. As a practical matter, indoctrinating involves certain conversation, but it does not involve the kind of conversation central to the activity of giving instruction. Thus, as the teaching conversation becomes less related to the pursuit of truth, it becomes less an activity of instruction and more a matter of indoctrination. We may represent these remarks schematically:

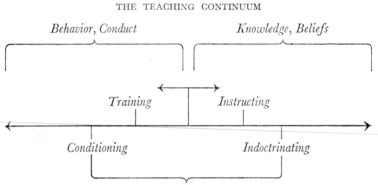

THE TEACHING CONTINUUM

*Behavior, Conduct*                    *Knowledge, Beliefs*

*Training*          *Instructing*

*Conditioning*          *Indoctrinating*

*The Region of Intelligence*

The diagram is not meant to suggest that the distinctions between conditioning, training, instructing and indoctrinating are perfectly clear and precise. On the contrary, each of these concepts, like the teaching concept itself, is vague. Each blends imperceptibly into its neighbor. It is as with the well-known case of baldness. We cannot say with precision and accuracy at precisely what point a man becomes bald. There is nonetheless a distinction, clear enough in its extremities, between a bald head and a hairy head. One might say that the difference is a matter of degree. But if the difference between conditioning and training or between instructing and indoctrinating is simply a difference of degree, then one must ask, 'What is it that differs in degree?' The fact is that instructing and indoctrinating are different in kind, but the respects in which they differ may be exemplified in different degrees. Thus, we may be uncertain in many concrete cases whether the conversation of a teaching sequence more nearly resembles instructing or indoctrinating. But it does not follow from this that the difference between them is obscure, that we are uncertain about it or that they differ only in degree. It follows only that in such specific instances the criteria that mark the difference, though perfectly clear in themselves, are neither clearly exemplified nor clearly absent.

A parallel example may suffice to make this clearer. To lie is to tell a falsehood with the intent to deceive. But now consider the following circumstances. Two brothers go to bed on the eve of one's birthday. He whose birthday is coming wishes to know what in the way of gifts the next day may hold in store for him. So he questions, prods, cajoles, and teases his brother to tell him. But he receives only the unsatisfactory but truthful answer from his brother that he does not know. And so the teasing continues and sleep is made impossible. The only recourse for the weary one is to invent a lie. It must, however, be a lie that is believable. It must satisfy and yet must be most assuredly a lie. And so he says what is most improbable, 'You will get a bicycle'. But now suppose they discover on the morning after that indeed the principal gift is a bicycle. The question might arise, did the brother lie or did he not? If the answer is 'Yes', the difficulty arises that what he said was in fact the truth. If the answer is 'No', the fact will arise that he intended to deceive. A case may be built for both answers, because in this illustration, the criteria for lying and for truth telling are mixed. The case is neither one nor the other. It does not follow, however, that the difference between lying and truth telling is obscure. Such examples show only that the criteria which mark the difference may be in more or less degree fulfilled. It shows there is a degree of vagueness present, a point at which we cannot decide.

And so it is in the present case. The concept of teaching, as we normally use it, includes within its limits a whole family of activities, and we can recognize that some of these are more centrally related to teaching than others. We have no difficulty, for example, in agreeing that instructing and certain kinds of training are activities which belong to teaching. We may have more difficulty, and some persons more than others, in deciding whether conditioning and indoctrinating legitimately belong to teaching. There is, in short, a region on this continuum at which we may legitimately disagree, because there will be many contexts in which the criteria which tend to distinguish teaching and conditioning or teaching and indoctrination will not be clearly exemplified. Thus, there is an area of uncertainty on this continuum, an area of vagueness neither to be overcome nor ignored, but respected and preserved.

Nonetheless, were we to extend this continuum, we would discover another region of agreement. For we would surely stretch a point too far were we to extend the line on the left and include such activities as intimidation and physical threat, or on the right and include such things as exhorting, propagandizing and just plain lying. The continuum would look like this:

*Thomas F. Green*

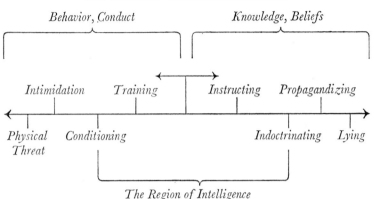

We would have to strain and struggle to include within the teaching family such things as extortion, lying and deceit. The point is not that such things *cannot* be included among the assemblage of teaching activities. The point is rather that to do so would require an extension and distortion of the concept of teaching. It is clear in any case that such activities are less central to the concept of teaching than conditioning and indoctrination, and that these are, in turn, less central than training and instruction. Thus as we extend the extremities of this continuum we depart from a region of relative uncertainty and enter a segment within which we can agree with relative ease. Lying, propagandizing, slander and threat of physical violence are not teaching activities, although they may be ways of influencing persons' beliefs or shaping their behavior. We know in fact, that these activities are excluded from the concept of teaching with as much certainty as we know that training and instructing are included. This shows approximately where the region of vagueness occurs in the concept of teaching. It occurs in respect to matters of behavior, somewhere between the activities of training and conditioning, and in respect to matters of knowledge and belief, it occurs somewhere between instructing and indoctrinating. The most central properties of the concept of teaching are revealed, in short, within the limits of what we have called the region of intelligence. Or, to put the matter in another way, we can say that teaching has to do primarily with the relation between thought and action.

It is a matter of no consequence that there have been societies which have extended the concept of teaching beyond this limit of vagueness and have thus included even the most remote extremities of this continuum. That propaganda, lies, threats, and intimidation have been used as methods of education is not doubted. But the conclusion warranted by this fact is not that teaching includes such activities, but that education may. Propaganda, lies, and threats are more or less effective means of influencing and shaping beliefs and patterns of behavior. It follows that teaching is not the only method of education. It does not follow that the use of propaganda, lies and threats are methods of teaching.

The concept of teaching is thus a molecular concept. It includes a congerie of activities. In order to more clearly understand the concept it may suffice to simply describe in schematic form what are the logical properties most central to this family of activities and to display in what respects other less central activities do or do not bear the marks of teaching. In this way we may gain in clarity without doing violence to the vagueness inherent in the concept. At the same time, we may avoid importing some obscure and *a priori* normative definition of teaching.

## The topology of belief systems

Such a topology of the teaching concept is partially displayed in the teaching continuum. In order the better to see what is implicit in this continuum, it is necessary, or at any rate useful, to introduce another topological model, or set of models, having to do primarily with the right-hand side of the continuum. That is to say, this topology has to do not with the structure of the teaching concept, but with the structure of belief systems. It is related to the concept of teaching, however, because teaching has less to do with *what* we believe and more to do with *how* we believe; and this contrast is best displayed in the structure of belief systems.[1]

This contrast between what beliefs we hold and how we hold them is not, however, altogether obvious. For it may seem, initially at least, that a person must either believe a thing or not, and that there can be no question as to *how* he believes it. A belief, after all, is either true or doubtful, precise or muddled, clear or confused. But these differences all have to do with the belief itself and not with the *way* it is believed. One might suppose there cannot be different ways of believing a thing as there are different ways of planting corn or skinning a cat. When a person believes something, he believes it to be true, and in addition to arriving at some decision on its truth, he does not need to decide also *how* to go about believing it.

There are, nonetheless, certain adjectives which appear in belief statements but which do not qualify the truth or falsity, clarity or precision of the belief. They have to do instead with the *way* we believe something. They delineate, as it were, a 'style' of belief. We can, for example, believe something strongly or not, with passion or not, for good reasons or not. Two persons may hold the same belief with a different measure of strength, with more or less adequate reasons, or on more or less adequate evidence. They may, on the contrary, believe different things with equal strength, reasons, or evidence.

These adjectives of belief style fall roughly into two categories. In the first, there are those which have to do with the way beliefs are held in relation to each other. In the second class are those words which describe the way beliefs are held in relation to evidence or reasons. To understand these differences, we have to recognize that people seldom if ever hold to a belief in isolation, in total independence of other beliefs. Each of us, in fact, possesses a whole system of beliefs, and we can understand that in this system there may occur different arrangements. Thus, two persons may hold to similar beliefs and yet they may hold them in quite different arrangements. Thus the order of one's beliefs is a property of belief systems conceptually distinct from their content, and this can be described as a contrast between the beliefs we hold and how we hold them.

For example, in the order of anyone's beliefs there are quite often identifiable relations of a logical sort. That is to say, there are always certain beliefs which people may tend to reject because they understand them to be logically incompatible with others they accept. The point is not that such beliefs *are* logically inconsistent, but only that they are thought so. Similarly, we can identify some beliefs which a person may tend to accept because he finds them implied by others he accepts or consistent with others he accepts. Given any three beliefs in a system we shall say that if C is held to as implied by B, then B is primitive in respect to C. But if B in turn is held to as implied by A, then B, which is primitive in respect to C, is derivative in respect to A. When a belief has the status of a primitive belief and is not itself held to be derivative from any other belief, then we may say it is a primary primitive belief.

In short, the concept of primitive and derivative beliefs is a quasi-logical concept. That is to say, it has nothing to do with the actual objective logical relation between beliefs. But it does have to do with the logical order they receive in a belief system. A primitive belief is one which is not itself questioned. In this respect it resembles a postulate. It is itself appealed to in determining the acceptability of other beliefs. A belief which is seen to be implied by a primitive belief will *tend* to be more acceptable. One which is seen to contradict a primitive belief will *tend* to be rejected. A primitive belief then has the status of an arbiter, so to speak, in determining which beliefs can be received and which must be rejected. But the important point is that this adjudicative function is performed on the basis of a logical claim. It is the claim that what is implied by a truth must be true; what is contradicted by a truth must be false.[2]

But this relationship between primary and derivative beliefs is not a fixed or stable one, nor is it the objective order which logicians may establish between propositions. It has to do with the logical order which beliefs receive in a system. It has long been observed that men have the untidy disposition to hold in logical relation beliefs which are in fact wholly independent. The objective order of beliefs discoverable through logic, is based upon their content and structure. It has to do with *what* is believed. But the order we are concerned to describe has to do with the order beliefs may be given. It can be described only as having to do with *how* they are believed.

The second point to observe is really a facet of what has been said already. It is simply that belief systems are in many respects not logical systems at all. When, for example, the theory of evolution is found by some person to conflict with some logically primitive belief concerning the authority of scripture, it is true that one or the other belief will *tend* to be rejected or modified; but we must ask *which* it shall be, the belief in evolution or the belief in the authority of scripture. And this question has to do less with the logical structure of a belief system than with its psychological or spacial order. It is not uncommon for students in the course of study to discover that they must alter certain of their beliefs and cancel out others altogether. The facts of social life and the order of institutions may conflict with one's idealized conceptions of the world. Some cherished myths regarding our national heroes may become shattered in the pursuit of the truth about our history. If one is to live in the company of others, some cherished standards of judging them may have to be abandoned along with some treasured estimates of one's self. It is often with respect to some beliefs an easy thing to change and with respect to others wholly beyond the realm of possibility. A belief which one person may be quite prepared to doubt, another may be incapable of questioning.

Thus some beliefs are more important than others, and the measure of their importance, in this sense, is not whether they are logically primitive but whether they are psychologically central. Thus, we can visualize a belief system as having a spacial dimension, as having the structure of a set of concentric circles. Within the core circle will be those beliefs held with greatest psychological strength, those which we are most prone to accept without question, and, therefore, least able to debate openly and least able to change. As we move from circle to circle toward the perimeter there will be distributed those beliefs which we hold with progressively less strength and are more prepared to examine, discuss, and alter.

Psychologically central beliefs do not cluster together because they are logically primitive. It is quite conceivable, in fact, that beliefs could be logically derivative and yet psychologically central. Beliefs which are quite independent in the logical dimension of a belief system may nonetheless be related by the fact that they are 'core' beliefs. Whether a belief is central or peripheral has, therefore, little to do with its content; it has to do not so much with what a person believes, as with how he believes it. Thus, the same belief may be psychologically central to one person and peripheral to another. The spacial location of a belief is determined not by its logical properties, but by the manner of its psychological possession.

A belief system is not a logical system. It is not at all uncommon that men hold strongly to certain beliefs which if ever set side by side would clearly conflict. But until they be set side by side, and their inconsistency revealed, there need be no problem in believing both. Indeed, two beliefs equally central psychologically, may be logically incompatible. Thus one may hold certain central convictions concerning matters of economics—that competition among men is the only basis for social progress, that individual initiative is the supreme requirement for merit, that a man is entitled to keep what he can secure, that if a person does not 'succeed', he has no one to blame but himself. Similarly, one may hold to a set of beliefs in matters of public morality—that only by cooperation among men can society be improved, that one must be charitable in assisting those who are less fortunate, that a good member of society is one who does not 'take advantage' of his neighbors.

Such conflicting sets of beliefs may all be held as psychologically central. This is possible because we tend to order our beliefs in little clusters encrusted about, as it were, by a protective shield which prevents any cross-fertilization among them or any confrontation between them. Thus we may praise the value of competition as an article of economic faith and the necessity for cooperation as a fundamental demand of social ethics. In this way we can hold psychologically central, certain beliefs which are at many points logically incompatible. This is perfectly possible provided we never permit our cluster of economic beliefs to influence our ethical convictions or permit our ethical beliefs to influence our economic thought. We can do this effectively by protecting certain clusters of beliefs by a hard coating as the germ of a seed is protected from the corrosive influences of the winter. This impregnable shield appears disguised as a belief itself. 'Ethics has nothing to do with business' or 'Religion ought to stay out of politics.' A student for example, may possess a religious faith which militates against the demands of inquiry. He may nonetheless, be a successful student provided he never permits his religious faith to influence his life as a student, and conversely never permits his life as a student to influence his understanding of his religion. Such a segregation of concerns can be accomplished by adopting certain beliefs. 'Matters of faith are beyond the reach of reason to appraise.' Or, again, it is not uncommon to find those who devote their lives to scientific study and yet hold to a religion which is fundamentally a matter of magic. 'Science is one thing and religion is quite another.'

We may therefore identify a third dimension of belief systems. First, there is a logical relation between beliefs. They are primary or derivative. Secondly, there is a relation between them which has to do with their spacial location or psychological strength. But there is a third dimension in every belief system by which certain clusters of beliefs are held more or less in isolation from other clusters and protected from any relationship with other sets of beliefs. Each of these dimensions has to do not with the content of our beliefs, but with the *way* we hold them. None of these dimensions need be stable. Indeed, the belief systems of different persons can be described in relation to the ease with which different clusters of beliefs can be related, the number and nature of the logically primitive and psychologically central beliefs, the ease with which they may move from center to periphera and back, and the correspondence or lack of it between the objective logical order of beliefs and the order in which they are actually held.

There is a second way of marking this distinction between beliefs we hold and how we hold them. It has to do not with the relation between beliefs, but with their relation to evidence or reasons. When beliefs are held without regard to evidence or contrary to evidence, or apart from good reasons or the canons for testing reasons and evidence, then we may say they are held non-evidentially. It follows that beliefs held non-evidentially cannot be modified by introducing evidence or reasons or by rational criticism. When beliefs, however, are held 'on the basis of' evidence or reasons, can be rationally criticized, and therefore can be modified in the light of further evidence or better reasons, then we shall say they are held evidentially.

This contrast between holding beliefs evidentially and non-evidentially corresponds closely to a fundamental point on the teaching continuum. It has to do with a conventional contrast between teaching and indoctrinating. This difference has nothing to do with the contents of beliefs. It is perfectly possible that two persons may hold to the same belief and yet one may do so evidentially and the other non-evidentially. It is possible, in other words, to indoctrinate people into the truth. The only problem is that they will not *know* that it is the truth. They will only know that it is a *correct* belief. That is to say, they will hold to certain true beliefs, but will be unable to give any adequate reasons for them, any clear account for them, or offer any sound evidence in their support beyond the logically irrelevant observation that they are commonly held beliefs. And yet we cannot be said to *know* that a belief is true, if we cannot give any reasons for it, any explanation of it or any evidence in support of it. In short, even though the beliefs one holds are true, one cannot be said to know they are true, if they are believed in this non-evidential fashion. They can only be known to be *correct* beliefs, and that is one of the features of beliefs held as a consequence of indoctrination.

But this contrast between teaching and indoctrination cuts more deeply. Consider the following context.[3] At some conferences there is a period set aside to lay out the work of the conference, to set the limits to be observed and the methods to be followed. It involves the presentation of decisions already arrived at and now presented as 'the ground rules', so to speak, within which the work of the conference shall proceed. A sales conference, for example, may be concerned with the study and discussion of a single method of selling, excluding all others from consideration.

Such a period is sometimes called an orientation period. But it may also appropriately, more accurately, but less wisely, be called a period of indoctrination because of the place and function served by debate. In such a period, persons may raise questions; there may be discussion and a certain amount of disagreement expressed with decisions arrived at. This process overtly resembles the process of debate carried on for the purpose of informing and arriving at decisions. But in this context questions are raised, information given and discussion permitted only for purposes of persuasion, never for purposes of *arriving* at conclusions.

Both teaching and indoctrination may involve debate, questions, discussions and argument. Both appear to involve instruction, and, in that respect, there is a striking resemblance between them. But there also is a great difference. In indoctrinating, the conversation of instruction is employed only in order that fairly specific and predetermined beliefs may be set. Conflicting evidence and troublesome objections must be withheld because there is no purpose of inquiry. The conversation of instruction is adopted without its intent, without the 'due regard for truth' so essential to instruction. Not every point on the teaching continuum, is therefore, equally a point where truth is significant. Indoctrination begins precisely where a concern for truth ends. In short, the intent of indoctrination is to lead people to hold beliefs as though they were arrived at by inquiry, and yet to hold them independently of any subsequent inquiry and therefore secure against the threat of change by the later introduction of conflicting reasons or conflicting evidence. The intent, in other words, is to produce persons who hold their beliefs non-evidentially.

That this is the intent of indoctrination is proved by the fact that the process of indoctrinating, unlike the process of teaching, is *logically* dispensable to success. Consider, for example, the following illustration.[4] Suppose we identify two persons, Adams and Barnes, neither of whom knows the identity of the discoverer of the American continent. Let us suppose that with Adams we present certain evidence, give explanations, enter into arguments, examine the statements of authorities, and finally Adams concludes that there are reasonably good grounds for the claim that the discoverer of the American continent was Columbus.

Let us use a different method in the case of Barnes. He is told to respond with the name 'Columbus' whenever asked for the identity of the discoverer of the American continent. He is then asked the question at intervals, rewarded for the correct answer and punished in some way for a wrong answer. In this manner, he may learn to respond correctly and without hesitation.

But could we say that Barnes had been taught that Columbus discovered America? Certainly not. One reason is that at no point in such a process need it be asserted that Columbus *did* discover America. We could say that Barnes had been trained to make a certain response, a response which, by the way, need not manifest intelligence, but we could not say he had been taught that Columbus discovered America. Indeed, he could have learned to make this response without having learned that Columbus discovered America. For this reason, we could not say that Adams and Barnes had learned the same thing, even though by certain observable measures they will appear to give the same response. What Barnes knows is how to respond. What Adams knows is that Columbus discovered America. What one knows is a skill; what the other knows is a truth—or at least a reasonably well-founded belief. But what is most important is that Adams has arrived at this knowledge or belief by a process which we call teaching, and he could not arrive at this truth or come to hold this belief as he does hold it, except by that process or by a process resembling it in certain important logical respects.

The creation of an evidential style of belief is inextricably and logically tied to the process of instruction, or to another process which closely resembles instruction. A non-evidential style of belief, however, is conceptually independent of the process by which

D                                                                                     35 beliefs are acquired. A belief is held non-evidentially when it is held quite apart from any reasons, evidence or canons for testing reasons and evidence; and, therefore, the process by which the belief comes to be held is logically a matter of no consequence. But when a belief is held evidentially, it is held always in relation to its grounds in reasons or evidence; and thus the process by which the belief comes to be held is logically decisive.

This is an extraordinarily important and far-reaching mark of difference between instructing and indoctrinating. It follows that insofar as teaching has to do with the acquisition of knowledge and beliefs held evidentially, it is an activity which necessarily involves instruction.

This does not imply that the way of knowing and believing aimed at in instructing can be achieved only in instruction. It does imply, however, that it can be achieved only by a process which resembles instruction in certain important respects. Study, for example, is an activity which aims at accomplishing the results of instruction; yet it does not require the presence of an instructor. Study, in short, is a method of learning and not a method of teaching. Although study is an activity more intimately related to learning than to teaching, it is nonetheless an activity which in its anatomy starkly resembles instruction. Study, as distinguished from other methods of learning—practice, drill, memorization—always involves asking questions, weighing evidence, giving and testing reasons, and so forth. The conversation of study, in short, is the same as the conversation of instruction. What is aimed at in teaching, insofar as it involves instruction, can also be accomplished by study. This fact we acknowledge when we speak of the need for independent study rather than the need for independent learning. In this way we acknowledge that study is another way of accomplishing precisely what is aimed at in teaching.

Suppose, however—to return to our example—that after extensive periods of instruction, Adams refused to acknowledge that Columbus was the discoverer of the American continent. Would it follow that we had failed in teaching? Not necessarily.[5] We would need to know *for what reasons* he refuses to assent to such a commonly held opinion. It may be, in fact, that the reasons for his judgment are better than can be offered for the more widely received opinion. He might say something like this: 'There seems to be good evidence for the view that Columbus was not the first European to set foot on the American continent. Indeed, it seems a well established fact that many years before Columbus' voyage, there were visitors to this continent of some Scandinavian descent. But the visits of these people seem not to have had the far-reaching historical consequences of

Columbus' discovery. If you consider the historical consequences of great importance, then one might say Columbus discovered America. But if you mean by that that this was the *first* discovery of America, then you would be mistaken.'

This kind of reply would not signal the failure of instruction. It would be evidence of singular success. Instruction is an activity which has to do not with what people believe but with how they believe it. It has to do not so much with arriving at 'the right answer' as with arriving at an answer on the right kind of grounds. It is no objection to point out the many areas of knowledge in which it is important to lead students to the right answer. For all that is usually pointed out is that there are many areas of knowledge in which the grounds of decision are decisive, and in which therefore there *is* a correct answer which it is important to know. Even, in mathematics how-ever, where a 'right answer' is often discoverable, a concern simply to lead students to that answer, or to equip them to find it, is a fundamentally defective kind of instruction. Even in such a formal science where certitude is common, we are concerned that students be brought to an evidential style of knowing. To focus simply upon securing a right solution without understanding the nature of mathematical operations is the mathematical equivalent of in-doctrination. Indeed, when indoctrination is seen to involve a certain style of knowing or believing, we can discover the possibility of indoctrination in nearly every area of human knowledge and not simply in those having to do with what we would more commonly call 'matters of doctrine'. In other words, when, in teaching, we are concerned simply to lead another person to a correct answer, but are not correspondingly concerned that they arrive at that answer on the basis of good reasons, then we are indoctrinating; we are engaged in creating a non-evidential style of belief.

There is one further curious fact to observe about the concept of indoctrination and its relation to a non-evidential way of holding beliefs. It has to do with the difficulty in identifying concrete cases of indoctrination as opposed to teaching. We have already suggested that there is an area of vagueness between instructing and in-doctrinating. The difference between them is clear, but the criteria that mark the difference may, in specific instances, be mixed. For example, a person who has received his beliefs by indoctrination will be able to give reasons for them, offer evidence, and in other ways display every mark of holding his beliefs in an evidential way. But this is an illusion, albeit an illusion to which each of us, in some measure, submits. A person who is indoctrinated can sometimes give reasons and evidence for his beliefs, because as a practical matter, reasons and evidence were necessary in the process of establishing

37

his beliefs. The difference, however, is betrayed in his *use* of reasons and evidence. He will use argument, criticism, evidence, and so forth, not as an instrument of inquiry, but as an instrument establishing what he already believes. He will display a marked incapacity to seriously consider conflicting evidence or entertain contrary reasons. That is to say, such a person will hold his beliefs as matters of ideology. It is indeed the characteristic of an ideology that it requires reason and argument, not for inquiry, but for defense. It requires reason as a weapon. This is not required for the defense of a belief held evidentially.

The point is that the differences between instruction and indoctrination, clear enough conceptually, are extraordinarily difficult to detect in specific cases. It requires, in ourselves, the capacity to discriminate between beliefs which are held evidentially and those which are not. To do this, we must not only have the capacity to detect sophistry in ourselves, but the courage to reject it when discovered, and the psychic freedom to follow where the pursuit of truth may lead. The detection of non-evidential beliefs in ourselves, therefore requires not simply the logical skill to examine and appraise the adequacy of reasons, but the psychic freedom to give up or alter those beliefs which are non-evidential. In short, the distinction between instruction and indoctrination, easy enough to grasp intellectually, is immensely difficult to detect in practice, because it involves nothing less than the most radical examination of our belief systems in their psychological dimensions. To possess such a capacity is a mark of rare courage and honesty.

This psychic difficulty corresponds to a certain interesting logical difficulty. It is a curious but quite understandable fact that it is both grammatically and logically impossible for a person to say of himself truthfully and in the present tense, that he holds his beliefs as a consequence of indoctrination. It is something which cannot be said. Suppose I walk into a room where I find someone lying down in an attitude of blissful sleep. I ask, 'Are you asleep?' Without hesitation, with clarity and firmness of voice, he answers, 'I am.' His answer is strong evidence that in fact he is not asleep. Similarly, if a person says with sincerity and conviction 'My beliefs *are* indoctrinated' (there is no satisfactory way of putting it) it must follow that his beliefs are no longer held as a consequence of indoctrination only, and he is already on his way toward an evidential style of belief. Indoctrination is successful only if people *think* they hold their beliefs evidentially and in fact do not, only when they use reason as a weapon under the illusion that they are seriously inquiring. Indoctrination then is the intentional propagation of an illusion. All of us live with this illusion to some extent. Insofar as teaching is directed at matters of knowledge and belief, it involves instruction and may be described as the effort to free us from this illusion to whatever extent that is possible. Teaching might be described then as the unending effort to reconstitute the psychic structure of our ways of believing. But in order to begin, instruction presupposes that there is already a certain kind of structure of beliefs. The death of innocence is needed before teaching can begin. At this point teaching and indoctrination both become intimately related to the formation of attitudes.

To say this, however, is merely to repeat an observation at least as old as Socrates' attempt at the moral reform of Athens, namely that the beginning of inquiry is the confession of ignorance and the ensuing willingness to follow where the truth may lead. This is an attitude, a disposition, which like most other attitudes can be described as the manifestation of a certain kind of belief system, a certain way of holding beliefs. He cannot be taught who is convinced there is no truth to be appropriated or none he does not possess already. But it takes no great fund of experience to observe how rare is the capacity to admit one's ignorance, to seriously entertain new ideas, alternative ways of doing things, and to change one's point of viewing the world. Every mind is fettered to some extent, ridden with presuppositions and stereotypes which stand in the way of mental freedom. Every man knows some point at which he cannot earnestly confess his ignorance. It would come as a personal affront; it would endanger the self.

These are the points which teaching cannot touch. For teaching, insofar as it involves matters of knowledge and belief, begins with posing questions to be answered or answers to be questioned. It begins by placing such matters in the open where they cannot be avoided. But there are those who cannot allow certain questions to be raised, who cannot permit certain doubts because they touch upon themselves too directly, threaten them too deeply. In proportion as such questions are greater and greater in number, in proportion as one's psychologically central beliefs are multiplied and segregated, teaching has less and less scope for success. Teaching is ineffectual in those whose minds are enchained by prejudice or who cannot face the questions which must be raised. Teaching aims to remove these fetters; it seeks by instruction to reconstitute the order of our beliefs so that even our psychologically central beliefs are evidentially held. But in this it presupposes already some measure of psychic freedom. For instruction to proceed, it must, in effect, find some foothold from which to push back the darkness and let in the light.

It is in this sense that the practice of teaching presupposes certain attitudes, the cultivation of which is at the same time the consequence of teaching. The attitudes it presupposes, constitute that

39

posture toward the self and toward the world which permits new questions to present themselves and new answers to be entertained. When a teacher can, in effect, find no foothold from which to proceed, he must try directly to change attitudes in order to begin teaching. The formation of attitudes is, in this sense, a precondition for teaching. It is also a consequence, however, insofar as teaching is concerned with the *way* we hold our beliefs. To the extent that it has this consequence, we may say that teaching is that activity which preeminently aims at enhancing the human capacity for action. It is concerned with the nurture of that state of being which we might describe as the posture of the pilgrim, the capacity, within limits, to tolerate an increasing measure of alienation, to be free to wander in the world.[6]

One of the clearest illustrations of the failure to teach, in this sense, is found in the Church. For in the Church, as in the political arena of our society, there are those who think the aim of teaching is to get people to hold certain specific beliefs even though the evidence does not always support them, though they are not believable to the person taught and cannot be defended on the basis of good reasons. The result of so-called Christian education is, sometimes from the perspective of the university, disastrous. Sometimes it destroys the possibility of teaching because it results in a non-evidential style of belief. There is learning in such education, but the kind of learning which results in holding beliefs so that henceforth further learning is made more difficult and further teaching rendered all but impossible.

No one who has long been a university teacher will fail to detect how often those students most at home in the Church, most articulate in matters doctrinal, are those whose minds are most bound and restricted and who are least able to learn or seriously inquire. They are often the ones least capable of doubt and most lacking in the courage to follow where the truth may lead them. They are, in short, often lacking in the moral courage which their lives as students require. Their education in the Church often has had the consequence of multiplying their 'core' beliefs by an endless list of prohibitions, and segregating their beliefs into such well protected and isolated clusters that neither facts nor reasons may penetrate. It is a strong indictment of the Church that in its education it often produces such a non-evidential style of belief.

It is a serious charge, however, not only because of its social consequences, but because it contradicts what it is the Church's task to affirm. Such education is a subtle form of unbelief within the Church itself. It is a denial of the view that men are justified by faith, in favor of the view that they are justified by their opinions. Education in and by the Church has often, as a consequence, had damaging results.

It is not, however, the presence of the faith which creates a non-evidential style of belief; it is its absence. Those whose minds have been enchained by their education, are men of little faith. To say that men shall abide in faith does not mean they shall abide in their opinions, not even in their opinions about God. To think otherwise would be to suppose that God loves men because of their beliefs. There may be those who entertain such a faith, but it is surely not the kerygma that it has been the historic concern of the Church to affirm. The man of faith should be the most fearless in the search for truth because he knows that in the end it is not decisive. Being freed even from that most worldly of all concerns, namely the concern for his own salvation, he may be fearless even in his search for the truth about God.

One must add, however, that the Christian Church is not the only party in the modern world guilty of fostering a non-evidential style of belief. Our schools, including universities, have often been barbaric in the same way. Some years ago, in his studies on dogmatism, Rokeach and others tested many college freshmen in the east and middle west.[7] They were concerned to study the belief systems of these students, not only *what* they believed but *how* they believed it. The results were astonishing. The test included a series of statements accompanied by a series of reasons. The students were to indicate the statements and reasons with which they agreed. Remarkable numbers agreed with such statements as the following: 'We ought to combat communism because communism means longer working hours and less pay', or 'Hitler was wrong because otherwise he wouldn't have lost.'

These are responses of persons who have been led to hold the 'right beliefs' but never have been taught good reasons for them. There has been learning which has resulted in the observable and verbal responses of the right kind, but for entirely erroneous reasons or for none at all except that such beliefs are 'correct'.

## The topology of enabling beliefs

This emphasis on an evidential system of belief is susceptible to misunderstanding in a dangerous way. It could be understood to imply that one should not have *any* passionate convictions. A belief held evidentially is amenable to examination, and therefore open to change in the light of better reasons and more substantial evidence. Thus the possession of firm convictions seems to conflict with the cultivation of evidential beliefs. He who has passionate convictions is to that extent and at those points no longer open-minded, and he who is at *every* point open-minded must be without any passionate convictions. He is that completely flexible man, whose placid and weak mentality marks him off as dangerous, because he thinks nothing is really very important.

An evidential belief style does not commit us to such a mentality. The problem is rather to seek closure of mind at precisely those points and on those matters which will permit us to be open to the evidence on all other matters of belief. The only beliefs, in short, which must be rejected are those which prevent us from being open to reasons and evidence on all subsequent matters. As Chesterton has put it in another context: 'There is a thought that stops thought. That is the only thought that ought to be stopped.'[8] He might have added that there are beliefs without which no beliefs can be warranted and these are the only beliefs which at all cost must be affirmed.

Such beliefs, in fact, ought to enlist our most passionate loyalty, for they are the ones which enable us to hold all other beliefs in an evidential way. For example, a thorough skepticism in regard to reason, a kind of complete anti-intellectualism, if held to as a deep conviction, would successfully prevent the examination of any subsequent beliefs. It could lead only to a non-evidential way of believing. On the other hand, a 'due regard for truth'—the belief that truth is powerful, attainable and to be treasured whenever identified —such a belief is indispensable if *any* belief is to be held evidentially. Such a conviction does not commit us to the naive faith that all men have a due regard for truth or are equally moved to dispassionately weigh and consider the evidence on important questions. Nor does it commit us to the truth of any specific belief. It commits us only to a certain *way* of holding beliefs, and that way is an evidential way. Indeed, a 'due regard for truth', understood in this way and passionately held to, is indispensable if we are to hold to *any* beliefs in an evidential way. A deep conviction concerning the value of truth is in this sense rationally defensible because without it there can be no rational defense of any belief whatsoever.

It is not, therefore, the aim of teaching to eliminate all passionate convictions. The aim, on the contrary, is to seek every possible assurance that our passionate convictions, our enabling beliefs, are also rationally or evidentially held. Such enabling beliefs may be open for examination, capable of refinement and elaboration, but under no conditions can they be exchanged for others. Their abandonment cannot be warranted on the basis of evidence or reasons, because they are precisely those beliefs without which we could not seriously entertain the evidence.

These comments also are susceptible to a dangerous misappropriation. At the point of enabling beliefs, there is only the most tenuous line between the fanatic and men of less singular devotion. For at this point, the difference between what is believed and how we believe it is obscured. How a person believes something can be reduced, at this point, to an account of what he believes. The actions of the inquisitor after all, may be defended on grounds of the most passionate regard for truth, a regard for truth so strong, in fact, that it becomes necessary to stamp out every trace of error that the truth may receive the recognition it deserves. The difficulty with the fanatic at every point, however, is that he confuses a due regard for truth with passionate concern to propagate certain *specific truths*.

But it may be answered, 'Is not a due regard for truth also a specific set of beliefs?' It is indeed. It is the belief that truth is attainable, powerful, and to be treasured. But the belief that truth is attainable does not entail the belief that we have attained it. Such a regard for truth does not permit us the illusion that we have appropriated more than a fragmentary vision of the truth. It does not permit us with ease to identify the truth. Rather, it places upon us the difficult and tortuous task of weighing with great care whatever beliefs we may regard as true, holding them always as open to challenge, and to change in the light of further evidence and fresh reason. In short, although a due regard for truth involves a passionate and unswerving loyalty to certain specific beliefs, although it involves a kind of fanaticism, it is an unyielding commitment to just those beliefs which will not permit the fanatic to develop.

It is at this point again that the Christian faith provides an interesting illustration. The Christian faith is often thought to be contained in certain doctrinal assertions. As such, it is commonly conceived to have more to do with *what* men believe than with *how* they believe. There is in this view a considerable burden of truth. But faith is not simply a matter of credal recitation; it is also a matter of fidelity. The fact is that *what* is believed in faith is precisely what is sufficient in order that all subsequent beliefs may be surveyed, examined, and held in an evidential way. What is believed, in short, has to do not so much with the beliefs we hold, as with the way we hold our beliefs. It has to do, in short, with the conditions without which we could not have a 'due regard for truth', i.e., the conditions which permit us to develop an evidential 'style of belief'.

For example, one of the greatest barriers to a free and fearless search for truth is the tendency of men to identify their ideas with themselves, so that one cannot attack ideas without attacking their author. The result is that in debate beliefs are held non-evidentially, and reason is used in the fashion required by ideology, not as an instrument of inquiry, but as a weapon for defense of self. A 'due regard for truth' then becomes extraordinarily difficult, and men find it virtually impossible to value the emergence of truth more highly than they value their own victory in debate. When we find such an attitude expressed in the practice of teaching, we recognize the authoritarian personality, the person who is less concerned that his words *be* truthful and more that they be regarded as the truth. Perhaps one ought to expect no more, for our beliefs are indispensable to ourselves; an attack upon them is an attack upon us.

This is, theologically speaking, the expression of man's unceasing effort to achieve salvation by works, to value his own ideas more highly than the truth, not because his thoughts carry a greater burden of truth, but simply because they are his. The man of faith is like any other man. He does not escape his condition, but along with others he may at least understand it, and understanding it place his hope elsewhere than in the fruits of his labor. For to walk in faith is to walk in the confidence that in death there is life, that beyond the death of self, there is hope for the freedom to think without any limitations except those imposed by the demands of thought itself. The quest for knowledge then holds no fears. Though it may displace one's ideas, it cannot endanger one's person. On the contrary, it can hold only inexhaustible surprises.

It is precisely the possibility of this kind of psychic freedom which lies at the heart of teaching. It is a due regard for truth which serves to distinguish the conversation of instruction from that of indoctrination. In indoctrination we are concerned primarily with *what* people believe and as a consequence we are concerned with *how* they believe it. In teaching, however, we are concerned primarily with *how* persons believe a thing and, therefore, can afford less concern with *what* they believe. If we adhere to the practice of teaching, we shall not be permitted a great anxiety over those who do not believe as we do, *provided* they can be led to a psychologically central regard for truth. For given that enabling belief, held with passionate conviction, it will follow that their beliefs, and our own as well, may be open to subsequent alteration in the face of reasons, evidence, and further reflection upon our experience. Apart from such beliefs, however, the hope that men's opinions may be changed by teaching is a hope in vain. Their beliefs will either be unalterable or else so easily changed as to fluctuate with every changing wind of doctrine or fashion of opinion. Without a due regard for truth, we must resort to indoctrination, force, or outright lies. With it, we may instruct. We may then say to men, in effect, 'Come, let us reason together.' A due regard for truth is an indispensable condition for that civilizing community in which not men but ideas are perpetually on trial.

Indoctrination, nonetheless, has a perfectly good and important role to play in education. There is nothing in these remarks which would suggest otherwise. Like the development of attitudes, indoctrination may be useful as the prelude to teaching. Just as we need not cut off the hand of every child or thrust one of every fifty into the street in order that they may understand the dangers of knives and highways, and learn to obey the rules established to protect their lives, so we need not offer reasons for every belief we think important for children and adults to hold. On the other hand, we have no warrant to inculcate beliefs for which there is no good reason or for which we can offer no good reason, and we must be prepared to offer reasons or evidence when they are requested. Though indoctrination may, in many contexts, be both good and necessary, it can never be justified for its own sake. It can only be justified as the nearest approximation to teaching available at the moment. Indoctrination, in short, may be sanctioned only in order that beliefs adopted may later be redeemed by reasons, only that they may be vindicated by teaching.

## Notes

1 The following account of belief systems is suggested by, but not derivable from nor identifiable with, the views of Milton Rokeach. In many ways this account goes beyond what Rokeach has done, and goes beyond it in a way he would find unacceptable. See his *The Open and Closed Mind*, New York: Basic Books Incorporated, 1960.
2 See Leon Festinger, *A Theory of Cognitive Dissonance*, Evanston, Illinois. Row, Peterson and Company, 1957. His thesis roughly is that when one receives a message which is dissonant with an established belief held by a person, then one or more of three different things may happen, either the message will be rejected and some reasons developed to justify its rejection, or it will be modified so as to become 'consonant' with the belief system and therefore suitable for internalization, or finally, the belief system itself may be modified so as to become 'consonant' with the message. Festinger is not always clear concerning the meaning of the terms 'consonant' and 'dissonant', but they are reminiscent of the logical notions of 'consistent' and 'inconsistent' (p. 2), and are actually given 'a more formal conceptual definition' (p. 3) in terms of negation and the phrase 'follows from'. Although his discussion lacks precision at the level of definition, there is no doubt that he is pointing to the fact that belief systems do have a logical structure of the kind I have tried to sketch.
3 The following illustration was suggested by a student of mine, Mr William Lauderdale.
4 Another student of mine, Mr Gerald Reagan, suggested this illustration, although to make a slightly different point.

5 Note, however, that a failure to get the 'right answer' in the case of Barnes would constitute a failure to succeed in teaching. Indoctrination aims at inculcating the 'right answer', but not necessarily for 'the right reasons' or even for good reasons.

6 The topology of teaching helps us to discriminate between those considerations which enter as a part of the teaching activity and those which enter only as presuppositions of the teaching act. For example, there are some views of teaching which focus upon the personal relation of teacher and student, emphasize the need for mutual trust and acceptance, and thus, stress in the teaching relation those matters having to do primarily with mental health and self-understanding. Such views tend to picture the teaching activity as primarily therapeutic. Such views have nothing to do with the teaching activity, though they have much to do with satisfying the conditions without which teaching cannot succeed or even begin. In short, they deal with the presuppositions of teaching and not with its substance.

This does not mean that such views are irrelevant to what teachers are concerned to do. For there are many actual settings in which teachers for psychological and institutional reasons, are called upon to forsake the task of teaching and attend to those matters which must be satisfied in order that teaching may begin. It ought always to be kept in mind that the 'office' of teacher often requires more than a talent for teaching. It requires also that one be now a counselor, now a clinician, now a friendly guide, and another time a public relations officer. To say that these activities have to do with the presuppositions of teaching does not mean they must temporally precede the activity of teaching. It means simply that though they are always involved in the 'office' of teacher, they are not logically central to the activity of teaching.

7 Milton Rokeach and Albert Eglash, 'A scale for the measurement of intellectual convictions', *Journal of Social Psychology*, xliv (August 1956), pp. 135–41.

8 Gilbert K. Chesterton, *Orthodoxy*, New York: John Lane Co., 1909, p. 58.

# Indoctrination and respect for persons

4

## William Heard Kilpatrick

The education thus far discussed is an education designed to free the whole personality of the learner for the fullest living, for the best and most independent exercise of all his powers, for the control of his own destiny. This alone we have counted true respect for the personality. It was further brought out that without such development the individual is not free in perhaps the most important sense, that true and effective freedom depends thus as much on inner growth, on the ability to use the mind effectively, as on the absence of external restraint. In fact, it might be said that a condition of inner slavery is the worst kind of slavery; such an individual has no wish to change his status, he even fights against his true freedom. To aid the individual, then, to the fullest use of his powers, to fullest intelligent and responsible self-direction and effectiveness, is to give the greatest possible respect to his personality.

But teachers have not always thus sought to respect the personalities of those studying under them; many today still act otherwise. In other words, teachers have too often cared more for the subject-matter they teach or the cause they represent than for human personality. In the early days of the Protestant Revolt, for example, both sides alike competed for proselytes, each side struggling to get control of as many youth as they could in the effort to fasten their respective doctrines upon the minds and hearts of the young under their care. It was only at a later date, under the democratic teaching of respect for personality, that men grew to the point of questioning such partisan indoctrination.

The term *indoctrination* just used demands a word of explanation. The word means, literally, implanting doctrines. When such implanting on an uncritical basis was the common practice of the school, and indeed one of its principal aims, to indoctrinate and to teach came to be but diverse ways of describing the same process. The term *indoctrination* then carried no derogatory implication, and this was until recently its recognized meaning and status. The *Oxford English Dictionary* (this part published about 1900) recognized no other meaning. But with the development of democracy and the coming of modern rapid change, it was increasingly felt that education could no longer be content with inducing uncritical belief, but must instead develop responsible thinking on the part of all as a necessary preparation for democratic living and citizenship and an unpredictable future. In this way the term *indoctrination* has been increasingly restricted to its derogatory implication of an improper inducing of uncritical belief.

There are, to be sure, some who still believe it right for parents and teachers to implant their own doctrines in the young under their care so that these doctrines will remain fixed beyond the possibility of later question or revision. These people accordingly use the term *indoctrination* with a favorable implication. Also, curiously enough, during the late war the American Navy adapted the term *indoctrination* to mean 'instruction in the fundamentals of military discipline, naval customs, and usage'. Naturally this interpretation carries no derogatory implication. And this naval use of the term has since been extended to other areas. So that the term is currently used in several different senses, the one here followed being, however, the more usual meaning in educational writing.[1]

That democracy must refuse and reject indoctrination in this prejudice-building sense would seem beyond question. Where competent opinion differs as to what to believe, for parents and teachers to take advantage of the child's ignorance and docility to fasten in him beyond recall their own chosen views is to enslave this child to those who thus teach him. Democracy and a proper respect for the child's personality must reject such enslavement as partisan exploitation of the individual's right to be educated to do his own thinking and make his own decisions.

This modern attitude of condemning such indoctrination is not limited to the present day. Dryden spoke definitely in 1687:

> By education most have been mis-led;
> So they believe, because they so were bred.
> The priest confirms what the nursery began,
> And thus the child imposes on the man.
>
> 'Hind and Panther'.

And further, at the 1807 dedication of Milton (Mass.) Academy, Rev. Thomas Thacher said: 'A Preceptor has no right to inculcate his peculiar sentiments in theology on the mind of the pupil'.[2] And Bronson Alcott is quoted as saying: 'The true teacher defends his pupils against his own personal influence.'[3] Professor Raphael Demos of Harvard has recently said: 'We *mould* material things into the pattern of human ends. But we do not *mould* human beings, and do not wish to do so. That way lies indoctrination, propaganda, the worst tyranny of all because it is tyranny over the human mind.'[4]

Various questions, however, properly arise in connection with what has just been said.

1. The child's education cannot wait until he is mature enough to think for himself. We have to begin from the first. Does this not force indoctrination upon us?

Possibly some indoctrination is thus inevitable with younger children, but even in these cases the ultimate intent should be to the contrary. For example, we will work as best we can to build the habit of truthfulness in the young child, and we must begin this before he can understand why lying is a bad social practice. But as soon as we can and as fast as we can we lead him to see the social reasons for truthfulness. The practice of honesty in the form of not stealing can be taught on a basis of understanding why earlier than truth-telling; for the child can easily understand how he would feel if someone should take his toys. In all cases where habits are desirable, we teach the habit even though the why has to come later. Even if there is controversy as to what is right, the parent or teacher will still teach his own best insight as to the proper habit. As soon as possible, however, the child, now grown older, should be helped to get a reliable understanding of what is socially and morally involved, so that he may be intelligent in his moral conduct. Ultimately, when adolescence has well advanced, the youth should be encouraged to review critically both his habits and the earlier accepted why of those habits and attitudes. He does this in order that he may now make both habit and reason really his own. Previously, he had learned them as a child, when he thought as a child. Now he must rethink them, to make them his own or to reject them or revise them on his mature level. If he does not do this, he will be living henceforth enslaved to his childish ideas.

2. A decade or two ago there was positive demand that the schools actively help build a new social-economic order. If this means that teachers should plan such an order and then by specific indoctrination raise up a new generation committed to the new order so planned, we cannot accept this program. Teachers as such have no proper or exclusive commission to plan such an order; and any attempt by indoctrination of the young to create such an order would of itself be a clear denial of the democratic process.

It does, however, seem a specific duty of the school to recognize that the existing social order demands a certain amount of continual remaking, and that the school accordingly has a correlative duty to have the young study, suitably to their age, the strengths and weaknesses of our civilization. And no custom or institution, however cherished, can claim exemption from such study and criticism. This means the free and untrammeled study of all pertinent controversial issues; but in such study the teacher's aim must be the upbuilding of the students to make thoughtful choices, not the

49

winning of them to his side of a partisan controversy. 'If any teacher, by the way in which he teaches, either wilfully or carelessly permits some bias or prejudice of his own, or even the inappropriate expression of his reasoned convictions, persistently to mar the process of fair-minded study on the part of those studying under him, he is to that extent damaging those students and in that same degree is manifesting his unfitness to teach.'[5]

3. While agreeing that indoctrination in other matters is wrong, some still feel that the case for democracy is different; for it we should indoctrinate. They claim (i) that, democracy being fundamental to our way of living, we should run no risk regarding it, but indoctrinate all in it from earliest childhood. They point further to the facts (ii) that our democracy is now threatened from without as never before and (iii), sad to say, that some of our own people do not even now fully accept democracy. From these considerations, they say, indoctrination of all is demanded.

To such a proposal the reply seems to be to agree to the three facts and assert that the conclusion does not follow. To teach democracy in undemocratic fashion, in a way to foster uncritical acceptance, would seem an odd way of fostering democracy. To indoctrinate a belief in democracy without including the reasons for democracy, and without building ability to think critically about it, is to make blindfolded adherents of democracy. Such people would not know the why of their practices or dogmas and consequently could not be trusted to apply the doctrines intelligently. When they grow up into active citizenship they might be easily induced, for example, to forbid the study of controversial issues in school. They might forbid the critical study of democratic doctrines and so prevent wise adaptation of these doctrines to new conditions that arise. In one word, such indoctrination would make blind dogmatists of democracy, quite unfit to carry on the democratic process in a changing civilization. That way lies fanaticism.

The conclusion of the whole matter, it appears, is that democracy and ethics must at bottom respect the personality of all concerned, to develop each as best possible toward more effective use of his mind and toward intelligent and responsible free play of intelligence. On this we must stand. Such respect for personality is indeed the most sacred thing among men.

In an earlier day practically everybody counted education to be exactly the process of fixing in the child what his guiding elders thought he should think and believe. The Alexandrian outlook proceeded rather consistently on this theory; and contending Western religions always have been—many still are—strong in practicing this kind of indoctrination. Under the influence of the Enlightenment and democracy, we began to see that to fix beliefs indelibly in the child is to enslave him to his teachers. In the degree that the child cannot, or will not, later re-examine such early implanted beliefs is he unable to think and decide for himself. He has then in very fact, been enslaved. And any teaching which does not expect to upbuild in him, as fast as he can manage it, the tendency and capacity to think for himself is to that extent failing to respect his personality and, specifically, to help him build the character needed for democracy. No teaching is ethically defensible which knowingly and willingly hides from any person any matter within his grasp which will help him to think more adequately. So to teach is to fail of the ethical and democratic demand to treat the individual always as end and never as means merely.

That there are difficulties here cannot be denied. As parent or teacher I have to make decisions for those under my care on matters that they are not yet ready to decide, but which—in some sense at least—cannot now be postponed. Some writers have therefore said that all education begins in indoctrination and can only gradually move away from it. It is true I have to make temporary decisions such that my educative methods at that point may, to the undiscerning, look like indoctrination. Perhaps at the very beginning the difference is in intent only: 'Do I or do I not mean by my teaching or other influence to indoctrinate this growing person to think as I decide?' If I mean not to indoctrinate him I shall, as soon and as fast as I can, explain the why of what I think and do, and let him in —as far as he is able—on the reasoning process at work. So from the earliest possible moment I bring him to expect reasoning to control both my thinking and his. And the older he gets, the more I shall expect him to act on reason and the more I shall help him to seek out the pertinent reasons and learn to obey them.

Curiously enough, some claim one exception to the rule against indoctrination, namely, that we must indoctrinate democracy, that this is too important a belief to leave to the choice of the immature mind. If we admit this one exception, then we must, in logical consistency, admit any other doctrine that the teacher or parent counts too important to endanger. It would be safer to say that democracy is so important that it must be understood and used intelligently and not applied blindly; and if it is to be used intelligently, it has to be learned thoughtfully. The practical answer would seem to be (i) that before our pupils can understand reasons for believing in democracy, we must none the less help them to live democratically, else they will not learn to respect each other or learn how to discuss intelligently, decide cooperatively, or execute with shared responsibility; but also (ii) we must, as soon and as fast as we reasonably can, have them consider the arguments for and against democracy and increasingly decide, each one for himself, on the merits of the case as he sees it, what he shall believe. To 'indoctrinate in democracy' is both a contradiction of terms and a denial of the very democracy we profess to be teaching.

To this argument, academic freedom is, for older youth, the corollary. Jefferson's two statements previously quoted well present the fundamental position here:

> I have sworn on the altar of God eternal hostility to every form of tyranny over the human mind. (Letter to Benjamin Rush, September 23, 1800)
>
> This institution [the University of Virginia] will be based upon the illimitable freedom of the human mind. For here we are not afraid to follow truth wherever it may lead, nor to tolerate error so long as reason is left free to combat it. (Letter to William Roscoe, December 27, 1820).

The statement put forth in 1941 by the N.E.A. Committee on Academic Freedom, also quoted earlier, seems to say well what is more precisely needed here:

> Academic freedom is . . . in essence the freedom to study and learn, and to share with others the results of study. . . . It is thus intended for the good of students and of the public rather than for the personal satisfaction of instructors. . . . This practice of intelligent study is necessary to the proper working of democracy as of no other kind of society. . . . The justification of academic freedom lies . . . in its inclusive and unbiased study. If any teacher, by the way in which he teaches, either wilfully or carelessly permits some bias or prejudice of his own, or even the inappropriate expression of his reasoned convictions, persistently to mar the process of fairminded study on the part of those studying under him, he is to that extent damaging these students and in that same degree manifesting his unfitness to teach.[6]

For the contrary view we have a D.A.R. official saying in 1923 that 'academic freedom of speech has no place in school, where the youth of the country are taught and their unformed minds are developed.'[7] And in keeping with this view an official of the Daughters of Colonial Wars in 1940 spoke in condemnation of a certain textbook then in common use, complaining that this book 'tried to give the child an unbiased viewpoint instead of teaching him real Americanism'. And she went on to say that 'all the old histories taught "my country, right or wrong"; that's the point of view we want our children to adopt.'[8]

These latter quotations bring us to the second of our two problems: controversial issues.

Certain conservatively minded people are strongly opposed to having the schools consider any really controversial issue. Some of this opposition springs from resistance to change and some from the fact that in the Alexandrian type of school these opponents had attended all teaching was authoritarian; the school set out dogmatically in the book or lecture what the pupil or student should learn. Consequently they can hardly conceive any other way of teaching.

There are to be sure various kinds and degrees of controversial issues. Some matters, like the multiplication table, are fixed beyond any question. All such we shall teach unquestionably, but understandingly; for it is intelligent persons and responsible citizens we wish to develop. There are other matters which school children have to take pretty much on authority, as the spelling of words and the facts of distant geography and history; but even in these, especially in such matters as geography and history, the wise teacher will seek as far as possible to make the pupils increasingly independent of the teacher, and, especially, independent of particular books, by helping them to learn to use various reference sources. For again, what we wish is to cultivate critical study and independence of thought.

There are still other matters which once were controversial but are now no longer so considered among competent teachers. We can conceive these once controversial issues on a scale: at one end, those most widely accepted by communities; and at the other end, those least accepted. As teachers we should deal differently with the different parts of the scale according to the temper of the community on the matter. Evolution, for example, is in some backward communities still rejected. In such a community we may decide to treat it as a truly controversial issue rather than as a matter no longer so taken (in this sense) by scientists. Instances of these once controversial issues are quite interesting. The earth we now know to be round, but it was not always so counted, as the Bible speaks of the 'four corners of the earth'. (Rev. 7:1). That the earth rotates daily on its axis and revolves annually about the sun was denied in 1633 by a group of church doctors: 'the doctrine that the earth is neither the center of the universe nor immovable, but moves even with a daily rotation, is absurd.'[9] That the earth is older than 4004 B.C. was once denounced—and still is by some—as antagonistic to revealed religion.

Finally we come to the really controversial issues, those issues concerning which a considerable number of thoughtful people hold contrary opinions. Most very live current problems may be expected to fall under this head. Some of these are so important that pupils or students of the proper age and development should study them, partly to understand the different positions taken and reasons therefor in order that each may form his own opinion, partly to learn, in the only possible way, how to deal intelligently with as yet unsolved social problems. In the degree that a problem is properly to be counted controversial will the true teacher refuse to let his own position prevent those under him from thinking fairly for themselves regarding it. The teacher must know that on such issues he is a public servant. He is not there to gain converts to his partisan cause; he is there to help those under his care learn to think reliably for themselves.

In the matter of controversial issues teachers must understand that, however or whatever they teach or refuse to teach, they are none the less necessarily promoting one kind of society in preference to all others. If they refuse to teach controversial issues in any effective way, they are thereby educating either to uncritical acceptance or to uncritical rejection of new proposals; either of these is an education to inferior citizenship. That many people prefer youth to be so educated is only too true. The true teacher, however, cannot yield to such a reactionary attitude; he must educate those under his care to the best independent thinking he and they can effect. To this conclusion we seem inexorably led by our study of the philosophy of educative method and democratic teaching.

## Notes

1 A fuller consideration of this meaning of this term is given in Rivlin and Schueler's *Encyclopedia of Modern Education*, 1943, p. 393.
2 Quoted in Elmer E. Brown, *The Making of Our Middle Schools*, New York: Longmans Green, 1902, p. 239.
3 *Webster's Dictionary of Synonyms*, Springfield, Mass.: Merriam, 1942, p. 728.
4 *American Scholar*, xv, p. 99.
5 National Education Association, *Principles of Academic Freedom*, Washington: N.E.A., 1941, p. 8.
6 *Ibid.*, pp. 4, 5, 8.
7 *Daughters of the American Revolution Magazine*, Washington, 57, p. 270.
8 *Philadelphia Record*, 20 February 1940.
9 Quoted in Karl Pearson, *Grammar of Science*, New York: Macmillan, 1911, p. 20.

# Indoctrination and moral education  5

## R. F. Atkinson

There is too little communication between academic moral philosophy and the philosophy of education. They are separate countries, and a citizen of the one finds himself an alien in the other. The language change is confusing, and it is hard to feel altogether confident of one's judgment of what is and is not worth saying once one has crossed the frontier. So, at any rate, it has come to seem to me. In the present paper what I have tried to do is to proceed, by way of a discussion of instruction and indoctrination, to the consideration of a prominent theme in recent moral philosophy whose implications for moral education are, it seems to me, insufficiently appreciated in much that is written on the topic. There seems still to be point in emphasizing the sense in which there are open options in morality and consequently in moral education.

### I

The distinction I have adopted the terms 'instruction' and 'indoctrination' to mark is clearly important in many educational discussions. What is less clear is how firm a distinction it is, and over what range of things taught it can be maintained. There would seem to be no great difficulty in drawing it with respect to academic and vocational education, but can it be drawn in the field of moral education? It is here that I, at least, am disposed to object most strongly to indoctrination, but I am not at all sure that there is a basis for instruction here either. There can, obviously, be instruction *about* morals: it is instruction *in* morals that is in question.

'Instruction' and 'indoctrination' are not the only, and may well not be the best pair of terms for the distinction intended. Sometimes 'education' is the term opposed to 'indoctrination', whilst 'instruction' is used for a rather direct sort of telling of people what is and is not so, a telling that smacks rather of indoctrination than education proper. Again, Scheffler, in his illuminating study *The Language of Education*,[1] adopts a much narrower usage for 'instruction' than I have elected to do. It is possible, of course, that there is here a difference between British and American usage. Such linguistic matters are not, however, of very great importance in themselves. The distinction required is simply a special case or reflection of that between the rational and the irrational or a-rational. It is that distinction applied to the teaching process.

'Instruction', though probably not 'indoctrination', is perhaps most naturally applied to theoretical teaching, to teaching *that* as opposed to teaching *how*. But the distinction we are concerned with can perfectly well be drawn with respect to teaching how, which cannot in any case be wholly separated from teaching that. Quite apart from the fact that, so far as language goes, it is very frequently a matter of choice whether we speak of teaching how or that, it is clear that academic teaching as ordinarily understood is not exclusively theoretical, nor vocational purely practical. Vocational training normally involves the mastery of some fact and theory, academic the acquisition of a variety of skills.

Instruction, then, is essentially a rational process, both at the giving and, in so far as it is successful, at the receiving end. It involves, for instance, providing adequate support, by way of proofs, reasons, evidence, whatever may be appropriate to the field in question, for the conclusions it is sought to impart. No higher degree of conviction is sought than is warranted by the nature of the support available. Not conviction by itself, but justified conviction, rational assent is the aim. The imparting and acquiring of an understanding of what is taught is consequently involved in its realization. Because of this, and in so far as it succeeds, instruction puts its subject in the way of making progress in the field by his own efforts. Indoctrination, on the other hand, need not. It is subject to no such restrictions. Conviction or assent is all that is sought, and any teaching procedure is acceptable provided only that it is or is thought to be effective in achieving this end. Understanding, awareness of the grounds upon which opinions ought to rest, is not required. If knowledge consists in justified (full) conviction, then the object and result of instruction may be knowledge; whereas of the man who is indoctrinated merely, although what he believes may be true and capable of justification, it will not be possible to say that he knows it.

With regard to teaching and learning how, the instruction/indoctrination distinction manifests itself as that between, say, training and drilling. The trained man only knows how to carry out certain routines which will, no doubt, in appropriate circumstances, be effective in producing the results. The former operates intelligently, whereas the latter does not. The trained man knows what he is about, knows not only the rules of procedure but also the reasons for them, and hence knows how to adapt the rules to non-standard conditions. The man who is merely well drilled has to make do with rules of thumb which he mechanically applies.

This does not pretend to be an account of teaching methods. I am not maintaining that teaching should or can consist entirely in instruction and training as I have described them. Even where the ultimate aims are knowledge and intelligent practice, it seems inevitable that some recourse will have to be had to non-rational teaching methods, that it will sometimes be necessary to try to impart information and techniques beyond the recipients' understanding, that there will be some learning by rote or drill. Nor, moreover, can anybody have a full grasp of all the information, techniques, etc., that he puts to use. We have all taken a vast amount on trust, and must continue to do so.

Instruction and indoctrination, training and drilling—this sort of distinction, whatever words may be used to express it, is, I believe, commonly taken for granted in discussions of the aims and practice of education. On what basis does it rest? Once the question is raised it becomes apparent that the distinction presupposes that there are clear criteria of truth, cogency, correctness in any field to which it applies. It is not required that there should be a body of established truths, facts, laws, practices, in the field, only that there should be criteria for determining what is and what is not acceptable. Instruction, training, is then a matter of teaching with due regard to the criteria appropriate to the field in question: indoctrination, drilling, the reverse. Accordingly, the more fugitive the criteria may be in a particular field, the harder will it be to distinguish instruction and indoctrination.

It is, moreover, on this basis easy to understand why we are inclined to discriminate morally between instruction and indoctrination. Since the process of instruction is governed by criteria which are in principle accessible to any rational person, it is, to use the traditional, imprecise, but perhaps sufficiently well understood language, a matter of treating a person as an end in himself: it is not putting him to use, exploiting him, treating him as a mere means, as indoctrination so clearly is. And further, so long as the instruction/indoctrination distinction can be drawn within a field, we have, as it were, ready-made, a basic for evaluating and regulating the non-rational teaching procedures that we may be obliged to use, whether for lack of time or competent teachers or because of the immaturity and/or incapacity of the taught. We can restrict ourselves to the inculcation of information and practices which could be the content of rational teaching and, with regard to the young especially, employ only those non-rational methods which do not or as little as possible impair the recipients' capacity for subsequent instruction and training.

Before turning to the main enquiry how moral education stands with regard to the instruction/indoctrination distinction, it might be worth while to take a look at two cases in which the need for such an enquiry has been overlooked—once very obviously, in the other case less so. No one can fail to see that in the following passage, which one must hope to be fairly untypical of ecclesiastical pronouncements on education, a relevant question has been begged:

> Every education system makes use of indoctrination. Children are indoctrinated with the multiplication table; they are indoctrinated with love of country; they are indoctrinated with the principles of chemistry and physics and mathematics and biology, and nobody finds fault with indoctrination in these fields. Yet these are of small concern in the great business of life by contrast with ideas concerning God and man's relation to God, his neighbour and himself, man's nature and his supernatural destiny.[2]

But John Stuart Mill's much weightier and in so many ways justly celebrated defence of the liberty of thought and expression suffers, it seems to me, from a similar defect. The chief ground on which Mill supports this liberty is that it is the necessary condition of people's acquisition and full understanding, which alone secures stable possession, of 'the truth'.[3] This is no doubt the case where truths of fact (scientific truths) are concerned, but the argument is meant to apply to thought and expression in morals, religion and politics too. It has to be asked, therefore, whether there are truths of anything like the same sort to be discovered in these fields. Mill in his essay betrays an altogether inadequate awareness of the possibility of radical differences among the various fields of enquiry, speculation and practical judgment. He appears to think that they can readily be placed on a simple scale of increasing complexity, running from mathematics, where 'all the argument is on one side', through natural philosophy (science), to morals, religion and politics. So very far is Mill from according any special status to moral 'truths', which presumably must by their nature have some specially close relation to conduct, that he allows that they, along with any other opinions, lose their immunity when so expressed as to be direct instigations to action,[4] as if people were to be allowed any moral opinions they liked so long as there was no danger of them or anybody else acting upon them. It may be that sense can be found for the idea of truths in morals, politics and religion, but unless and until it has, nobody is entitled to advocate liberty of thought and expression in these fields on the ground that it is a necessary means to securing the truth.

## II

Is there then a firm enough basis for drawing the instruction/ indoctrination distinction with respect to moral education? In many treatments of the topic attention is directed on to the contrast between direct moral teaching by explicit precept on the one hand, and reliance on example, on the candid discussion of moral issues as and when they arise in the teaching of other subjects, on the other. On the face of it at least, this contrast relates primarily to the method of moral teaching, whereas the present concern is with its content, or rather with the question whether there is a possible content for moral instruction. It is true that indirect methods of moral teaching, in so far as they engage the attention and judgment of the taught, to that extent differ from indoctrination as described above. All the same our question about the content of moral education remains to be answered.

What then is there to teach in morals? Not, it is clear, information in any ordinary sense, nor practical skills. As to the latter, moral progress is frequently understood in contradistinction from the acquiring of such skills as are necessary or helpful for achieving economic or social success, and, even if one takes more presentable candidates like promoting other people's welfare, there is no getting round the fact that immorality is never viewed as a matter of lacking or losing a capacity. Incapacity is indeed a defence against charges of immorality. And as to moral information—what could this be? Take any moral position and its opposite can be maintained without logical error or factual mistake. It can, of course, be taught and learnt (is a possible object of knowledge) that a certain moral position is held by certain people, but, whatever adequate grounds for holding a moral position might be, it is clear that this is not among them. There can be moral teaching, instruction in, as opposed to instruction about morality, only if there are criteria of truth, cogency correctness, in the field. Are there such criteria?

Manifestly it is impossible even to list all the more important sorts of answer that have been given to this question. All I shall attempt is to illustrate a type of view which seems to be dominant among contemporary philosophers of a, very broadly, empiricist or, less happily, linguistic persuasion. There is no one who seriously entertains the hope of being able to establish a substantial moral criterion, a touchstone of moral truth. The possibility of formulating a criterion for applying the term 'moral' is, of course, another and less momentous affair. Morality, it is asserted or conceded, cheerfully or sadly, is a field in which there are irreducibly open options.

It has to be recognized, of course, that the difficulties in the way of establishing a moral criterion are inherent in the empiricist position, which excludes, among other things, the possibility of recognizing necessary or self-evident (non-tautological) truths in morals. And further, it is not at all impossible that contemporary empiricistically minded moral philosophers have operated with an unduly simple notion of what a moral criterion could be. It can be a matter of great difficulty to find words to express the ideas people have of what is and is not morally acceptable, ideas which are very often much more complex and subtle than the 'principles' to which lip-service is paid, and which are quoted as examples in the moral philosophy books. But the obstacles to establishing a moral criterion are not problems of formulation. Morality is not unique in that its first principles are not susceptible of proof. What distinguishes morality from the formal and natural sciences is that in it different and opposed first principles are readily conceivable, and are in fact accepted by morally serious people.

Although contemporary moral philosophers differ from Hume on many important matters they are with him on the point of present concern. Hume in effect suggested that, provided no errors of logic or fact were made, any moral position was as much or as little reasonable as any other. Conduct is reasonable or otherwise in so far as it does not tend to achieve the satisfaction of the agent's desires. But desires themselves cannot be reasonable or unreasonable. ''Tis not contrary to reason to prefer the destruction of the whole world to the scratching of my finger'.[5] The way Hume expressed his insight is highly exceptionable. It is simply untrue, now and in Hume's day, as he did in fact rather oddly notice, that such terms as 'reasonable' and 'rational' are never applied to desires of ends.[6] But this leaves the substantial point untouched. Choice of means can be reasonable or rational in a sense in which choice of ends cannot. Mistakes can be made about means in a way they cannot about ends. Agreement is achievable in principle about the means to given ends, as it is on any other matter of fact. There is not the same basis for agreement on ends.

The historical Hume had many other observations to make about morality, and started some lines of thought which lead away from the view described. It is, however, this possibly somewhat over simple interpretation of him that has been remembered and reflected in current moral philosophy. Stevenson, for instance, follows Hume on the main point. He too, despite some few appearances to the contrary, maintains that there can be logically irreducible differences on moral matters. He is prepared to allow that moral judgments may be held to be 'true', but it turns out that he regards this as merely an idiomatic, perhaps debased usage in which the word

functions simply as a mark of assent.[7] He does not hold that disagreements whether a moral judgment is true can be settled in
principle. And, although Stevenson is willing to talk of people
arguing from matters of fact to moral judgments, and of their
offering factual statements as reasons for moral judgments, he has
scruples about applying the term 'valid' to such arguments.[8] Even
if ordinary usage permitted this application of the term, it would be
misguided to go along with it for fear of suggesting that the quoting
of factual reasons somehow served to establish a moral judgment.

Moral teaching would presumably be regarded by Stevenson as a
matter of influencing attitudes and, rather promisingly, he distinguishes between rational and non-rational (persuasive) methods of
effecting this,[9] and again between moralists and propagandists.[10]
Hopes of finding here a basis for the instruction/indoctrination
distinction are soon dashed, however. The discussion of moralists
and propagandists consists mainly in pointing out that the terms
overlap in application and consequently give scope for persuasive
definitions. The distinction between rational and non-rational
methods of influencing attitudes is equally disappointing. It turns
out to be the distinction between influencing attitudes by operating
on beliefs and influencing them direct, i.e. by overtly emotive talk.
The former procedure can indeed be called giving reasons for a
moral judgment, but this needs to be interpreted in the light of
Stevenson's doctrine that *any* belief about *any* matter of fact which
is *causally* efficacious in influencing attitudes may be adduced as a
reason.[11] It is not a very impressive species of rationality that Stevenson finds room for in morality. It is a rationality that has lost all
connection with truth or correctness, as they are ordinarily understood. Opposed conclusions can be reached from the same premises
by equally rational methods. The emotive theory of ethics, of which
Stevenson is perhaps the most thorough and serious exponent, is, it
is true, now largely abandoned, in part because it seems to allow too
little scope for rationality in morals. More fashionable views, though
from within the tradition they appear very different from Stevenson's, do not, it will transpire, differ significantly from his on the
point at issue.

Hare, in a by now well known passage in his *Language of Morals*,[12]
gives an account of what he calls justifying a moral decision completely by showing that it is in line with a way of life to which one is
committed. This need not be conceived as a simple exercise in deduction, a matter of mechanically applying general principles to
particular cases. It is explicitly recognized that our principles are
made what they are by, and are modified in the light of, our decisions
in particular cases. But once a decision has, so to say, been fitted into

a complete pattern of living, the view is that there is no more to be said by way of justification of it. Different and opposed ways of life are held to be possible and, as Hare recognizes, the question arises whether the choice of a way of life is to be considered completely arbitrary. Manifestly it cannot be justified in the way that a decision is justified by being referred to a way of life. Hare denies that such choices are necessarily arbitrary on the grounds that a person considering what is involved in the choice of a way of life may be considering *everything* that could conceivably bear upon the matter, and that a choice consequent upon such comprehensive deliberation cannot correctly, i.e. in accordance with usage, be called arbitrary or unfounded. In so far as these words connote haste or inadequate consideration of relevant matters then Hare is undoubtedly correct. But this should not be allowed to obscure the fact, which of course Hare does not deny, that opposed choices of ways of life may be equally well-founded and non-arbitrary. It follows that opposed decisions in particular cases may be equally susceptible of 'complete justification'.

No recent moral philosopher has found a way round the point that irreducible differences are possible in morality, that 'justifications' in this field have the remarkable property of failing to exclude opposed alternatives. Such writers as Toulmin[13] and Baier,[14] for instance, do no more than reduce the emphasis given to the point, and perhaps even obscure it by conventionalist manoeuvres. And the most thorough discussion of the topic that has appeared, by Taylor in *Normative Discourse*, though it is clearly intended to advance the discussion beyond the point at which Hare left it, seems in the end to amount to no more than a more elaborate restatement of Hare's position.[15]

In this work Taylor undertakes to specify the necessary conditions, which are I suppose held to be jointly sufficient, for the choice of a way of life to be rational. There turn out to be three of them, those of freedom, enlightenment and impartiality.[16] But, it transpires, we can never in practice know that these conditions have been fulfilled. We do not and never will know that one way of life is rationally preferable to another.[17] It is moreover allowed that there may be irreducible differences among people's rational preferences.[18] Indeed in one place Taylor explicitly asserts that it is a 'fundamental error' to overlook or deny the 'element of decision' which underlies all normative, and hence all moral, assertions.[19]

If, with Hume, we emphasize the distinction between appraisals of means and appraisals of ends, we are likely to come to think that the former can be 'objective' in a way the latter cannot. If, somewhat similarly, we make much of the distinction between proximate and ultimate justifications, between justifications *within* a certain accepted framework and justifications of the framework itself, we can hardly fail to conclude that completeness is achievable in the former case in a way it cannot be in the latter. The setting of questions about justification in morality so far determines the answers to them that it is natural that attempts should from time to time be made to see whether they cannot be set differently. Such writers as Dewey[20] and Myrdal,[21] for example, have in their different ways, and perhaps not always with sufficient attention to the logic/ psychology ambiguity of questions about the ways we think and argue, tried to break out from the means/ends, fact/value frameworks. Peters' recent discussions of moral education (1959 and 1962)[22] will bear examination from this point of view. Not that he was, as I understand him, so much concerned with questions of justification as with emphasizing the possibility of appraising the manner of education as well as its aims and content. It is all the same worth enquiring whether this re-direction of emphasis affects the matter of justification.

Peters' central contention is that the more general problems of education are not means/ends problems at all. Mill's *Logic* (Book vi, chap. 12),[23] first published over a century ago, is perhaps the classical statement of the view that all practical problems have this form, but Mill is followed in all essential respects by so recent and philosophically sophisticated a writer as O'Connor.[24] Such scepticism as O'Connor expresses in chapter 5 of his book about the adequacy of the education/applied science analogy does not derive from any doubts about the appropriateness of applying the means/ ends category here, but rather from his doubt whether the social sciences have developed to a point at which they are clearly of more use to the educator than is commonsense, 'psychological' lore. Peters is much more radical. The more general aims of education, such objects as 'self-realisation', 'character', 'citizenship', are, in his view, neither goals nor end products. Like 'happiness' they are high-sounding ways of talking about doing some things rather than others and of doing them in a certain manner. Statements about the aims of education are better to be understood as expressing views about *how* rather than *what* we should teach, views about the procedure rather than the content of education. Values are involved in education less in the shape of goals or end products than as principles implicit in certain manners of proceeding.

I have no doubt that this distinction between values as ends or goals and values as rules of procedure is a useful one, and that Peters is right in suggesting that some educational pronouncements, though ostensibly about *what* is to be taught, are better conceived as

63

pronouncements about *how* any subject matter should be taught. No doubt, too, moral education can be thought of as a matter of teaching people a manner of conducting their practical lives, rather than as one of teaching them substantive principles of conduct. Such a shift of emphasis might well furnish a basis for co-operation in moral education for people who are divided with regard to substantive principles of conduct. It is moreover possible that some of the stress one finds in discussions of moral education on the importance of indirect methods, example as opposed to precept, should be interpreted as a somewhat confused way of making a point like Peters'. That is to say, it might be interpreted not as it appears to be intended and as I suggested above, as a view about the method of teaching a given subject matter, but rather as the view that the problem is to teach people how to grapple with the 'subject matter' for themselves, to teach them how to go about making practical decisions and not to present them with practical conclusions. 'Character' in 'character training' could then be understood in the third of the senses distinguished by Peters in the works referred to, the sense in which it refers to the *style* rather than to the *content* of a person's rule-following.[25]

My one worry here is that such an attempt to exhibit the problems of moral education in a fresh light may distract attention from the fact that there are substantial moral issues calling for decision. By all means let us consider the manner as well as the matter, both in teaching and practical life. But we must not forget that there are choices to be made about the manner too. As with all other practical choices, there are no rules laid down to make them for us, though we can decide to adopt whatever rules commend themselves to us. Nor is there any method given, though we can decide to adopt one.

### III

It might well be thought that the impossibility of establishing an ultimate moral criterion has received at least as much emphasis as it deserves in recent moral philosophy. I have, however, been struck by the absence of much reflection of it in most of the discussions of moral education I have seen. There is undeniably a widespread belief in the importance of moral education, and some attention is given to questions of method and approach, but it seems to be assumed that there is no room for serious dispute about what is to be taught. This assumption—but perhaps it is really a conspiracy of silence—needs very little consideration to be seen to be quite extraordinary. There is obviously widespread disagreement on the moral issues of daily life, on the 'details' of morality, and, as I have tried to show, there is little enough reason to suppose that a greater measure of agreement can be reached on fundamentals.

This reluctance to take account of the possibility of moral conflict may, in Britain, be partly explicable on historical grounds. Morality seems most usually to be thought of as an appendage of religion, as that part of the teachings of the various religious bodies which can be regarded as common ground. Rather elaborate suggestions, which have in the main been carried out in the public educational system, are made in both the Spens (1938)[26] and Norwood (1943)[27] Reports for maintaining religious instruction and practice in the schools in the face of denominational disagreements. No need for any such arrangements with regard to moral teaching seems to be envisaged. I suppose it is feared that any serious consideration of morality might reopen the denominational quarrels of the past. Hence the constant lip-service to platitudinous ideals, whose bearing on any concrete issue of daily life is left wholly obscure. Hence the air of complete unreality that infects discussions of morality from official or otherwise respectable sources. Hence too the absurd public outcry when some prominent figure makes a candid observation, allows it to be known, say, that he is aware that there are conscientious and serious people who dissent from some article of the 'official' sexual code. To judge by what is said in public, a great many people in Britain have not grasped the possibility that people may differ in their views of what is right and ought to be done, and not merely in the extent to which they live up to or fall short of what the one 'true' view would require of them.[28]

I am very far from thinking that the point I have been pressing is the only important point about morality. Indeed I think moral philosophy may in recent years have been unduly preoccupied with questions of ultimate justification, and that the more recent reaction, change of emphasis, is to be welcomed. On the other hand, however obvious and familiar it may be to some, the point remains an important one, which needs to be taken account of, not least in connection with moral education.

## Notes

1 I. Scheffler, *The Language of Education*, Springfield, Illinois: C. Thomas, 1962, pp. 76–7.
2 Quoted by J. S. Brubacher, *Eclectic Philosophy of Education*, Englewood Cliffs, New Jersey: Prentice-Hall, 1951, p. 326.
3. J. S. Mill, *On Liberty*, 1859, Chapter 2.
4 Mill, *op. cit.*, Chapter 3.

5  D. Hume, *A Treatise of Human Nature*, 1739–40, Oxford, 1888.
6  Compare P. Edwards, *The Logic of Moral Discourse*, New York: Free Press, 1955, pp. 127–8.
7  C. L. Stevenson, *Ethics and Language*, New Haven, Connecticut: Yale University Press, 1944, p. 169.
8  *Ibid.*, pp. 153–4.
9  *Ibid.*, Chapter 6.
10  *Ibid.*, Chapter 10.
11  *Ibid.*, p. 114.
12  R. M. Hare, *The Language of Morals*, New York: Oxford University Press, 1952, p. 69.
13  S. E. Toulmin, *Reason in Ethics*, New York: Cambridge University Press, 1950.
14  K. Baier, *The Moral Point of View*, Ithaca, New York: Cornell, 1958.
15  P. W. Taylor, *Normative Discourse*, Englewood Cliffs, New Jersey: Prentice-Hall, 1961.
16  *Ibid.*, pp. 165–75.
17  *Ibid.*, p. 174.
18  *Ibid.*, p. 175.
19  *Ibid.*, p. 249.
20  J. Dewey, 'Theory of valuation', *Int. Encyc. Unified Science*, II: iv, University of Chicago Press, 1939.
21  G. Myrdal, *Value in Social Theory*, trans. P. Streeton, New York: Harper, 1958.
22  R. S. Peters, *Authority, Responsibility and Education*, New York: Taplinger, 1960, and 'Moral education and the psychology of character', *Philosophy*, Vol. xxxvii, No. 139, January 1962.
23  J. S. Mill, *A System of Logic*, 8th ed., 1898.
24  D. J. O'Connor, *An Introduction to the Philosophy of Education*, London: Routledge & Kegan Paul, 1957, p. 7.
25  Peters, 'Moral education and the psychology of character', p. 43.
26  'Spens Report', *Report of the Special Committee on Secondary Education*, London: H.M.S.O., 1938.
27  'Norwood Report', *Curriculum and Examination in Secondary Schools*, London, H.M.S.O., 1943.
28  The recent 'Newsom Report', *Half Our Future*, London: H.M.S.O., 1963, I am glad to see, does show at any rate some awareness of the possibility of moral disagreements in the staff room.

# Indoctrination
# and doctrines

6

## Antony Flew

Recently the School of Education in the University of Manchester sponsored a series of public lectures in the philosophy of education, a series now published as a book edited by T. H. B. Hollins.[1] Such a venture would in any case, in its British context, have been fairly unusual. But it so happens that this one may well turn out to be something of a landmark, since the organizers succeeded in drawing contributions from several well-known British analytical philosophers—a group previously notorious for its disdain toward the whole area. The present paper is primarily concerned with the concept of indoctrination and with what can and cannot be done through the analysis of this idea. But it so happens that two of the papers in that volume make contentions about the nature of indoctrination, and two others bear on this indirectly: the first two are 'Education and Indoctrination', by Mr John Wilson, and 'Adolescents into Adults', by Mr R. M. Hare; the second two are 'Against Utilitarianism', by Mr Alasdair MacIntyre, and 'Aims in Education: Neo-Thomism', by the Most Reverend G. A. Beck, Roman Catholic Archbishop of Liverpool. It therefore becomes possible to present what we have to say in the form of close commentary on the argument of the papers by Hare and Wilson.

The disadvantages of such a method of presentation are obvious. But they are, I think, outweighed by compensating advantages. First, at the present stage—or, indeed at any stage—of the development of the philosophy of education one could surely do with more close discussion. The very fact that we shall be concerned with the details of what has been said, rather than with its general drift, or with the approach which it exemplifies, must make a prior familiarity with the original lectures, which cannot reasonably be taken for granted, less necessary: the points at issue will become sufficiently obvious from the passages quoted. Second, this starting from a given landmark text makes it easier to work in more general suggestions, which transcend the particular object case of the concept of indoctrination, about what can and cannot reasonably be expected from the analysis of the concepts of education. Third, the outline view, which is all I have positively to offer here, was in fact developed, and can best be understood, as a synthesis of Wilson's thesis with Hare's antithesis.

F

I therefore proceed immediately, in section I, A, to give summaries of the views first of Wilson and then of Hare. Next, in I, B, I indicate, rather more discursively, what I take to be the positive contributions of Hare and Wilson. The whole of section II is devoted to criticism of Wilson. But all its four subsections raise in this particular context issues of more general interest: II, A considers the relations, and his confusions, between logical mapwork and practical prescription; II, B examines what Wilson offers as paradigm cases of indoctrination, urging that two out of the three are instructively unrepresentative; II, C, argues that the consensus upon which, rather oddly, he hopes to base a programme of radical reform does not in fact obtain; and II, D takes up briefly two points which, though fairly important, are less central to Wilson's argument. The whole of section III is devoted similarly to Hare. But in this case all three subsections bear upon a single comfortably neglected truth: that there can be no satisfactory treatment of at least this part of the philosophy of education which refuses to face and to come to terms with the disagreeable fact that there are fundamental differences of ideology.

In section IV we return to the idea that indoctrination might be a matter not of evidence and content, nor of aim, but rather of methods or manner. Here, in subsection IV, A, it is argued that the actual impossibility of teaching certain sorts of critical thinking in certain ways is not theoretical but practical, although, of course, not a whit the less important for that. In subsection IV, B, it is argued that if there is, or is to be, a sense of *indoctrination* which refers to methods and manners of teaching, then this should be regarded as secondary and seen as having, perhaps, a wider range of possible application than the primary sense. Finally, in section V, I make rather damping suggestions about the scope and promise of logical geography in this particular neck of the woods.

## I The positive contributions of Wilson and Hare

*A. Summaries*

For Wilson, what makes an educational practice indoctrination is the inadequacy of the evidence for, or the actual falsehood of, the doctrines which the indoctrinator endeavours to inculcate. He says:

> The concept of indoctrination concerns the truth and evidence of beliefs. . . . If we are to avoid indoctrination, therefore, the beliefs we teach must be rational. They need not be certain . . . it may only be that the general weight of evidence is in their favour. They *may* be certain, or they may be highly

probable, or probable, or just likely on the whole. What they
*must* be is backed by evidence: and by 'evidence' of course
we must mean publicly-accepted evidence, not simply what
sectarians like to consider evidence . . . (p. 28)

Against this Hare contends that the essence of indoctrination does
not lie in either the falsity of, or the insufficiency of the evidence for,
the doctrines. Instead it is to be found in the aim of the indoctrinator.
As Hare sees it, Wilson has considered only 'two possibilities: a
distinction on the basis of *method*, and a distinction on the basis of
*content*.' (p. 47). Since, very reasonably, Wilson wants to distinguish
indoctrination, as a bad thing, from education, as a good thing, and
since he also, and equally reasonably, wants to allow that various
more or less coercive or nonrational methods of instruction are sometimes proper, it seems that the issue has somehow to depend on the
content. But 'this,' Hare urges, 'will not do at all' (p. 48). He intro-
duces a third option, a distinction on the basis of *aim*.

The educator is waiting and hoping all the time for those whom
he is educating to start *thinking*. . . . The indoctrinator, on
the other hand, is watching for signs of trouble, and ready to
intervene to suppress it when it appears, however oblique and
smooth his methods may be. (p. 69)

Again, the aim of the educator is to work himself out of a job, to
'find that he is talking to an equal, to an educated man like himself—
a man who may disagree with everything he has ever said; and,
unlike the indoctrinator, he will be pleased.' (p. 70)

## B. *Their contributions*

Now I certainly do not claim to be myself able to provide a complete
philosophical account of the concept of indoctrination. What I hope
to do is to bring out certain fundamentals, and I hope, in particular,
that that still future full account will have to find room for ideas
about *both* content *and* aim. Justice has somehow got to be done:
not only to what should be the very obvious point that the object of
indoctrination is to implant unshakable beliefs; but also to what is
apparently less obvious, that the beliefs concerned surely cannot be
of just any kind at all.

On the first of these points, the cynic might suggest that the
essence of every variety of teaching must really lie in the aim rather
than effects achieved; inasmuch as we professional teachers—and
we university teachers most of all—are notoriously willing to claim
that we have been engaged in teaching without encouraging, much
less insisting on, any officious enquiries into the effects actually

produced by our activities.² This cynical suggestion is in part grounded on the fact that the word *teach* can be used as both a task and an achievement verb.³ The term *indoctrination* apparently embraces similar possibilities of equivocation: between, on the one hand, the task or the attempt simply, and, on the other hand, the task or the attempt successful. But Hare's point is different and in no way cynical. It is a matter of one possible aim as opposed to another, rather than of the task as opposed to the achievement.

On the second of the two fundamental points, it is well to begin, very simplemindedly by stating that the concept of indoctrination refers to the implanting of doctrines. The reiteration of the root word *doctrine* may suggest, beneficially, the notion of a limitation on the possible content. The lack of provision for this is, I think, a defect in Hare's story, a defect which has somehow to be made good. For, surely, it would be artificial as well as harsh to accuse some ideologically Nothingarian primary school teacher of engaging in indoctrination if the only grounds which you proposed to advance, were that she was struggling, by wholly traditional methods, to implant the multiplication tables into the none too malleable minds of her pupils, and that, in defiance of Hare's liberal ideals, she would be very much more surprised than pleased if any of these pupils were ever later to inform her that her teaching here had been, in substance, incorrect.

Again, suppose that we had—would that we did have!—an effective and painless means of teaching anyone—even me—to speak fluent French; sleep-training would be the very thing. Now this unhappily still unavailable technique for teaching someone *how* to do something would presumably involve the simultaneous imparting of a lot of associated beliefs *that*:⁴ I can scarcely become able to say this, that, or the other in French without, at the same time, coming to believe that whatever happen to be the correct French expressions are, indeed, just that. Yet the inculcation of beliefs of this sort, even by such imaginary nontraditional means would not, I think, naturally be labelled or rebuked as *indoctrination*.

These two examples show that Hare's account in terms only of aims cannot be adequate. Nevertheless the deficiency cannot be made good simply by insisting that the question of indoctrination only arises where doctrines are to be taught, and by then specifying that a doctrine is merely a belief which, if not false, is at least not known to be true. For suppose that there actually were errors in the multiplication tables with which our primary school teacher was trying to drill her class, or that some of the French being pumped into a sleeping brain was in fact plumb wrong. Then the faults involved would not be indoctrination; they would be arithmetical incompetence or malicious dishonesty. Before we can speak of indoctrination we have to be dealing with the imparting of beliefs, whether true or false, which either themselves are, or at least which are closely connected with others which unequivocally are, of that subsort, whatever it may be, which can correctly be described as doctrinal. Although it may perhaps be true that whatever may count as a doctrine in this context is either false or not known to be true, the cases considered do seem to indicate that it is not every false or not known proposition which can, as such, qualify.

Indoctrination in a 'newly emerging country' begins, therefore, not when children are exposed—as happens too often, even in happier lands—to teachers who are either uneager to be instructed about the errors of their teaching, or just plain incompetent, or both. Rather it occurs when, for instance, a commission of all too competent people is set up with powers to inspect all libraries at every level and with a mandate to 'work out a system to ensure the removal of all publications which do not reflect the ideology of the party, or are antagonistic to its ideals.'[5] The quotation comes from the official terms of reference, as recently approved by the government of Ghana; and the move constitutes, I am afraid, a major step on the road from an authoritarian to a fully totalitarian regime. It should be chastening—especially perhaps to those inclined to mistake intellectual ability to be the supreme educational value—to reflect that the chairman of this committee of ideological censors is Dr W. E. Abraham, the first African to be elected to a fellowship of All Souls and presently, Professor of Philosophy in the University of Ghana.

Again, if any teaching or misteaching of French were to constitute indoctrination, it would have, I think, as a necessary, though not as a sufficient, condition to be somehow tied up with something wider and more ideological. This requirement could be satisfied if the occurrence or nonoccurrence of particular word roots in French was thought to bear on some politico-racial question as to whether the French are Aryans, or on the thesis—which was at one time regarded as essential to Christianity—that Hebrew was the world's original language.[6] (It might even be allowed to be sufficient if the wider doctrine involved was that of some purely academic school or party.)

## II Difficulties in Wilson's view

### A. *Logical mapwork and practical conclusions*

We turn to Wilson's paper. The first point arises almost before he begins. Following Ryle, he describes what he is about to do in neo-Humean terms. It is an exercise in logical geography:[7] we are going to

> map out the area of meaning of a particular concept, and sketch
> its logical geography by contrasting it with other concepts,
> paying attention to borderline cases where we are in doubt,
> considering model cases which we know to form part of
> the concept's geography, and so forth. (p. 25)

This can be an excellent image for characterizing one fundamental kind of philosophical activity. It is no longer apt when the philosopher ceases simply to describe the situation as it presently is and proceeds to suggest ways in which it might be improved. Mapping is indeed a prudent prelude to prescription. But the moment we start to change the landscape we cease to be mere mapmakers; and, of course, why ever not? In the words of that Master Mapmaker of modern philosophy, the late Professor J. L. Austin: 'Essential though it is as a preliminary to track down the detail of our ordinary uses of words, it seems that we shall in the end always be compelled to straighten them out to some extent.'[8]

This general point may be especially relevant when we are dealing with a notion like indoctrination. Whereas its occasional running mate *conditioning* is, in the relevant sense, derived from a technical expression with a classical and standard definition,[9] *indoctrination* is a word of an unspecialized vocabulary. It is not, however, one of the commonest or most concrete terms, although it is one which is widely fought with and over. All these are reasons why we ought in this case to be more than usually ready to recognize, if that is what we find, that the philosopher's task here does not end with mapping. The odd thing is that Wilson, having thus himself proclaimed mapping to be his aim, at once goes on to say that he is doing something which in fact cannot consist with the limitations determined by his chosen image. He writes:

> Suppose that we could teach four-year old children all their
> mathematical tables while they were asleep, or by hypnosis? Or
> suppose that a boy could master A-Level physics simply by
> having an electric charge passed through his brain-cells? Is
> this indoctrination or not? I want to make it very clear at this
> point that the answer here is logically arbitrary. We can say
> yes or no as we choose. (p. 26)

Wilson then proceeds to advocate that we should say 'No'. It will be clear from what I have said already that the answer is not, in Wilson's sense, 'logically arbitrary', and that it has to be unequivocally 'No'. (But see also IV below.) The further point still to be made is that, if and in so far as normative advocacy is required, the proceedings cannot be embraced under the expression *logical mapwork*.

## B. Paradigm cases

The next occasion for comment is Wilson's initial list of standard examples.

> The model cases of indoctrination are obvious: brainwashing people to believe in Communism, teaching Christianity by the threat of torture or damnation, forcing people by early training to accept social roles as in Huxley's *Brave New World*.
> (p. 26)

The first of these three is, as a standard example, unexceptionable. But notice Wilson's later reproach to 'educationalists in our society' who 'enjoy themselves in letting off steam about the colour bar and race prejudice, though these are not forms of indoctrination which we normally practice in England' (p. 39.) We take this occasion to recall Dr William Sargant's well-known study of 'the mechanics of indoctrination, brain-washing, and thought-control'.[10] For there is throughout that book a salutary insistence on the analogies between political and religious instances: 'some of the most obvious similarities are often ignored because either the religious . . . or the political . . . is accorded official respect at the other's expense.'[11] It is also just worth remarking that the colour bar, as opposed to some justificatory theory, is not even a possible subject, much less a form of, indoctrination.

Wilson's third example seems rather less central. For the ideology of *Brave New World* is, in fact, remarkably thin. Hypnopaedia is used to drum in, by endless reiteration:

> Alpha children wear grey. They work much harder than we do, because they're so frightfully clever. I'm really awfully glad I'm a Beta, because I don't work so hard. And then we are much better than the Gammas and Delta. Gammas are stupid. They all wear green, and Delta children wear khaki . . .[12]

Extreme ideological poverty would seem to make this case at best peripheral. It is surely significant that Huxley himself talks not of indoctrination but of conditioning. Consider the boast of the Director of the 'Neo-Pavlovian Conditioning Rooms' after the nightmare demonstration on the crawling babies:

> They'll grow up with what the psychologists used to call an 'instinctive' hatred of books and flowers. Reflexes unalterably

conditioned. They'll be safe from books and botany all their lives.[13]

This particular employment of conditioning would, of course, have been wholly deplorable. But we must not allow the thought of it so to upset us that we confuse what are really two different ideas. A wholehearted and systematic programme of indoctrination and man-shaping would very likely involve a certain amount of conditioning. Professor R. S. Peters gives reasons for thinking that very little could be instilled by conditioning in a strict sense. No doubt as regards true and false beliefs this is correct. But a person aiming to mould a man to a predetermined way of life will be concerned not only with beliefs but also with Peters' own admitted exceptions, 'certain positive and negative reactions'.[14] This is where conditioning may come in.

Such man-shaping by conditioning may or may not be good or bad. But it is certainly not always and necessarily a means of indoctrination. It might, for instance, be an excellent thing to implant in our children both an aversion against the dirty and dangerous practice of smoking and a strong inclination to perform, on appropriate occasions, what Huxley called Malthusian drill: we should certainly have a deal less bronchitis and lung cancer and far fewer unplanned pregnancies if we could and did. But, be that as it may, such shaping could scarcely be said to constitute indoctrination, except, perhaps, in so far as it was integrated with, and was an expression of, an ideology. The same applies, as we hinted earlier, to 'the colour bar and race prejudice'; if what is implanted is simply dislike for people of alien pigmentations and a desire to stick to the company of those of your own, then this, deplorable though it would be, could not count as indoctrination; the question of indoctrination arises only when someone is taught to believe a lot of endorsing nonsense about racial superiority. With appropriate alterations the same applies in the case of the inclination, or the aversion, to contraception.

This brings us, very smoothly, to Wilson's second case: 'teaching Christianity by the threat of torture or damnation'. The reference is both perfunctory and confused. Here, and later, Wilson seems disinclined to apply his ideas specifically and concretely to the teaching of religion. He too should take to heart his own rebuke to educationalists letting off steam against only the locally unfashionable forms of indoctrination. His special interest is, apparently and fashionably, sex. The paragraph which begins with that rebuke ends by remarking how deplorable it is 'if children are taught to regard sex as something to feel guilty about' (p. 39). He considers that our sort of society is, distinctively, 'guilt-ridden in matters of sex and sensual enjoyment generally', an insight which is supposed to be a mark of the 'sociologically aware' (p. 40). Others might allow themselves to give weight to such merely quantitative evidence as that of illegitimacy rates rising, or at best not declining, despite the ready accessibility of (some kinds of) contraceptives. Such people might think that what is now needed most is not so much less guilt in these intrinsically gorgeous enjoyments, but, rather, more prudence, more responsibility, and more concern about possible human consequences.[15] However, this unsophisticated response no doubt fails to take proper account of the not so crudely detectable ongoings of the unconscious mind: 'more or less people may, at least consciously, side with D. H. Lawrence; but sex remains a matter of guilt' (p. 45).

Wilson seems here to have followed the bad example of MacIntyre, by lapsing into a sociological jeremiad to which all quantitative evidence and all possible proposals for reform are taken to be, or are subtly made, irrelevant. I have not now anything further to add to Hare's firm but kindly mockery of such unimproving indulgence (pp. 55–6). But if we are prepared to consider figures, and if we do want to attend to whatever sorts of indoctrination are most common in Britain today, then it is very hard to find any serious rival to the religious for the first place. Certainly if we are to apply either Wilson's criterion of evidential inadequacy or Hare's criterion of the teacher's response to adult rejection, or some combination of the two, then the teaching of religion must obviously be at least a strong frontrunner.

For the distinctively religious doctrines which are supposed to be taught as elements in religious knowledge are, if not false, at least not by any ordinary standards known to be true. It should indeed seem not just unwarranted but also inconsistent to push such doctrines as knowledge when you yourself propose to characterize the belief that they are true as faith. (A good example this, incidentally, of the way in which a philosophical issue—in this case one in the philosophy of religion—may have some bearing on questions of educational procedure.) Now one may perhaps discount as in practice frequently half-hearted and generally ineffective the Religious Instruction (R.I.) which is under the 1944 Act, presently provided in the great majority of ordinary, wholly tax-financed British schools. But one cannot similarly wave away the activities of what is, in terms of the numbers of children involved, a large partly or wholly private sector.

This sector consists in all those schools which are, whether in a stronger or a weaker sense, denominational. The classification being employed here cuts across those usually found in political and administrative talk about schools, for it lumps together almost all the so-called Public Schools and the various sorts of Church Schools within the state system. From this standpoint Keele Church of England Primary and the Jesuits' Stoneyhurst are both equally denominational schools.[16] Of course we can, within the sector thus marked out, find not only some variety of denominations but also very great differences in the amounts of time and energy devoted to the implanting of doctrines, and in the methods adopted and the measures of success achieved. Nor must one assume, simply because some institution was originally a religious foundation, that those who now man and maintain it must in fact share the aims and priorities of the founders. It, is at least doubtful whether most of those who send their children to Public Schools, or those, like myself, who staunchly defend their right to do so, are as concerned for the godly upbringing of their children as were the men whose generosity is commemorated on special school occasions. Yet when all such qualifications have been made, there is still no getting away from the fact that what, on Wilson's criterion or Hare's or a blend of the two, must count as religious indoctrination is a major feature of the British educational scene. For doctrines which are, surely at least, not known to be true are regularly being taught as if they were, in institutions whose present main aim is to produce unshakeable convictions of the truth of these doctrines. To focus on what is by many tests the most important case, none—least of all the Roman Catholic authorities themselves—would claim that their Church would continue to make the efforts which it does to maintain and to extend its school system in the extremely unlikely event that it ceased to be effective in producing Roman Catholics.

Having thus located the most formidable hornet's nest, we proceed to give it a stir. Wilson spares us the familiar general boast often (though, I am told, incorrectly) attributed to St Ignatius, and gives as his religious standard example the more particular 'teaching Christianity by the threat of torture or damnation'. This is a bad case of inadequate and confused specification. The expression 'the threat of torture' is presumably to be construed as referring to those this-worldly means of securing religious conformity which were, in less constricting times, employed by the Inquisition: an institution which it is nowadays thought to be bad form to mention; just as, and perhaps also for the same reasons as, it is apparently bad form to make pointed and possibly salutary comparisons between the different degrees of religious liberty conceded by the governments of Spain and Poland. But talk about damnation cannot be treated as if it were simply an eschatological substitute for such temporal torments.

Two differences are relevant. First, claims about damnation are part of, and not external to, the content of Christianity: precisely this, or perhaps its cause, is what salvation is to save you from. Hence strictly speaking, no one can be coerced by this threat unless he already believes some of the required doctrine. Second, damnation is not something which can be inflicted by one man upon another: it is God who damns, or, perhaps more nicely, God who initiates and sustains the arrangements under which a man can bring about his own damnation. Consequently, spokesmen for the Roman Church are able to think of themselves not as people threatening nonconformists with an eternity of anguish but, rather, as prophets giving warning of a danger altogether outside their own control. The detachment cannot, nevertheless, be complete. For the system also insists that its God is infinitely good, and it therefore requires the adherent to endorse as perfectly splendid whatever cosmic arrangements that God may choose to make.[17]

The upshot is that Wilson, in his account of what he offers as a model case of religious indoctrination, has mixed up both threats of torture in this world, with warnings against the danger of damnation in the next, and the employment of inadmissible means to secure agreement, with the teaching of what is, in some form, a fundamental Christian doctrine. The result is that Wilson contrives both to make it sound as if religious indoctrination was very much a thing of the past and to suggest that a kind of doctrine which is both logically and psychologically important to Christianity is really old hat.[18] Wilson thus fails to do justice to either the actual extent of the phenomenon or the nature of the claims of those who support it. (I concentrate here and elsewhere on the Roman Church as locally the most important from the present standpoint. But, of course, the same or similar doctrines are also taught by some Protestant groups and by some other religions, such as Islam.)

## C. Incorrectly assumed consensus

Both faults reappear in his persistent assumption of a consensus which does not in fact obtain (pp. 26 ff.)—an assumption which somehow develops into the idea of a desperate struggle of an elite of educators fighting to bring light into the surrounding darkness (pp. 42–6). This assumption, *and* this transition, are mediated by confusion in the reference of the term *we*. There are two cases which it is most important to distinguish: in the first case it refers to the users of English whose usage may be taken as determining the concept of indoctrination; in the second case to those, of whom I am one, who in general share Wilson's liberal ideas and ideals. The membership of the two classes is not the same. By failing adequately to distinguish the two sorts of reference Wilson is misled to think that logical geography is able to do more than it can. There is a general and happy regularity in the usages, and hence the uses, of the different words in a language: there must be or we could not call it one language. But there is not necessarily and always anything like the same fortunate degree of unanimity in the acceptance of ideal practical norms among those who share the same language or who, having different languages, share the same concepts. The logical geographer must, therefore, exercise especial care in dealing with those concepts which may contain built-in the notion of approval or disapproval.[19]

*Indoctrination* is certainly one. Wilson and Hare both take it that disapproval is built-in, that indoctrination must, as such, be a bad thing. I am inclined to think that this is now the dominant use, and myself to follow it, although it was not always, and is not everywhere now. (It could in Milton's prose works be a good thing, and the United States Army presumably approves of what it itself describes as its indoctrination courses.) However, in so far as indoctrination is to be taken as essentially bad, normative disagreements involving this notion are likely to appear as disagreements about the instances to which it may properly be applied. People will agree about the connotation but dispute over the denotation. The typical challenge is then to ask why it is supposed to be indoctrination when they do it, but not, apparently, when you do it. The typical response is to urge that the discrimination is not, after all, arbitrary or unfair. There really is some relevant difference between the two instances —some difference, that is, other than the morally irrelevant one that in the one case it is their lot and in the other case it is yours or, perhaps, ours! It is, as Hare has recently been insisting so powerfully, this which constitutes the fundamental dialectic of moral argument.[20]

If you take indoctrination to be necessarily bad, and if, with Wilson, you take it to consist in teaching as known the sort of thing which really is not or cannot be known, then you should expect any conflicts to appear as disagreements about what, or what sort of is or is not known. So we—here the editorial we—are not surprised to find that it is precisely such conflicts as this which Wilson is concerned curiously to minimize. The argument runs:

> Religious, political and moral beliefs are *uncertain* in a sense in
> which mathematics and Latin grammar are not uncertain . . .
> Many people regard their religious and moral beliefs as
> quite certain . . . But faced with the fact that, however strongly
> convinced people are about these beliefs, nevertheless different

people believe different things, we are prepared—with some reluctance—to place them in a special category. (p. 27)

This agreement, which Wilson calls 'the truce', is broken before it is made. For even between the same covers the Archbishop states: 'The first function of Christian education, then, is to impart a knowledge of God and of God's revelation . . . ' (p. 125 *n*). This is, of course, not an innocuous claim to teach as religious knowledge uncontentious facts about what people have believed and practised as their religions; it is the breathtaking assertion that the basic beliefs of Christianity, and of Roman Catholicism in particular, do constitute, without qualification, knowledge. Compare, classically, Cardinal Newman's discourse on 'Theology as a Branch of Knowledge', in which he concludes, baldly:

> Religious doctrine is knowledge, in as full a sense as Newton's doctrine is knowledge. University teaching without theology is simply unphilosophical. Theology has at least as good a right to claim a place there as astronomy.[21]

I certainly do not wish to dispute Wilson's tacit assumption that these claims are false. Indeed I have elsewhere deployed argument to show that this is so. The point here is that contentions which have been and still are widely, persistently, and respectably urged cannot simply be brushed aside as intellectually negligible. For a philosopher of education to do this is as reprehensible as it is unrealistic to ignore that in Britain they also have formidable institutional expression, with substantial state support. (In other countries, of course, other doctrines: within 'the socialist bloc'—the Clause Four countries—the corresponding, equally untenable, claim is that Marxism-Leninism is a science; and elsewhere again it is the Koran which embodies the supposedly revealed truth.)

### D. *Two misconceptions*

Two other occasions for comment in Wilson's paper can, and must, be treated briefly. One of these is not perhaps directly relevant. But the misconceptions are too popular to pass altogether unremarked. Wilson states: 'The human situation is tragic, and original sin an incontrovertible fact, in the sense that at a very early age the infant child has met with immense difficulties in facing reality . . . ' (p. 36). Reinterpretations on these or similar secular lines may be all very well so long as everyone realizes how very far indeed they are from the prior and technical sense of *original sin*: 'the result of a sin committed, in actual historical fact, by an individual man named

79

Adam . . . a quality native to all of us only because it has been handed down by descent from him.'[22]

It is, naturally, in this sense that the Archbishop would have us endorse 'the statement made in a leading article in *The Times Literary Supplement*-that the fact that man so often sees and approves the better but follows the worse can be explained only by the fact of Original Sin' (p. 123). Yet on this reading the thesis that original sin is the only plausible contender is plainly preposterous. If, on the other hand, *original sin* is to be construed either in Wilson's sense or, more straightforwardly, as involving only the uncontentious idea that we are all of us often or always more inclined to do what we should not than what we should, then this fact of original sin cannot be an explanation; it is itself the fact to be explained.

The second of the two remaining points is more relevant, although probably less interesting. Wilson says, very sensibly: 'if a child kicks up a row when there are adults in the room who want a quiet conversation, it is plainly right to shut him up—if necessary by force' (p. 36). But the reason given is:

> To allow the child to go on making a row under such circumstances is just as much indoctrination as to stop it making a noise in its own play-room, because it presents the child with a false picture—a picture of lunatic adults who are willing to stop talking just because some kid is screaming . . . (p. 36).

This will not do: first, for the obvious but disagreeably slick reason that if the adults are in fact willing to be thus child-dominated then the picture is not false at all; second, for the deeper reason that, as we have been urging all along, indoctrination requires doctrine. Simply to stop a child from making a row, whether in our drawing-room or in his play-room, has nothing to do with it, though questions about indoctrination might well arise if we proceeded to offer reasons. (The reasons might perhaps be 'God likes little children to be seen and not heard' or 'Modern psychology has shown that inhibition is always harmful'.)

This is something which Wilson said himself on the previous page: 'In the interests of philosophical clarity we ought, perhaps, to remember that, strictly speaking, the mere process of getting someone to *do* something is not indoctrination' (p. 35). Unfortunately he gets carried away by a notion of 'the proper function of education—for the educator to act as an intermediary between the child and reality, clarifying and interpreting' (p. 35). At this level of abstraction philosophical clarity goes by the board.

## III Difficulties in Hare's view

### A. *Alleged refutation of Wilson*

The first point I want to make on Hare's contribution concerns his
argument against Wilson. Hare radically repudiates Wilson's whole
project of developing an analysis in terms of 'the content—what is
taught' (p. 48). He gives us a shot of realism by quoting the Archbishop, commenting:

> These Roman Catholics . . . will no doubt all think that they are
> sane and sensible, and that they are in touch with reality
> (perhaps they will add, 'natural and supernatural reality').
> So when these children have been duly indoctrinated and
> turned into good Roman Catholics, the parents will claim not
> to have offended against Mr Wilson's canon . . .
>    If we distinguish indoctrination from education in terms of
> their content, we are bound to reach this impasse (p. 49).

It is difficult to discover what on earth makes Hare think that
these considerations constitute a refutation. For it must surely be
perfectly obvious that the mere fact that some group denies a charge
cannot be, by itself, sufficient to show that that charge is false. Are
we supposed to assume that any suggested analysis has to be ruled
out unless, besides squaring with the connotation of the term, it also
has the power to generate instant agreement about the denotation?
On the contrary, where, as with *indoctrination*, one is dealing with a
word which has a use in ideological controversy, and which is taken
to have a dyslogistic meaning built in, then precisely what we ought
to expect is that, in so far as the connotation is agreed, the denotation
will be disputed. If we are going to call the possibility of such further
disputes an impasse, then every proposed analysis of any such term
is likely to end in a similar impasse. The true moral to draw from
this case of the recalcitrant Catholics is not that Wilson's criterion of
evidence and truth of content must be irreparably wrong, but that
there are bound to be conflicts over its application. This is what we
ourselves were indicating earlier, in a slightly different context,
when we protested at Wilson's complacent dismissal of claims to know
what he (and I) believe not to be known (II, C).

### B. *Ideological indoctrination and moral education*

Immediately after the last sentence quoted above, Hare continues:
'to make the distinction in this way is to say that there is a *right*
content—a *right* doctrine—and furthermore, that the teacher is the

man who knows what it is' (p. 49). Considered as objections to Wilson's proposed analysis of indoctrination these are very curious things to say. For one thing, it is clearly unsound to infer that because there is a right doctrine, someone must know what it is. Perhaps it does seem as if the Archbishop is at one point inclined to argue in this way (pp. 124–5 *n*). But Wilson's strong emphasis on sufficient and publicly admissible evidence surely indicates that this is not one of his temptations.

Again, unless we are supposed to be accepting some extreme positivist claim about the literal nonsensicality of all ideology, there is nothing to wring the withers about an alleged implication of there being a right doctrine. Even on such an extreme positivist view— which there is no decisive reason to think that Hare holds—all the meta-doctrines, which assert that the various competing systems constitute true theories, must be false; and that this is so must be the right meta-meta-doctrine.

The true story seems to be that Hare has here already forgotten the contentions about ' "natural and supernatural" reality' mentioned only two or three sentences previously. What he is apparently now thinking of is, perhaps exclusively, moral norms; and to these, at least on his view, the notions of truth and falsity in their primary senses may very well not apply.[23] The same concentration on morality, and on the teaching of moral thinking, marks Hare's whole paper. For the attempt to analyse the concept of indoctrination this is in one way unfortunate. The sort of belief system which constitutes the content of indoctrination typically carries, or is thought to carry, normative implications. Yet any norms as such are precisely not claims about what *is* but about what *ought* to be the case. Norms, therefore, provide a possible content for indoctrination only to the extent that they are, wrongly, thought to be and presented as a kind of fact.

What Hare most wants to show is how morality and moral thinking may be taught without indoctrination; and this must involve eschewing the presentation of norms as if they were not norms but some special kind of fact. This is an extremely important enterprise, especially in a country where it seems to be part of 'the conventional wisdom' to take it for granted that morality somehow presupposes religion. It is also an enterprise which has an indirect bearing on our present concerns. For if it can be clearly and distinctly shown that moral education need not involve indoctrination, then one of the main reasons for insisting that indoctrination in some form is unavoidable will be removed; and hence one of the main reasons against insisting that indoctrination must be, as such, bad.[24] Devotion to this enterprise nevertheless does distract and distort

Hare's analytic vision. To be engaged in showing, in one particular case, that and how something is dispensable is not the most direct way of explicating what, in general, that something is.

## C. *Inescapable ideological conflict*

We have already noticed how Hare's supposed refutation of Wilson apparently mistakes it that an adequate analytic criterion of indoctrination, notwithstanding that the word is to be read as dyslogistic, must both express the accepted connotation and at the same time produce consensus on the denotation. Such marvellous power is not, of course, possessed by either Hare's account of morality and moral thinking or his present application of this to the questions of moral education: and yet this is no reason at all for thinking that they are wrong.

Let us quote the Archbishop again: 'Only when we know what man *is* can we say what he *should* strive for, what sort of society he *should* live in, what institutions *should* serve him' (p. 109: italics supplied). There is, apparently, only one other option besides that favoured by the neo-Thomist:[25]

> Is man a glorified animal, expendable in the service of others, or in the service of the State; a part only of the whole, and subject to the whole? . . . Or is man a person with a rational spiritual nature, destined for immortality . . . an end in himself with an eternal destiny? (pp. 109–10).

In this second and approved case, 'Man is not self-caused or self-sufficient. He is expected to live his life under the Maker's instructions' (p. 115). These instructions, one might not unfairly add, seem to have been communicated most legibly, sometimes even exclusively, to the Archbishop's own organization.

The quotations given bring out, what Hare knows perfectly well, that Roman Catholics seem to be, as such, committed to the view that true norms express the Maker's instructions; and the comment should remind us that the contents of some of these proposed norms are most unlikely to commend themselves to the secular moralist. The point of these reminders is to underline that ideological conflict is here inescapable. Confronted by the teaching of morality as conceived by the Archbishop, Hare would surely, as he hints (pp. 48–9), want to condemn it as indoctrination. Equally obviously this condemnation could scarcely be acceptable to the Archbishop. So if the inevitability of such ideological confrontations is to be called an impasse and is to be considered to constitute a decisive disqualification of Wilson's suggested criterion of indoctrination, then, by parity

G

of reasoning, the same must presumably apply to Hare's account of morality and moral reasoning, to Hare's programme for moral education, and to Hare's own proposed criterion of indoctrination too.

If the Wilson criterion is accepted, then the ideological conflicts will, as we have seen (II, C), tend to present themselves as disagreements about what is and is not known. But if instead it is urged that the criterion should be the educational aim, then this is still no charm to make fundamental disagreements disappear miraculously. They will simply emerge in slightly different forms. It will be contended that Hare's educational ideals are unacceptable, or that indoctrination is not, after all, always deplorable, or, most probably, both. Thus it may be suggested that the true aim is to produce not just educated people but educated Catholics; and in so far as this involves indoctrination, then perhaps there need be no objection to that.

Hare's refusal to allow as relevant here any distinctions between the different epistemological status of various sorts of proposition leaves his position wide open to a very effective counterattack from 'These Roman Catholics . . . ' (p. 49). Anyone who finds it hard—as many of us will—to accept the suggestion that the ideal teacher must 'be pleased' if one day he finds that his former pupil has become 'a man who may disagree with *everything* he has ever said' (p. 70; italics mine), must become to that extent more prepared to accept that, in so far as every departure from this ideal involves indoctrination, then indoctrination really cannot always be a bad thing. Consider the argument:[26]

> Every educational institution makes use of indoctrination. Children are indoctrinated with the multiplication table; they are indoctrinated with love of country; they are indoctrinated with the principles of chemistry and physics and mathematics and biology, and nobody finds fault with indoctrination in these fields. Yet these are of small concern in the great business of life by contrast with ideas concerning God and man's relation to God . . . The Catholic educator makes no apology for indoctrinating his students in these essential matters.

No doubt if the point were put to him, Hare would insist that he did not himself italicize *everything*, and that, of course, he did not intend the word to be construed quite so strictly. But such a defence is no help in the present case. For if *everything* is not to be taken as meaning, literally, everything, then there has to be some criterion for determining what is and what is not to be included. And now it becomes extremely difficult to discern what this is to be if it is not to involve any Wilsonian reference to the content of, or to the available reasons for believing, the propositions originally taught.

## IV Secondary and primary senses of 'indoctrination'

In section I we said that we were going to urge that an adequate analysis of the concept of indoctrination would have somehow to do justice to two points: that indoctrination must presuppose the aim of implanting beliefs, and that the beliefs to be thus implanted must be of a certain sort. I have tried to develop and to support these contentions, although I have not been able to offer any satisfactory specification of the sort of belief which has to be involved. In the cases where the word is employed to carry unfavourable overtones it is probably right to list a third element in its meaning: that the doctrines to be implanted, as if they were matters of known fact, must be either false or at least not known to be true.

### A. Indoctrination: unacceptable means or manners of teaching

At this point it might be objected that some people do sometimes speak of indoctrination, meaning something unfavourable, where what is being put across is not sufficiently ideological to be unselfconsciously labelled as a doctrine, and even when the content is actually known to be true. The idea then is, presumably, that what is wrong with this teaching is neither its content nor its aim, but that propositions are being instilled by improper methods or in some inept manner. Indoctrination is thus to be contrasted here not so much with leaving them alone as with teaching them by the right means or in the correct way. Perhaps, it might be urged, we were too hasty in insisting that—always supposing that this were to be practically possible—it would be all right to 'teach four-year old children all their mathematical tables while they were asleep, or by hypnosis' or to enable a boy to 'master A-level physics simply by having an electric charge passed through his brain-cells' (Wilson, p. 26; quoted and discussed in II, A above). Really, these means, if they were to become available, would constitute indoctrination, and as such they would be educationally inadmissible.

Certainly we may have been too hasty simply to insist—always granting Wilson's suppositions—that these means would not be necessarily improper. But the reason is not that this conclusion would be unwarranted on these suppositions, but that there is something more which needs to be said about the suppositions themselves. Wilson was apparently supposing—and we followed him in this— that the new methods would produce not just a parrot capacity to regurgitate propositions learnt by heart, but an understanding know-ledge. He asks us to 'suppose that a boy could *master* A-level physics simply by having an electric charge passed through his brain-cells' (italics mine).[27] There is no doubt that this is a difficult supposition: one is inclined to say that it must be impossible to bring about this sort of result in this sort of way. Maybe it is. But, if so, the question is what kind of impossibility is involved. It is only if it is conceptual that the supposition becomes illegitimate.[28]

The answer is that the difficulty, or the impossibility, is, in fact, practical rather than theoretical. For the criteria of understanding refer to the present and to the future, not to the past. What settles questions about whether people do or do not know and understand is what they can or could do or say *now;* and not at all how they have got themselves, or been got, into the position of being now able or unable to say or to do the appropriate things on the appropriate present occasions.[29] So it seems that we cannot rule out suppositions, such as that made by Wilson, on the grounds that if—per impossible —it had been produced in this unorthodox way, it could not con-ceivably be genuine knowledge and true understanding. On the other hand it is as well to emphasize, as being of enormous practical importance, the contingent fact that many—perhaps most—of the most admirable educational ends cannot be produced by a con-strictive, authoritarian, and nonrational pedagogy. It is sufficient here just to remind ourselves, for instance, of the classical censures upon 'a cloistered virtue' in Milton's *Areopagitica* and of modern emphases that both morality and science are essentially self-critical and antiauthoritarian.[30] Although it may be logically essential that moral and scientific thinkers should possess these character-istics, it is not by the same token necessarily essential that the appropriate dispositions should have been acquired in some approved manner.

## B. *Indoctrination: implanting false or dubious doctrines*

From the standpoint of our present concern with the analysis of the concept, or concepts, of indoctrination, the moral would appear to be that if, and in so far, as people wish to apply the term to certain means or manners of teaching, then their usage should be regarded as involving a secondary sense. In the primary sense, we have sug-gested, indoctrination, where it is taken to be a bad thing, is a matter of trying to implant firm convictions of the truth of doctrines which are in fact either false or at least not known to be true; usually, of course, though not necessarily, the indoctrinator himself believes mis-takenly that the doctrines in question are both true and known to be true. In the secondary sense indoctrination would be a matter of trying, in any sphere whatever, to implant beliefs, even those which are true and known to be true, by certain disfavoured methods. And the general objection to indoctrination in this sense would presumably be that such methods are in some way incompatible with the production of a proper understanding of what is taught and of a critical appreciation of its logical and epistemological status.

The link between the two concepts might then be provided by this last complex idea. The development of the second notion, and a corresponding emphasis upon the differences in the logical and epistemological status of the different sorts of things which are taught, is likely to have an especial professional appeal to philosophers. For one of the main concerns of philosophy is the examination of precisely this sort of question about various kinds of proposition and the sorting out of the often unhappy and confused diplomatic relations between disciplines.

## V The limits of pure logical geography

But though the development of such a secondary concept of indoctrination would surely be educationally worth while, as well as congenial to the professional interests of philosophers, my own final suggestion is that there may not be all that much more logical geography to be done in this area. It is one thing to describe an existing concept as determined by present usage; it is another to develop a new, albeit related, notion demanding its own corresponding usage. A consideration of the usual contexts and manner of employment of the term *indoctrination* would scarcely lead us to conclude that what we have already in our hands is either a very sharp or a very complex intellectual tool. Indeed it may well be that in developing our own preliminary sketch for an account of what we have called the primary concept we have in fact already crossed unwittingly the here very elusive line between description and prescription. We may thereby have provided a notion rather more precise than that determined by present standards of correct usage for the term *indoctrination*.[31]

Be that as it may, what certainly would be wrong would be any idea that a sound logical geography must possess the power to dispel ideological conflicts. Such differences are not always and necessarily, either in practice or in principle, intractable. But they are there; and the philosophy of education has got to recognize and to come to terms with this fact. It is indeed precisely because we are not all agreed, precisely because there are such fundamental and such vital differences about how and what and with what aims we should

87

teach our children, that our educational theorists are so apt to produce for us the vacuous or ambiguous formulae of pseudo reconciliation: what Professor Stephen Wiseman robustly dismisses as 'too much pap and not enough roughage' (p. viii). For these are differences which, sometimes for good and respectable reasons, many of us wish to minimize. But in philosophy, where the aim is clarity, this will not do.

## Notes

1 T. H. B. Hollins, ed., *Aims in Education: The Philosophic Approach*, Manchester University Press, 1964. Each quotation from this book will be followed by the number of the page where it appears. Italics not in original will be so noted.
2 My Keele colleague, Mr Alan Iliffe, who, thanks to the generosity of the Nuffield Foundation, was enabled to do a thorough study of the workings of our Foundation Year was, I believe, the first person to be appointed by a British university to engage in full-time research into university teaching. Fortunately this belated good example is now being followed elsewhere in Britain.
3 Compare Israel Scheffler, *The Language of Education*, Springfield, Illinois: Thomas, 1960, Chapter IV.
4 For the contrasts and connections between knowing *how* and knowing *that*, see Gilbert Ryle, *The Concept of Mind*, London: Hutchinson, 1949, and New York: Barnes & Noble, 1949, Chapter II.
5 Reuter report, quoted in the *Bookseller* 5/xii/64. I owe this reference to the Librarian of the University of Keele.
6 See, for instance, A. D. White, *A History of the Warfare of Science with Theology*, New York, Dover: 1960, Chapter XVII.
7 See Gilbert Ryle, *op. cit.*, Introduction: and the first *Inquiry*, Section I, Compare my *Hume's Philosophy of Belief*, London: Routledge & Kegan Paul, 1961, Chapter I.
8 J. L. Austin, *Philosophical Papers*, Oxford University Press, 1961, p. 181.
9 I. P. Pavlov, *Conditioned Reflexes*, New York: Dover, 1960, Chapter II.
10 William Sargant, *Battle for the Mind*, Rev. paperback edition; London: Pan Books, 1959.
11 *Ibid.*, p. 128; compare p. 142 and passim.
12 Aldous Huxley, *Brave New World*, London: Chatto & Windus, 1952, p. 34.
13 *Ibid.*, pp. 28, 30.
14 In a paper to appear in a volume of essays in the philosophy of education, edited by Peters himself.
[*The Concept of Education*, London: Routledge & Kegan Paul, 1967, p. 13—ed.]
15 See, for instance, the articles on 'Illegitimacy, Family Planning, and the L.C.C.' and less certainly reliable, 'Sex at School' in *Family Planning*, vol. xiii, No. 4 (January 1965).

16 Obviously I am not here employing the criterion by which all
children given a Roman Catholic baptism become, by that very fact,
Roman Catholics. To use this criterion may be theologically correct,
or polemically convenient, or both, but it is not educationally
realistic. There were in January 1960, 683,528 children on the registers
of Roman Catholic schools in England and Wales. See table
on pp. 166–7 of *Catholic Education* 1960–61, published by the Catholic
Education Council for England and Wales.

This is also as good an occasion as any to remark that that
reluctance of educational thinkers to recognize paradigms of
indoctrination in their own backyards—a reluctance which, as we
have seen, Wilson himself both displays and rebukes—is not confined to one side of the Atlantic. John Dewey even goes so far as to
offer a definition of indoctrination by which it becomes logically
improper to speak of such a thing in a religious context: 'I shall take
indoctrination to mean the systematic use of every possible means
to impress upon the minds of pupils a particular set of political
and economic views to the exclusion of every other.' *Education Today*,
New York: Putnam, 1940, p. 356. No doubt this definition should be
seen in its context of a prime concern with and for the American
Public School system; and of a period when there was no question
of pumping tax money into parochial schools outside that system.
Yet it is nevertheless remarkable that Dewey should have had
nothing to say anywhere in that book about the significant
proportion of all American children whose parents withdrew them
from the public system in order to have impressed upon their
minds one particular set of religious views to the exclusion of every
other.

17 So that those who, taking the traditionally literalistic view of some of
these supposed cosmic arrangements went on to give their support
to cruel punishments and judicial torture on the grounds that God
himself punishes with eternal torment were not necessarily being
untrue to their religion: their chosen ideal of goodness was, on their
own account, albeit perhaps at one remove, the Supreme Torturer.
On the other hand, since damnation is thought of as in this way
God's own work, it was entirely possible for men, who might in a
purely human context have been humane, to feel themselves required to use every available means—torture included—to save whom
they could from unspeakable eternal catastrophe. See for instance,
A. D. White, *op. cit.*, Chapter XI (iii), especially pp. 361 ff.
Compare W. E. H. Lecky, *History of Rationalism in Europe*, New
Edition; London: Longmans Green, 1890, Chapter IV, passim, but
especially Vol. i, pp. 311 ff.

18 For an authoritative statement of what the Roman doctrine actually
is see, for instance, G. D. Smith (ed.), *The Teaching of the Catholic
Church*, London: Burns & Oates, with Imprimatur, Second Edition,
1952, Chapter XXXIII. This chapter, by Dr J. P. Arendzen,
was originally published separately as *The Treasury of the Faith*:

No. 33, *Eternal Punishment* (London: Burns & Oates, and again with Imprimatur, 1928). It is important not to be misled by the remarkable fact that there are nowadays some who, while generously unable to relish this particular treasure or to worship a God thus characterized, nevertheless wish to continue to be Roman Catholics. See, for a most striking instance, Mrs Magdalen Goffin, in M. de la Bedoyere (ed.) *Objections to Roman Catholicism*, London: Constable, 1964.

19  See, for instance, M. B. Foster, 'We in Modern Philosophy', in *Faith and Logic*, ed. B. Mitchell, London: Allen & Unwin, 1957, and J. O. Urmson, 'Some Questions concerning Validity', in *Essays in Conceptual Analysis*, ed. A. Flew, London: Macmillan, 1956.

20  R. M. Hare, *Freedom and Reason*, Oxford University Press, 1963, Section 6.

21  *The Idea of a University*, G. N. Schuster, ed. New York: Image Books, Doubleday Company, 1959, p. 80. It would have given Hume the greatest pleasure had he been able to read Newman's description of the author of the first Inquiry as 'this acute, though most low-minded of speculators' (p. 78).

22  The quotation comes from the Catholic Truth Society translation of Pius XII's Encyclical *Humani Generis*. The original Latin will be found in H. Denzinger, *Encheiridion Symbolorum*, Herder: Freiberg in Breisgau, Twenty-ninth ed., 1946, § 3028: compare, for the Tridentine definitions, §§ 787–792. I make no apology for choosing to refer to such authoritative sources: notwithstanding that after I had given an earlier version of the present paper as a public lecture in the University of London I was accused by a practising Roman Catholic of misrepresenting the Roman Catholic position by so doing. This odd reaction provides another instance of the phenomenon, remarked in Note 18 above: the existence of people who are practising Roman Catholics despite the fact that they cannot stomach some of the doctrine.

23  See R. M. Hare, *op. cit.*, passim.

24  This does seem to be at least a main reason why, for instance, I. B. Berkson insists that education cannot but involve indoctrination. See his *The Ideal and the Community*, New York: Harper, 1958, pp. 253–64.

25  Both the only two options recognized by the Archbishop involve exactly that idea which Hare is most concerned to reject, the idea that norms have to be provided for us. Compare also MacIntyre who, though he has recently rejected the notion of God as the provider, seems still inclined to cast society, albeit not 'our society', as in this respect the understudy for God. MacIntyre writes: 'The failure of both our society and our education lies in its inability to discover ends, to discover purposes which can furnish a sufficient reason for our activities and so render these activities reasonable and satisfying' (pp. 1–2). This neo-paternalism reminds me, frivolously, of the story of the woman who went into an ironmonger's and said: 'I am looking

for a vice for my husband.' She was told: 'But surely, madam, he can manage that for himself?'

MacIntyre's conclusion is prefaced by the personal statement: 'Last year a student whom I knew well had a breakdown as a result of taking seriously the question, "What am I studying for?" The chain of reasons had no ending' (p. 1). This student's endless chain of questions was, presumably, merely symptomatic. For had the trouble been, as MacIntyre presents it, purely intellectual, then his philosophy tutor must have been grievously at fault in not insisting, with Hume, that: 'It is impossible . . . that one thing can always be a reason why another is desired. Something must be desirable on its own account, and because of its immediate accord or agreement with human sentiment and affection'. (See Appendix I of the second inquiry.) I may perhaps here refer to my 'Tolstoy and the Meaning of Life', in *Ethics*, Chicago, LXXIII, 2 (1963); a consideration of the logic of such symptomatic questions in the context of a similar personal breakdown.

26 W. I. McGucken, *The Catholic Way in Education*, Milwaukee: Bruce Publishing Company, 1937, p. 60 reprinted as Reading 292 in J. S. Brubacher (ed.), *Eclectic Philosophy of Education*, Englewood Cliffs: Prentice-Hall, 1951. Brubacher himself takes indoctrination as a not necessarily obnoxious method or manner of teaching, but then insists that it is questionable whether this is legitimate where what is taught is controversial. See his *Modern Philosophies of Education* 3rd ed.; New York: McGraw-Hill, 1962, pp. 204–7.

27 Wilson does not himself insist similarly on mastery in the case of the four-year olds to be taught 'all their mathematical tables while . . . asleep, or by hypnosis'. But the same distinction could be applied in this case. See, for instance, the Ginn & Co. advertisement printed in *The Times Educational Supplement* some years back: 'Real understanding of early number combinations up to 9 plus 9 and 18 minus 9 is what the Infant Teacher should aim at, contends Dr Fleming, author of *Beacon Number*. One Headmistress, who previously believed her pupils should be drilled in mechanical number operations, is now converted to Beacon Number, and delighted with their intelligent and systematic progress . . .'

28 It is interesting, in more than one way, to compare again Aldous Huxley. The Director of Hatcheries and Conditioning is explaining: 'These early experimenters were on the wrong track. They thought that hypnopaedia could be made an instrument of intellectual education'. But this was wrong. 'The experiments were abandoned. No further attempt was made to teach children the length of the Nile in their sleep. Quite rightly. You can't learn a science unless you know what it's all about. Whereas, if they'd started on moral education, which ought never, in any circumstances, to be rational . . .' (*op. cit.*, pp. 32–3).

29 The fact that the same applies in the special case of present knowledge of the meanings of words involves that great care is needed in

so formulating an Argument of the Paradigm Case that it can be employed without question-begging against a really radical philosophical scepticism.

30 See, for instance, R. S. Peters, *Authority, Responsibility and Education*, London: Allen & Unwin, 1963.

31 For suggestions of yet another view of the logico-geographical situation see 'Instruction and Indoctrination', by my colleague Mr R. F. Atkinson in *Philosophical Analysis and Education*, ed. R. D. Archambault, London: Routledge & Kegan Paul, 1965; New York: Humanities Press, 1965. [Paper 5 in this volume—ed.]. However, Atkinson's main concern, like Hare's, is with moral education and with the nature of morality. He tells me that when it comes to indoctrination as such his own view would not be all that different from mine.

# Indoctrination and democratic method    7

## Willis Moore

The topic of indoctrination, which Mr Flew says[1] is a novel subject
for British educators and philosophers,[2] is one with which Americans
are quite familiar. It has been a major item in the long standing
debate over public versus church related schools, with supporters of
the former charging the administrators of the latter with the bad
practice of indoctrinating their students with religious dogmas. In
the decades spanning World War II many Americans, impressed
with the seeming success of the European dictatorships in molding
the minds of their youth through the method of indoctrination,
boldly advocated that we likewise indoctrinate American youth with
the core ideas of democracy.[3] The opponents of indoctrination as a
method of teaching, in secular or church related schools, have been
those educators who adhere to the liberal philosophy associated with
the name of John Dewey. In the American debates over this issue
definitions of key terms, including that of indoctrination, have
emerged and, perhaps because of the pervading influence of the
ideas of Dewey, have gained general acceptance in our country.

'Indoctrination' came to be described as a one-sided or biased presentation of a debatable issue, a presentation designed to 'assure a
favorable outcome for a predetermined point of view.'[4] It was seen
as 'education by imposition' and through the use of propaganda
devices, including censorship, and as an integral working feature of
absolutistic and authoritarian systems.[5] These liberal educators
asserted that this mode of teaching rests upon the assumption that
only a few members of any society are capable of thinking for themselves, the rest being dependent upon the few for guidance.

To this authoritarianism Dewey and associates opposed the
systematic liberalism of Western democracy as inherited from
Milton, Locke, Paine, Jefferson, Mill, and others and proceeded to
outline the method of teaching they believed to be consistent with
this liberalism. Human beings, including students, are essentially
rational and thus potentially capable of making adequate decisions
for themselves. It is the function of the schools, the press, and other
teaching agencies to improve and implement this rational capacity
in youth, not to restrict or inhibit its growth. The development of
this latent capability requires a free learning situation, with all
relevant alternatives for dealing with issues being presented fairly,

93

objectively, and in the light of significant consequences. The role of the teacher in the schoolroom should not be that of a sovereign, a dictator, or a god but, rather, that of a fellow investigator working cooperatively with the student in search of the most workable solution of the problems before them. For this method of teaching they tended to reserve the term 'education'.

'Indoctrination' and 'education', so described and contrasted, were identified as the teaching methods naturally growing out of, and used by, authoritarianism and democracy respectively. In thus sharpening the contrast between these methods, liberal educators were frankly forging tools for sensitizing fellow Americans to the danger of using an authoritarian method even in a worthy cause. They argued that in the long run this method is ineffective; for ideas and attitudes thus inculcated, not having been fastened in terms of reasons, are easily dislodged and lost. Also, of course, persons allowed to practice an authoritarian method are likely to be contaminated by its use and to become increasingly authoritarian in other areas of operation. The means is constitutive with respect to the end; authoritarian methods tend to create authoritarian products; so they wanted no part of it.

Adherents of the philosophic method of language analysis, however laudable they might think the cause to have been, would be quite critical of the liberties the Americans seem to have taken with existing usage of 'indoctrination' and other key terms. The Americans involved were admittedly less convinced than are language analysts of the sacred character of existing language conventions, but they would defend their manipulation of meanings in this instance as merely making sharper and clearer meanings already evolving in these directions. 'Indoctrination' had long been so intimately associated with the practice of restrictive inculcation of religious beliefs that it had absorbed much of the connotative flavor of the authoritarian institution it served. 'Education', on the other hand, at least in America, had been increasingly linked with and influenced by the less restrictive public school situation in which a pluralistic society insists that all its ideological facets be fairly reflected.

The pragmatic philosophy, or instrumentalism, as Dewey called it, to which the American opponents of indoctrination adhered does not encourage, even discourages, reverence for any institutional form, including language usage. Where the proponents of language analysis are inclined to limit their efforts to the description of the logical geography of a word, treating their findings as revelatory and authoritative in philosophic debate, the associates and followers of Dewey are so concerned with the character of the referent situation that they tend to treat language as an adjustable tool properly subject to whatever re-fashioning might render it a better instrument for dealing with problems in a situation only more or less adequately reflected in language. So, if the terms 'indoctrination' and 'education' have been somewhat manhandled in the American debate, these liberal Americans would not be likely to worry over the violence done usage. Mr Flew seems to be approaching the pragmatic position in the closing paragraphs of his essay where he admits that he may 'have in fact already crossed unwittingly the here very elusive line between description and prescription.'[6]

The current argument among our British colleagues as to whether 'indoctrination' should be defined in terms of aim, content, or method, or some combination of these, could hardly occur in the context of contemporary American philosophy of education. For better or for worse, Dewey's type of outlook, and the accompanying derogatory definition of indoctrination, have so permeated American educational thinking that we automatically deal with this concept in terms of method only. This is a perfectly natural outcome of the political debate of the World War II period which had so much to do with shaping its meaning. Americans were not then divided on either the aim or the content of political education. Both sides wanted to inculcate democracy in American youth and to strengthen its adherence to the democratic way of life. They differed, rather, on how to do this, on method, with some advocating the indoctrinative tactics of the Nazi party while others, the liberals, insisted on the use of the free, objective procedures long identified with the public schools of America. So, in America 'indoctrination' has come to mean strictly a method of teaching.

Admittedly, and particularly from the Deweyan type of outlook, this American usage is no more sacred than any other and does not have to be followed by anyone else or retained by those who now adhere to it. There *is*, however, an argument for everyone adopting it. It serves to highlight and to focus attention upon a most significant difference in possible ways of structuring the educational situation. Since modes or techniques of teaching are a central concern of the profession of education key terms so defined as to call attention to real differences in the area have great instrumental value for philosophers of education. Moreover, since the two modes thus singled out for contrast may be shown to have evolved from and to reflect the nature of two sharply conflicting political philosophies, one of which British and Americans join in supporting and one of which they abhor, the current American usage would seem to have much in its favor.

Mr Flew favors a definition of 'indoctrination' in terms of content, an act whose aim is to implant a belief which is either false or dubious[7] but he does recognize a 'secondary sense' of the term as referring to the implanting of a belief 'by certain disfavored methods'.[8] This latter meaning is roughly the American usage I have been describing. He seems to have been most strongly attracted to the first definition because of the root meaning of the word 'indoctrination' as implanting a *doctrine*, that is, a belief of some sort[9] an obvious reference to content. A philosopher who emphasized the etymology of a term as against current or developing usage would decide as Mr Flew does, but even he is uneasy about this decision as is made evident by his half-hearted endorsement of the 'secondary sense' indicated above and by his admission that he hopes to do justice to the topic in some 'future full account'.[10]

Although I have long been a partisan of the liberal approach to educational matters associated with the name of John Dewey[11] and still believe the American usage, arrived at in the manner and for the purpose described, to be useful and justified in contemporary philosophy of education, I have never been able to accept the theory in its entirety. I therefore welcome the recent publication by the Manchester University Press of the little book *Aims in Education*[12] as affording us the opportunity, as it has Mr Flew, of re-examining the language and the structure of the teaching situation.

In associating 'indoctrination' with authoritarian political philosophy and practice, particularly as these were exemplified in the Nazi regime of Germany, American liberals so stigmatized the term that none of them was willing to admit that this method of teaching has any legitimate use whatever. Since reflection shows us that even in our democratic society the inculcation of reaction and value patterns does and must begin before the child is old enough to be motivated by reason, the liberals had to ignore such teaching, define it away, or try to abolish it in practice. Some such teaching was written off as mere conditioning. The early learning of morals, for example, was explained as unconscious social osmosis, something not properly an object of our concern. The more extreme liberals, as 'progressive' educators, took the bull by the horns by advocating a nearly total permissiveness in the earliest learning situations, thus eliminating indoctrination in teaching by doing away with teaching.

It has always seemed clear to me that complete permissiveness on the part of the adult with respect to the pre-rational child is both impossible and unwise. The child naturally models his behavior and, within limits, his consequent value reactions on that of others, chiefly of adults. Only by isolating him from other persons, especially from adults, could we keep him from learning in this way. These observed patterns in others, even where no intentional teaching is done, are 'authoritative' for the child; and he is being 'indoctrin-ated' in terms of what he imitates where no reasons are furnished him for doing so. I see no reason for ignoring or trying to prevent the occurrence of this kind of learning or for giving it such a name as conditioning or absorption by social osmosis in order to separate it sharply from education of conscious and intentional sorts.

I should further contend that this natural imitative process is valuable, even essential, as giving the child a head start in living in terms of behavior patterns presumably tested and adopted by more mature persons. If a child had to learn every behavior item for him-self through trial and error, he would be hopelessly bogged down from the beginning in a world as complex as ours. Even lower animals exemplify the primitive wisdom inherent in imitative learn-ing. The extension of such indoctrination to intentional direction of the behavior of the immature into what the adult has learned to be safe and value producing paths is a necessary concomitant of the longer period of immaturity that constitutes one major difference between the human and the non-human infant.

What I propose, as a modification of the older liberal theory of education, is that we frankly admit that learning necessarily begins with an authoritative and indoctrinative situation, and that for lack of time, native capacity or the requisite training to think everything out for oneself, learning even for the rationally mature individual must continue to include an ingredient of the unreasoned, the merely accepted. The extent to which every one of us must depend, and wisely so, on the authoritative pronouncements of those who are more expert than are we in most of the problems we face is evidence enough of the truth of this contention. It would seem to be more in accord with reality to consider the 'indoctrination' and the 'educa-tion' of the earlier liberal educators to be the polar extremes of a continuum of teaching method along which actual teaching may move in keeping with the requirements of the situation. With infants in nearly everything and with mature, reasoning adults in very little, the teacher will use indoctrinating procedures. Between these two extremes the proper mixture of the one method with the other is appropriately determined by the degree of rational capability of the learner with regard to the subject-matter before him and the degree of urgency of the situation.

Some liberals may here charge that I have given away the whole cause of liberal education, that in allowing, in theory, this much indoctrination and authority I have gone over completely to the authoritarians. This charge I deny. In terms of the theory I have presented we can make a workable distinction between what the Nazi regime did and what we democrats propose in the way of

97

teaching procedures. 'Education' we can treat as the *ideal* method, to be embodied in practice in the maximum possible degree, and 'indoctrination' as a non-rational but necessary ingredient in the teaching process, to be held to the very minimum required by circumstances.

The supporting philosophies of man whence flow these two methods of teaching provide the basic distinction we seek. The liberal believes in a latent rationality in every normal infant, a capacity for reasoned decision-making that, under careful cultivation and through practice, can be enhanced and developed. The authoritarian holds that the vast majority of mankind remain indefinitely juvenile in their responses,[13] hence indefinitely in need of restrictive guidance and management in all important areas of behavior. Most liberals feel, moreover, that man is innately either biased in favor of the good and the right or, at worst, neutral with respect to them. The authoritarian suspects man of a bias in favor of the evil and wrong or that he is possessed of an original sin from which only a miracle can save him. In short, where the liberal is optimistic in regard to man's learning to think correctly and do right the authoritarian is a pessimist in both matters. The difference between the two philosophies and consequent methods of teaching should be seen not as the absolute white versus black of the older liberalism but as one of degree only, yet a very significant degree.

The teaching situation arranged by the liberal will differ markedly from that set up by the authoritarian. The liberal educator will encourage the student to reason to conclusions for himself, even regarding such seemingly settled items as basic scientific principles and the multiplication table. He will try to help the student to develop the habit of looking for the reasons for accepted conclusions. The liberal teacher will encourage the critical attitude, the questioning stance, the tendency to balance possibility against possibility, alternative against alternative. He will so teach that his students will not only be not afraid but even eager to subject to critical review what was taught them before they were capable of being critical, including what he has himself sponsored or endorsed. The liberal educator will teach, as Hare puts it, with the possibility in mind that he will some day discover that he is talking 'to an educated man like himself—a man who may disagree with everything he has said . . .'[14]

The authoritarian will attempt so to structure the teaching situation that certain basic truths are absorbed by the students and retained indefinitely against all opposition. This means that these items must not be subjected to criticism that a juvenile mind cannot throw off. Alternatives must not be mentioned; or, at least, they must not be put in too favorable a light. The cards must be stacked in favor of these 'truths'; and this means that the teacher must use censorship, propaganda, and indoctrination, even with persons the liberal would regard as capable of thinking for themselves. The most important teachings must be so deeply embedded in the mind and habits of the student that his mentors will not have to worry about his deviating from them in later life. It is the authoritarian assumption that if the student is so taught that he develops a habit of expecting reasons for whatever is presented him he may some day ask for reasons where it is unwise or impossible to give them to him; hence there is a tendency in authoritarian education to stress data, facts, and to neglect evidence or justification for these. The authoritarian educator would consider his efforts to have failed in the instance of any student who comes finally to doubt his teachings or differ with him.

Thus modified and made more realistic the liberal definition of 'indoctrination' is a useful instrument for helping us characterize and distinguish two common classroom methods of dealing with issues. In this form it seems to accommodate a number of the common meanings attributed to it by Mr Flew and the persons participating in the symposium he refers to.[15] Its content is some debatable idea or issue, in the broad sense of the term a doctrine, as Mr Flew contends. The aim of the indoctrinator is quite different from that of the educator, as Mr Hare asserts; and the techniques or methods involved in its use are different from those advocated by the liberal educator as ideal, as Mr Wilson and Mr Flew in his secondary sense contend. This definition, as explained above, allows us to treat indoctrination as, under certain circumstances, justifiable and even inevitable, thus removing the topic from the jurisdiction of the black versus white kind of thinking, which is rarely, if ever, appropriate in a value situation.

## Notes

1 Antony Flew, 'What is Indoctrination?' *Studies in Philosophy and Education*, iv, Spring 1966, 281–306. [Paper 6 in this volume. All references to Flew refer to this volume—ed.]

2 Flew, p. 67.

3 For example, see Erika Mann, *School for Barbarians*, New York: Modern Age, Inc., 1938, p. 45.

4 John S. Brubacher, *Modern Philosophies of Education*, New York: McGraw Hill Co., 1950, p. 201.

5 *ibid.*, p. 202.

6 Flew, p. 87.

7 *ibid.*, p. 85.

8 *ibid.*, p. 87.

# Indoctrination and freedom

# 8

## John Wilson

Since Professor Flew rightly takes me to task[1] for the linguistic carelessness of an essay intended more to stimulate a lay audience than as a piece of scholarly philosophical analysis, and since I imagine readers will be more concerned with the subject than with the in-fighting, perhaps the most profitable thing I can do is to re-state some aspects of my view more precisely, referring to those parts of Flew's paper to which my points apply; for though Flew's analysis is a good start, he would be the first to admit that it does not solve all the problems.

### I Illiberal practices

Of course Flew is right to distinguish indoctrination from condition-ing[2] and both these must be distinguished from straightforward force. Roughly, if I illegitimately (whatever this may mean) persuade a child to think that God will punish him for masturbating, this is indoctrination; if I give him a feeling of fear and repulsion about it, this is conditioning: if I tie his hands behind his back, this is force. Our worry about all these practices is that they diminish freedom. This worry, incidentally, is not removed by saying that children are small, ill-informed, irresponsible, etc.: for the same arguments could be applied to backward Africans, those with I.Qs of ninety, extreme neurotics, and so forth. A child of, say, twelve is certainly a person; and if we are not going to treat him as an end in himself, we must be able to justify it. No phrase like 'in his own best interests' will do the job: it can only be done by some kind of contract or mandate theory. But this is a separate problem.

### II How does indoctrination diminish freedom?

It is peculiar to indoctrination that the will of the person is not directly overridden. Someone conditioned may say: 'I have an irresistible feeling of repulsion about doing X, although I know it is perfectly all right to do it.' Someone physically forced, or command-ed under the threat of force, may similarly remain free in his beliefs and even in his feelings. But the indoctrinated person sub-scribes to a *belief*. For the concept of belief, more is required than that a person should utter certain words and behave in a certain way. He should be able to offer some sort of reason, however bad, for his belief; and it should be intelligible.

One might now feel inclined to ask 'How is indoctrination logically possible?' For a moral belief, or any belief for which the believer has reasons (not just causes), is something which you can (logically) only accept for yourself. The notion of 'making someone agree to something', or 'making someone accept something', may seem logically incoherent. The rough answer to this is that indoctrinated beliefs are those which a person thinks that he has accepted freely, for good reasons, but which in fact he has accepted when his will and reason have been put to sleep or by-passed by some other person, who has some sort of moral (as we significantly say) hold over him by virtue of his authority or some other power-bestowing psychological factor. The indoctrinated person, as Sartre would say, is in a state of self-deception: he is sleepwalking or in extreme cases double-thinking. His belief cannot be totally irrational, i.e. non-free and non-reasoned, otherwise it would not be a belief—and perhaps some utterances which we take to be beliefs are not really so; but it is irrational to the extent that it is indoctrinated. (It may be irrational because he is stupid or misinformed or neurotic: what characterizes indoctrination is that another person has deliberately tried to implant the belief.)

## III Aim, method, or content?

From one point of view none of these candidates will do, at least as the sole criterion. Aim alone will not do because it is conceivable that one might think it right to indoctrinate children with certain myths in order to give them a secure framework in which to grow up; and however liberal the overall aim or intention, it would still be in-doctrination ('Daddy will stop anything nasty happening to you', 'Mummy will always be there', even 'Jesus will protect you'). Method alone will not do because you can implant beliefs by illegiti-mate methods, but this only counts as indoctrination in certain cases (where the beliefs might be called *doctrines*, as Flew rightly says).[3] Content alone will not do because there is presumably a legitimate or non-indoctrinatory way of teaching the content, e.g. of morality.

But from another point of view all three enter into indoctrination. If it is characteristic of indoctrination that authority replaces reasons and facts, then the aim is (at least for that particular occasion) to stop the person thinking for himself. The method must be illegitimate, since it is intended to supplant the reason-and-fact method which we take to be correct; and the content must be such as would be correctly taught by a different, non-indoctrinatory method. Method and content go very closely together here (see II above): it is not merely contingent that those areas which involve free commitment—pre-eminently morality, politics, and religion— offer model cases for indoctrination.

More important than a dispute between these three, I believe, is a good phenomenological account of indoctrination and (more widely) of rational or sane thinking in general as opposed to rationalized or compulsive thinking. One reason why the borderline between indoctrination and other kinds of compulsive thinking is so hard to demarcate is that there are all sorts of ways in which we can compulsively direct another person's thinking. Granted, inculcation of feeling is conditioning and inculcation of beliefs is indoctrination. But what are we to say of the sets of descriptions which we make available to children and the built-in implications of value which parts of our language inevitably contain? Suppose we describe certain behaviour as 'dirty', 'uncivilized', or 'inhuman', or say of some misfortune that 'these things are sent to try us'. It is we, or our neighbours, who teach children to *see things in a certain way* via the descriptions and language we offer them. Is this indoctrination or not? I should be inclined to say that this question has to be settled, in any particular case, by empirical psychology and that the test is 'Does this way of seeing things, this sort of language, increase or diminish the child's rationality, in the sense of his appreciation of and control over reality?' This question is extremely vague, but I do not see how we can avoid it.

## IV Religion

Thus I cannot be so confident as Flew[4] about the position of religion vis-à-vis indoctrination because I am not at all clear (who is?) exactly what religious beliefs are supposed to *be*. In so far as they are false and unreasoned empirical beliefs, or authoritarian moral and unreasoned ones, then Flew is right; but suppose they are ways of seeing the world? Then, as with any other language-system which is logically self-contained (including the system of empirical statements, of formal logic, and of mathematics and many others), one must ask whether this is profitable or not. Nor must we expect the same kind of profit as we get from other systems: e.g. increased powers of prediction. Seeing your mother as somebody special, seeing a painting as more than splodges of paint, seeing the world as friendly—all these stand in need of justification. And the test of mental health, which might perhaps be broken down into such constituents as freedom to act, awareness of the outside world and of one's own desires, etc., seems the only possible one. Thus it may be that some way of seeing the world which Flew would call religious—some metaphysic—is for young children psychologically desirable. What I have said here is far too brief; and with many of Flew's strictures on religion, I wholly agree. Only, we cannot judge religion as a whole until we are clearer about what it is. And I do not think, *pace* Flew, that what some religious believers *say* religion is necessarily constitutes a good guide.[5] I should want to know much more about how it works psychologically and socially. Thus the merits of the idea of original sin may be considerable as against, say, a D. H. Lawrence-type liberalism and the 'prior and technical' religious sense of 'original sin' may not affect this.[6]

## V Sex

Flew says something *ad hominem*, though I do not think particularly *ad rem*, about sex.[7] I have expressed my views more fully elsewhere.[8] No doubt we all have our unconscious axes to grind. But it is perhaps just worth saying that it is no accident that the topic of sexual morality is, as he says, 'fashionable'. It is in this area rather than in the religious, that the contemporary challenge to authority is most obvious. The area seems to me an improvement, because it is more likely than the religious to lead challengers to an examination of the psychological facts which lie at the root of the notions of challenge, authority, indoctrination, and many others.

## VI Context and motivation

In view of what I have said in section IV above, it seems to me that the contexts of communication in which we deal with children, and our own motivation (particularly our unconscious motivation), are crucial to the notion of indoctrination, and to education in general. Beliefs are rarely, if ever, wholly rational and cannot be wholly irrational. We might rather be inclined to picture a scale, at one end of which we placed really solid cases of indoctrination, where beliefs were as divorced as they can logically be from facts and reason. At the other end one might put such contexts as philosophical discussion and psychoanalysis, where the aim is wholly clarificatory and non-authoritarian, where the method consists in trying to free each other from particular troublesome ways of seeing the world, or from descriptions which bewitch us, and where there is a sense in which the content does not exist at all. Or at least, such things are supposed to happen. Whether they do depends largely on whether the analyst lives up to these ideals.

## VII 'Logical geography'

This last point ties in, curiously, with what Flew says about 'mapping'.[9] Since philosophy is non-authoritarian, there is a sense in which the philosopher is not entitled to prescribe for others. He may, I suppose, suggest in the interests of clarity that we should all agree to a certain usage; but the only way in which he is 'compelled to straighten things out', or even entitled to do so, is by clarification. But as Professor Wisdom pointed out long ago, clarification can be achieved by different methods. There are times when a paradox which violates normal usage ('Moral judgments aren't judgments at all'; 'We are none of us ever really free'; 'We can't help indoctrinating') may help to clarify and times when we need to keep our feet firmly on the ground. There is no general rule about which times are which: it all depends on the state of mind of the person you are doing philosophy (or psychoanalysis) *at*. It is in this sense that philosophy is therapeutic. Philosophers have not got to choose between trying to 'change the landscape' and being 'mere mapmakers'. They effect changes precisely *by* being mapmakers: that is, by offering someone descriptions which he recognizes to be, in terms of his own ends, better: that is, clearer, less conflicting, and less worrying.

### Notes

1 Antony Flew, 'What is Indoctrination?', *Studies in Philosophy and Education*, iv, Spring 1966, pp. 281–306. [Paper 6 in this volume. Page references refer to this volume—ed.].
2 p. 70 *et seq.*
3 p. 70.
4 p. 75 *et seq.*
5 e.g. pp. 76–7.
6 pp. 79–80.
7 pp. 74–5.
8 John Wilson, *Logic and Sexual Morality*, Harmondsworth: Penguin Books Ltd, 1965.
9 pp. 71–3, 87–8.

# Indoctrination and religion

## Antony Flew

The Editors have invited me to comment upon papers by Professor Willis Moore[1] and Mr John Wilson,[2] papers which were both in their turn provoked by a polemical article of mine.[3] I needed no second summons. I propose to comment on several specific points in both papers, and to take issue with some. But this rejoinder also has a more general theme. For Wilson's comeback, and even perhaps Moore's paper too, provide yet further unintentional illustration of the reluctance to accept and to come to terms with the fact that, certainly in Britain and surely in the U.S.A. also, the most widespread and the most successful programme of indoctrination is that of the schools which maintain their separate and independent existence precisely in order to inculcate belief in the doctrines of the Roman Catholic Church. Any philosophy of education which is to be in our countries adequately relevant and realistic has got, as I urged in my original article, to face this fact.[4]

## I Moore exposes a liberal flank

The first thing I want to say in response to Moore's paper—and it is pleasant to be able to begin on this note—is that he surely exaggerates any differences which we may have about language. For I certainly do not believe in 'the sacred character of existing language conventions'[5] not if this would involve, as it presumably would, holding that there is no room for considered changes for the better. I take this first opportunity to correct any false impressions that I am one of those philosophers—if such there be—content 'to limit their efforts to the description of the logical geography of a word, treating their findings as revelatory and authoritative in philosophic debate.'[6] Indeed Austin himself would have been happy to assent to Moore's proposal, in the spirit of Dewey, 'to treat language as an adjustable tool properly subject to whatever refashioning might render it a better instrument.'[7] Austin put forward a very similar idea, expressed with different emphasis and in another image, in the passage which I cited from his classic 'A Plea for Excuse.'[8] The differences, if there have to be differences, will be in the degree of importance attached to the study of existing usages and uses, and in how exclusively such study is justified by reference to the possibilities of reform. The common ground, in terms of the mapwork image, is that our linguistic maps should be taken always as descriptive and not as categorically prescriptive; but that even the most radical and emancipated reformer will use as his starting point the best available representation of how things presently are.

My second comment is to say how illuminating I found Moore's account of the background of the discussion in the U.S.A.: 'For better or for worse, Dewey's type of outlook, and the accompanying derogatory definition of indoctrination have so permeated American educational thinking that we automatically deal with this concept in terms of method only'; and 'So, in America "indoctrination" has come to mean strictly a method of teaching.'[9] Yet even in this American context I still want to suggest that such a notion is too crude to be adequate to the complexity of the issues involved. For, surely, we cannot out of hand dismiss basic differences of logical status in the content of what is taught as irrelevant to the questions of how, if at all, these different sorts of thing ought to be taught?

There is, for a start, the world of difference and, as I think Moore is tacitly recognizing, educationally relevant difference between, on the one hand, the development of values and, on the other hand, the teaching of matters of fact. Again, considering only factual or would-be factual propositions there is a whole spectrum of equally relevant difference: between those at one extreme which can, on the best possible evidence, reasonably be said to be known; and those at the opposite extreme for which, whether or not they happen to be true, there is no evidence at all. If as a result of a great debate in World War II and after, American educationalists really do now through force of habit think of indoctrination as a matter only of method, then it is perhaps unprofitable to try to break this habit; and prudent regretfully to accept that, according to their usage, the American meaning of the word 'indoctrination' would be exactly as Moore says it is. Americans in that case would or will have to find some other means to allow for such vital differences of logical status among the various things taught. (Incidentally, in view of what Moore says, it begins to seem odder than ever that in 1940 Dewey should actually have defined 'indoctrination' in such a way that it could occur only with economics and politics, and never with religion.)[10]

The hint of hesitation enters the penultimate and prepenultimate sentences of the previous paragraph because Moore, immediately before telling us how 'in America "indoctrination" has come to mean strictly a method of teaching', himself makes an essential reference to what I have here been calling the logical status of the content of the teaching: ' "Indoctrination" came to be described as a one-sided or biased presentation *of a debatable issue*, a presentation designed to "assure a favourable outcome for a predetermined point of view." [11] If and in so far as the confrontation between indoctrination and education has indeed been confined to the teaching of debatable issues, then this tacit restriction surely needs to be made explicit; while even allowing that it has in fact not been observed in the past there are nevertheless reasons, and these reasons which should appeal as strongly to Moore as to me, why it needs to be introduced for the future.

The crux is that if you make no such restriction, but instead insist upon a concept of indoctrination which refers to method only, then you weaken the liberal position by exposing a flank to the objection that some considerable measure of indoctrination is practically un-avoidable. This objection becomes the more serious since in any general debate one is forced to recognize the strength of the popular misconception that differences of degree or quantity, because they are as such not differences of principle, cannot really matter. Moore should not be surprised if he finds, as he fears he will, that: 'Some liberals may here charge that I have given away the whole cause of liberal education, that in allowing, in theory, this much indoctrination and authority I have gone over completely to the authoritarians.'[12] This would, of course, be an unfair charge; for, while construing indoctrination as referring only to methods, he is very firm that this 'non-rational but necessary ingredient in the teaching process' must 'be held to the very minimum required by circumstances.'[13] But the liberals, of whom I certainly count myself as whole-heartedly one, are surely wise to fear the practical consequences of his concession that while ' "Education" we can treat as the ideal method . . . "indoctrination" . . . ' is a 'necessary ingredient in the teaching process'. On the other hand, as Moore insists, once granted this interpretation of the term 'indoctrination' the position of the 'more extreme liberals'[14] is untenable: honesty compels 'that we frankly admit that learning necessarily begins with an authoritative and indoctrinative situation, and that . . . even for the rationally mature individual must continue to include an ingredient of the unreasoned, the merely accepted.'[15]

The right way to meet these points, without dangerously exposing the liberal flank, is by introducing into the concept of indoctrination some appropriate essential references to content; or, as the case may be, by recognizing that these are already there. This is, in effect, what I was urging earlier in my criticism of Hare's idea of a definition solely in terms of aim:[16] when I suggested that the notion must be limited first to the presentation of debatable issues; and then further perhaps to the would be factual, as opposed to the purely normative.

Once some such limitation, or limitations, have been made it ceases to be necessary to allow that any indoctrination at all is inevitable.

Consider again in this rather different context the passage from *The Catholic Way in Education*, quoted previously: 'Every educational institution makes use of indoctrination. Children are indoctrinated with the multiplication table; they are indoctrinated with love of country; they are indoctrinated with the principles of chemistry and physics and mathematics and biology, and nobody finds fault with indoctrination in these fields. Yet these are of small concern in the great business of life by contrast with ideas of God and man's relation to God. . . . The Catholic educator makes no apology for indoctrinating his students in these essential matters.'[17] It is simply false to suggest that either the multiplication table or the fundamental principles of chemistry, physics, and biology are evidentially on all fours with Roman Catholic—or any other—positive doctrines about God; whilst a refusal to discern any radical difference between the teaching of facts and the inculcation of values would prejudice the claim to be doing any sort of disciplined philosophy. But as soon as we both recognize these distinctions and allow for them within our concept of indoctrination, then our liberal position is no longer so easily turned; for now, on this more sophisticated interpretation of the word 'indoctrination', it is at least very far from obviously true that every educational institution does and must 'make use of indoctrination'.

There seems to be no reason, other than the presently irrelevant present distribution of political power, for thinking that the teaching of some reasonably disputatious doctrines as if they were known facts is inevitable. No doubt it is true, as the Hierarchy obviously believes, that without the present systematic indoctrination of the children the strength of the Roman Catholic Church would spectacularly decline; and this itself is, surely, a devastating confirmation of our contention that neither its nor any other positive doctrines about God can be rated as known and manifest truths. Even if it were the case—and I do not myself admit that even this is proved—that democratic institutions somehow presuppose the general acceptance of some similarly disputatious would be factual beliefs, it still would not follow that it is in the interests of such deservedly cherished institutions either necessary or prudent to indoctrinate our children with these congenial beliefs. We might consistently and properly insist, with Dewey and his followers, that: 'The means is constitutive with respect to the end; authoritarian methods tend to create authoritarian products. . . . '[18]

*Antony Flew*

## II Wilson's second thoughts

Since Wilson arranged his second thoughts under a series of sub-headings it will be convenient for me to follow by making my comments in the same order; though not always under the same headings.

### A. Why 'we' worry

One of the many grounds of complaint against Wilson in my earlier paper concerned a confusion over the reference of the term 'we'. My first objection to his rejoinder focuses upon the same word. He writes: 'Roughly, if I illegitimately (whatever this may mean) persuade a child to think that God will punish him for masturbating, this is indoctrination: if I give him a feeling of fear or repulsion about it, this is conditioning: if I tie his hands behind his back, this is force. Our worry about all these practices is that they diminish freedom.'[19] The first of these two sentences does perhaps constitute a helpful beginning for the explication of the differences between indoctrination, conditioning, and force. But in the second Wilson is once again appealing to a consensus which does not in fact obtain. Not only is it, quite obviously, not the case that everyone is worried about diminutions of freedom, but some of us have additional or alternative objections to each of the practices specified. To the first I myself would still persist in objecting upon the simple-minded and old-fashioned ground that there is no sufficient reason for thinking that the belief in question is in fact true; and this altogether without prejudice to the possibility of raising some further objection once the nature of the illegitimate means of persuasion supposed is revealed. It is disappointing to see Wilson here apparently abandoning the best thought of his earlier contribution: 'The concept of indoctrination concerns the truth and evidence of beliefs, and our objection to it is basically that in the realm of belief we must put truth, evidence and reality first, and other considerations second.'[20]

### B. Beliefs without reasons

Wilson writes: 'For the concept of belief more is required than that a person should utter certain words and behave in a certain way. He should be able to offer some sort of reason, however bad, for his belief; and it should be intelligible.'[21] These two claims about belief are baldly stated, not argued; as if it were just obvious that both equally are true. Certainly intelligibility, in a straightforward non-technical sense, is essential to belief. For it would scarcely do to say that someone believes that a mishmash of nonsense syllables is true; and to believe something must be to believe that that something is true. But it is a bit difficult to think up any reasons why Wilson should believe that a true believer must as such be able to give reasons; unless—incredibly—he is somehow mistaking a necessary condition for counting a belief as rational for a necessary condition for allowing it to be any sort of belief at all.

This difficulty makes one think that Wilson ought to have paused for a moment to consider what sort of reason he could himself offer for this particular belief about belief. It might perhaps be urged that the concept of belief is so connected with those of having and giving reasons that a creature incapable of either giving or having reasons could not properly be said to hold any beliefs. But, even if this is right, it still would not show that there logically could not be a particular belief held without any reason at all; although it certainly is hard—especially perhaps for philosophers—to credit that anyone who believed anything could in fact be quite unable to offer something which would at least pass as a supporting reason, however bad.

Again, it might be put: not, as Wilson says, that 'Beliefs are rarely, if ever, wholly rational and cannot be wholly irrational';[22] but rather that reliefs may be, and often are, entirely irrational but cannot be wholly non-rational. The burden of the latter claim would be that to believe at all, either rationally or irrationally, is necessarily a prerogative of a rational, as opposed to a non-rational, animal. Those who have picked out man as 'the rational animal' have not, as Russell delights mischievously to suggest, intended by that token to deny the notorious facts of human bigotry, stupidity, and superstition: for non-rational creatures must be incapable of such intellectual delinquencies. But none of this has any tendency to show that a candidate would have to be disqualified as a belief if its assertor proved to be quite unable to proffer any supporting reason, however wretched. If anything it suggests the contrary. Nor is Wilson's strongly counter-intuitive thesis made more immediately acceptable by his own observation that it might appear to make indoctrination logically impossible: 'The notion of "making someone agree to something" or "making someone accept something," may seem logically incoherent.'[23]

In the absence of any supporting argument the only way I can throw further light on Wilson's position is by comparing it with Mr Alasdair MacIntyre's bizarre contention that 'part of our concept of having a belief or making a choice is that beliefs and choices cannot be produced or altered by non-rational means'; a contention which MacIntyre—with none of that slight embarrassment which one seems at this point to detect in Wilson—categorically insists must

carry the consequence that 'the concept of causing people to change
their beliefs or to make moral choices, by brainwashing or drugs, for
example, is not a possible concept'.[24] Since I have recently discussed
this along with other more plausible associated ideas at length elsewhere[25] I will confine myself now, however reluctantly, to the unkind observation that MacIntyre's paradox—that strange false fruit
of philosophy—would lighten the load of many an apologist labour-
ing to defend the indefensible.

## C. *Aim, method, or content*

Wilson under this head urges that 'none of these candidates will do,
at least as the sole criterion'.[26] I gladly agree. But he continues:
'Method alone will not do because you can implant beliefs by
illegitimate methods, but this only counts as indoctrination in
certain cases (where the beliefs might be called *doctrines*, as Flew
rightly says). Content alone will not do because there is presumably
a legitimate or non-indoctrinatory way of teaching the content, e.g.
of morality.'[27] With the first of these statements I can again happily
agree. But the second seems to be in two ways unfortunate: first,
because the example of morality is at the very least eccentric to indoctrination; and, second, because unless doctrines are essential to
morality, it becomes uncertain whether there is any example to
make exactly Wilson's point.

My reason for jibbing at Wilson's example is sufficiently indicated
in a passage of my original paper: 'The sort of belief system which
constitutes the content of indoctrination typically carries, or is
thought to carry, normative implications. Yet any norms as such are
precisely not claims about what *is* but about what *ought* to be the
case. Norms, therefore, provide a possible content for indoctrination only to the extent that they are, wrongly, thought to be and
presented as a kind of fact.'[28] If this is right, and I am by no means
completely sure that it is, then the claim that God punishes masturbation is—as Wilson says—a possible subject for indoctrination;
whereas the simple, and simply unacceptable, prescription that
masturbation is wrong is not.

But if for any reason Wilson's chosen example of morality cannot
serve then there seems to be no adequate substitute available. For if
Wilson's own first thoughts were right—and no contrary argument
has been presented in this Journal—then 'The concept of indoctrination concerns the truth and evidence of beliefs . . . in the realm of
belief we must put truth, evidence, and reality first . . . we must
grade our teaching to fit the logical status of the beliefs which we are
putting forward . . . if they are totally uncertain they must not be

taught at all—at least in the sense that we must not persuade people to adopt them.' If doctrines are, as Wilson then thought, essentially uncertain then there surely can be no 'legitimate or non-indoctrinatory way of teaching' them (as certain). To insist once more on what is locally the most important case: it necessarily must be indoctrination to teach would be factual religious beliefs as religious knowledge; unless these beliefs themselves—as opposed to the beliefs that they have been and are believed many—do themselves constitute knowledge.

## D. Religion

In his original paper Wilson had no doubts but that religious indoctrination is possible, and does occur; though he preferred not to give it the prominence due to what is locally most important. Instead he chose to concentrate on sex—this perhaps being the most convenient way 'to stimulate a lay audience'[29] as well as to encourage 'an examination of the psychological facts which lie at the root of the notions of challenge, authority, indoctrination, and many others.'[30] But he has since developed unnerving doubts: 'because I am not at all clear (who is?) exactly what religious beliefs are supposed to *be*.'[31]

He continues: 'In so far as they are false and unreasoned empirical beliefs . . . then Flew is right; but suppose they are ways of seeing the world? . . . with many of Flew's strictures on religion, I wholly agree. Only, we cannot judge religion as a whole until we are clearer what it is.'[32] The entire paragraph, I confess, strikes me as a scandalous example of the diversionary misuse of a proper philosophical sophistication. In the first place, I did not pass any strictures on religion in the abstract and as such, nor, I think, did I offer any judgments upon religion as a whole; and Wilson, significantly, makes no attempt to show that I did. In view of the enormous variety of beliefs and practices which may correctly be characterized as religious any such wholesale treatment would obviously be utterly misguided; not but what Wilson might be thought to be himself involved in some similar sort of essentialist error, when he expresses his unclarity about 'exactly what religious beliefs are supposed to *be*'.

Second, and more subtly, there are of course—as Wilson might perhaps have credited me with being aware—various special dimensions of complexity here. Certainly there are some people none of whose religious beliefs either do, or are intended to, express facts either about this world, or about a world to come, or about a Super-Power in and or behind the world.[33] But equally certainly, and both relevantly and immeasurably more importantly, the central and distinctive doctrines of traditional Christianity are intended by the orthodox to be in some way factual; notwithstanding all the attendant logical difficulties.[34] And what I was, and am taking, as for us the outstanding paradigm case of indoctrination is not the teaching of religion in general—any religion, anywhere, anytime. It is the enormous and generally effective effort made in our own two countries now by a particular highly traditional Christian Church, which seeks to fix in the minds of children an unshakeable conviction of the truth of its specific distinctive doctrines.

It is indeed difficult to understand what relevance Mr Wilson sees in his philosophical perplexity about 'exactly what religious beliefs are supposed to *be*.' For surely he would not want to pretend that the logical difficulties which, for example, beset most straightforward doctrines of a future life render them ordinarily unintelligible; and hence not really doctrines after all; thus eliminating them as possible contents for indoctrination?[35] Such a move would be insufferably sly, smirking, and evasive; and it is not one which I should wish to attribute to anyone unless it was quite clear that he was making it. Fortunately in Wilson's case this does not seem to be the move which he entertains.

The crux is that such doctrines are at worst unintelligible only in a special strict technical sense; which is nothing to the present point. For it is not at all impossible but rather somewhat common for human beings to believe that which involves self-contradiction or is logically vicious in some other way and which, therefore, may be said to be senseless in the philosophers' strict sense. But as Wilson himself rightly insists (see B, above) nothing can rate as a belief at all unless it is in some ordinary weak lay sense intelligible. And of course intelligibility of this weak sort is the only sort of intelligibility that need be required of something before it may be viewed as a possible belief and hence as possible content for indoctrination. (Incidentally, it is perhaps just worth remarking that, in considering what is essential to belief, the appeal is and must be to correct ordinary usage; since Wilson indicated no peculiar or technical sense, and hence specifies no other standard. Since this is the case, Wilson's suggestion that 'perhaps some utterances which we take to be beliefs are not really so' is very curious indeed.[36] It is reminiscent of Marshal Saxe's question as to whether we have any guarantee that the planet we all call Uranus really is Uranus.)

Now on the other hand, a toothless religion of the sort indicated by Wilson—just one of the ways of seeing the world—a religion which neither had, nor was intended to have, nor was thought to have any factual content, could scarcely raise a question about indoctrination; and therefore cannot be directly relevant. No doctrines; no indoctrination![37]

# Notes

1 Willis Moore, 'Indoctrination as a Normative Conception', *Studies in Philosophy and Education*, iv, Summer 1966, 396–403. [Paper 7 in this volume—ed.]
2 John Wilson, 'Comment on Flew's "What is Indoctrination?" ', *Studies in Philosophy and Education*, iv, Summer 1966, 390–5. [Paper 8 in this volume—ed.]
3 Antony Flew, 'What is Indoctrination?', *Studies in Philosophy and Education*, iv, Spring 1966, 281–306. [Paper 6 in this volume—ed.]
4 Flew, pp. 73–7. [All references to Moore, Flew, and Wilson are to this volume—ed.]
5 Moore, p. 94.
6 *ibid.*, p. 94.
7 *ibid.*, p. 95.
8 Flew, p. 72.
9 Moore, p. 95.
10 See note to Flew, p. 89.
11 Moore, p. 93 (italics supplied).
12 Moore, p. 97.
13 *ibid.*, p. 98.
14 *ibid.*, p. 96.
15 *ibid.*, p. 97.
16 Flew, pp. 81–5.
17 Flew, p. 84.
18 Moore, p. 94.
19 Wilson, p. 101.
20 'Education and Indoctrination' in T. H. B. Hollins, ed., *Aims in Education: The Philosophic Approach*, Manchester University Press, 1964, p. 28.
21 Wilson, pp. 101–2.
22 Wilson, p. 104.
23 *ibid.*, p. 102.
24 ' "Commitment and Objectivity": a Comment' in *The Sociological Review Monograph No. 3: Moral Issues in the Training of Teachers and Social Workers*, University of Keele, 1960, p. 91.
25 'A Rational Animal' in J. R. Smythies ed., *Brain and Mind*, Routledge & Kegan Paul, 1966.
26 Wilson, p. 102.
27 *ibid.*, p. 102.
28 Flew, p. 82.
29 Wilson, p. 101.
30 *ibid.*, p. 104.
31 *ibid.*, p. 103.
32 *ibid.*, p. 104.
33 See, for instance, R. B. Braithwaite *An Empiricist's View of the Nature of Religious Belief*, Cambridge University Press, 1955. It should be noted that though this may correctly delineate the true nature of the

suFlew*Antony Flew*

emasculated and civilized faith of a Kingsman, that faith is quite
certainly not the Faith of the Saints and of the Fathers.

34 See, for instance, the discussions on 'Theology and Falsification' and
'Death' in A. Flew and A. MacIntyre, eds., *New Essays in Philosophical
Theology*, London and New York: S. C. M. Press and MacMillan,
1955. Also *ibid.*, passim.

35 See, for instance, the discussion on 'Death' mentioned above; also
the introduction to A. Flew, ed., *Body, Mind, and Death*, New York:
Macmillan, 1964.

36 Wilson,`p. 102.

37 I referred in my first article to the shocking case of Professor Abrahams,
sometime Fellow of All Souls' and later philosopher in council to
the Convention People's Party of Ghana. He had accepted the
Chairmanship of an official Commission formed 'to work out a
system to ensure the removal of all publications which do not reflect
the ideology of the party, or are antagonistic to its ideals'. I cannot
forbear to mention that, as a result of the recent coup removing the
Nkrumah dictatorship, Professor Abrahams has now himself had to
serve a spell of preventive detention: during which, one hopes, he
pondered afresh the first duty of all holders of political power—
that of ensuring the possibility of their own removal by peaceful and
constitutional means.

# Indoctrination and intentions

# I O

## J. P. White

### 1. Introduction

When I used to teach 'Liberal Studies' to Technical College students, I used to find myself in a dilemma. I had given up history teaching in a Grammar School because I did not want to teach about May Day in Shakespeare's England to the young boys or the causes of the Hundred Years' War to sixth-formers. I began to teach, among other things, about the rise of the Labour Party and the origin of the Welfare State. But, at the same time, I felt that I was treading on dangerous ground. How far was I getting my students consciously or unconsciously to share my own political beliefs, however carefully I stuck to the 'facts'? And if they did come to share them was I not indoctrinating them, not educating them? In my very selection of topics to include these political issues was I not doing with different content what a planner of a history syllabus in Soviet Russia does— and wasn't this indoctrination? I thought back to what my head master had told me after a disastrous lesson on sex I had given to a class of fourteen-year-old boys in a Secondary Modern School when I first taught: 'I've always said so, and I'll say it again, lad: you can teach anything you like in school, as long as you keep off just three things: religion, sex and politics.'

History teaching in schools is one area where the question 'Is this indoctrination?' is notoriously apt to arise; another is religious education. But there are two further contexts in which it appears, in one of which the question is likely to be aired by certain moral philosophers, and in the other by certain educational theorists. The first of these is the moral education of the very young child. Children are brought up to obey moral rules. They cannot be given reasons for following these rules, for any reason that might be provided would be incomprehensible to them. So they have to be made to follow the rules by non-rational means, e.g. by fear of the withdrawal of their mother's love if they are disobedient. The question is: is this non-rationally based moral 'education' indoctrination? Green[1] argues that it is. Indoctrination is marked, for Green, by a person coming to hold a belief unintelligently, that is, without evidence. 'Indoctrination', he says, 'may be useful as the prelude to teaching (i.e. teaching which is rationally based)[2] . . . we need not offer reasons for every belief we think important for children and adults to hold.' Atkinson,[3] on the other hand, holds that one must distinguish between two sorts of 'non-rational teaching procedures that we may be obliged to use ... because of the immaturity and/or incapacity of the taught'. We are instructing, not indoctrinating, if the non-rational beliefs which the child learns, *can* be justified, and if they are inculcated in such a way as not to impair, or impair as little as possible the recipient's capacity for subsequent instruction and training. But if the beliefs are unjustifiable we must be indoctrinating. So, for Atkinson, the crucial issue in early moral education is the objectivity or otherwise of moral judgments. 'There can be moral teaching, instruction in, as opposed to instruction about morality, only if there are criteria of truth, cogency, correctness, in the field. Are there such criteria?' Hare[4] differs, yet again, in giving a negative answer to the last question (there are no objective moral judgments; the latter depends on 'decisions of principle' which each must freely make for himself) while claiming that early moral education is not indoctrination, as long as the teacher's aim is not to 'stop the growth in our children of the capacity to think for themselves about moral questions' (p. 52). Briefly, then, Green holds all early moral education to be indoctrination, independently of the question whether moral judgments can be known to be true or false; Atkinson holds that it is indoctrination only if they cannot be known to be true or false; and Hare holds that it is not necessarily indoctrination even though they cannot be known to be true or false. I do not want to examine these positions here, although I shall do so later; I merely want to indicate the philosophical controversy that can arise over questions of indoctrination in the moral sphere.

The other area of interest in indoctrination comes from the controversy between 'child centred' and 'traditional' theories of education. One of the charges of the former way of thinking against the latter is that the traditional teacher merely tries to implant items of information into some pupils' minds, without letting them discover this information for themselves. For some child-centred theorists, any attempt the teacher makes to get children to learn things, is labelled 'indoctrination', and one is indoctrinating when one is getting children to learn up geographical facts for rote reproduction, or when one is teaching algebra by 'chalk and talk'.

The above examples are enough to show that there is considerable room for clarification on what is meant when one talks of 'indoctrination'. The confusion surrounding the word is further increased by reports from Russia and China about indoctrination programmes based on 'brainwashing' techniques. Is not indoctrination, after all, some sort of tampering with and restructuring of the brain as

Sargant presents it in 'Battle of the Mind'? If so, what is the connexion between brainwashing of this sort and the forms of so-called indoctrination which we have just examined? Are the other examples of indoctrination not examples at all, because they do not rely on brainwashing techniques? Or do they, in some subtle way, involve brainwashing? What, after all, is brainwashing?

## 2. The ambiguity of 'indoctrination'

Questions about indoctrination tend to arise in the sorts of contexts which I have mentioned, but it is not clear that in every case when people talk about indoctrination, they mean the same thing. It will be helpful to distinguish here a number of different intentions which a parent or schoolteacher might have in getting children to learn things. We can distinguish the intentions that:

(i) the child should learn words or phrases that he is able to repeat by rote.

(ii) the child should believe that a proposition 'p' is true. This is different from (i) in that in (ii) the child must *understand* what 'p' means. The child in (i) may learn to repeat the words 'I ought not to steal' without understanding what stealing is. (This is not, of course, to deny that rote learning *excludes* understanding, but merely to affirm that it does not *require* it). But the child in (ii) cannot believe 'p' if he does not know what it means.

(iii) the child should believe that 'p' is true, in such a way that nothing will shake this belief.

(iv) the child should believe that 'p' is true, if and only if he has come to see that there are good grounds for believing it. This implies the intention that the child reject 'p' if he comes to see that there are no good grounds for believing it.

Both (iii) and (iv) are compatible with (ii); but they are incompatible with each other; for the teacher with intention (iii) intends so to fix 'p' in the child's mind that the later production of good grounds for rejecting 'p' will not lead the child to give up 'p'.

Some, but not all, of the controversies about indoctrination have arisen because all three intentions (i), (ii) and (iii) have been used as defining attributes of indoctrination—and some uses of the term cover (iv) as well.

(i) Those who claim that a teacher is indoctrinating because he is merely getting his pupils to learn things by rote, are defining 'indoctrination' in terms of intention (i).

(ii) Those who argue, like Green (above, p. 117), that early moral education must be indoctrination because the teacher is getting the child to believe that he ought to behave in such and such a way

J. P. White

without giving reasons, define 'indoctrination' as a non-rational way of trying to achieve intention (ii).

(iii) Those who deny that early moral education is indoctrination as long as the teacher has no intention of getting the child to believe unshakably that he ought to behave in such and such a way, are not really at issue with those of Green's persuasion, because they define 'indoctrination' in terms of intention (iii).

(iv) For those child-centred theorists who hold that all attempts to get a child to learn anything (as distinct from letting him 'discover' things) are forms of indoctrination, the term is broad enough to cover all four intentions.

The word 'indoctrination' was often used in the past to refer to teaching generally: to indoctrinate a person was merely to get him to learn something. In this century the word has taken on more precise meanings. It now usually refers to particular *types* of teaching, distinguished by different intentions that some teachers have in mind, e.g. to get children to learn by rote, or without reasons, or in an unshakable way—intentions that were not clearly distinguished in the past when the word was used more widely. As different educationists tend for different reasons to disapprove of one or more of these intentions, the word has come to be used pejoratively in most cases. (But not in all: the American Army clearly approves of the Indoctrination Courses it arranges for its troops, although it is not clear in what sense 'indoctrination' is to be taken here.)

### 3. Intention, method and content as criteria of indoctrination

Teachers who are worried about indoctrination in schools today are not on the whole worried because they are teaching children to learn by rote; neither do they mean by 'indoctrination' any sort of 'formal' teaching. Like myself, in my history teaching days, they have in mind, as paradigm cases of indoctrination, communist systems of 'political education' or, perhaps, the teaching of religion in Roman Catholic schools. I want to argue that 'indoctrination' in this sense is definable solely in terms of intention (iii). Indoctrinating someone is trying to get him to believe that a proposition 'p' is true, in such a way that nothing will shake that belief.[5] Definitions in terms of the sort of proposition which is taught (content) or in terms of the methods of teaching 'p', will not do. To show this, I would like now to consider in detail some attempts which have been made to define 'indoctrination' otherwise than in terms of intention (iii) alone.

(a) John Wilson[6] implicitly denies that the indoctrinator need have *any* intention of getting a person to believe anything. (For him indoctrination is distinguished by the *content* of what the pupil comes to believe: the beliefs are uncertain, not in the sense that they cannot be 100 per cent proved, but in the sense that there is no publicly acceptable evidence for them. Religious, political and moral beliefs provide, for Wilson, paradigm cases of beliefs that can be indoctrinated.) He argues that if a child kicks up a row when there are adults in the room who want a quiet conversation and we don't make the child shut up, this 'is as much indoctrination as to stop it making a noise in its own playroom, because it presents the child with a false picture—a picture of lunatic adults who are willing to stop talking just because some kid is screaming'. Here, notice, we need not have the intention of presenting the child with a false belief —we may just intend to make it stop screaming. The false belief that the child gets may be an unintentional result of our behaviour.

But *is* this 'indoctrination'? If so, the term becomes so wide as to be meaningless. For if whenever a person comes to have a false belief 'y' as a result of my acting on intention 'x', I am indoctrinating him, then I may be indoctrinating someone whenever I act on *any* intention. Wilson's case is one of neglect, rather than of indoctrination. To say that it is one of neglect is to say that the adults responsible for the child *did not do* what they ought to have done (i.e. shut him up). At least a minimal necessary condition of something's being indoctrination is that it is an activity: the indoctrinator must be *doing* something. Now, we normally distinguish one activity from another in terms of the agent's intention.[7] We can say that a person raising his arm is engaged in one activity rather than another, say signalling rather than doing P.T., not from observing his bodily movements (which may be the same in both cases), or from looking at the results of what he is doing (in both cases a taxi may draw up), but only when we know what intention he has in mind. Since indoctrination is an activity, it can only be distinguished from other activities in terms of the particular intention the indoctrinator has in mind.

(b) A second argument that intention (iii) is not a necessary condition runs as follows. *Some* indoctrinators may have the intention of fixing their pupils' beliefs so that they are unshakable, but not all. For many indoctrinators—e.g. of Marxism or of Roman Catholicism —have themselves been indoctrinated. They believe that the doctrines that they hold cannot but be true. Therefore many of them are fully prepared to accept rational discussion of these doctrines in their teaching, for they do not believe that such discussion could ever undermine them. If asked to describe what their intentions are in teaching, they say that they are trying to get their charges to think for themselves and deny that they are trying to rivet unquestionable beliefs into the mind. That is, they claim that they are motivated by intention (iv), not intention (iii). Yet however what they are doing might be described from within the religious or political system in which they are working, if viewed from outside the system, they would rightly be called indoctrinators. We would call them this not because they have intention (iii), but because of the particular subject matter which they are teaching: it is because they are teaching religious and political *doctrines*, that we call them 'indoctrinators'.

Not all arguments that the content of what is taught is important in deciding whether or not this is a case of indoctrination deny the importance of a particular intention as an additional criterion. We shall examine just such an argument in a moment. But what of arguments like the present one, which claim that the indoctrinator need not have any particular intention? One criticism of it, as it stands, is that it assumes that the teacher's avowed intention is necessarily his real intention. But is it conceivable, that his avowed intention is also his real intention? If so, then if any of his pupils questions a fundamental proposition of the doctrine, like 'There is a God' or 'The course of history is predetermined', he will not fob him off with specious argument or use non-rational techniques of persuasion to get him to believe the proposition, but will try to explore with the pupil whether there are any good grounds for it. But if he is as open-minded as this, would we, seeing him from outside the system, say that he is indoctrinating? If so, then there seems no reason why the philosopher of religion or of politics, who is also concerned to explore whether or not there are good grounds for the propositions mentioned, should not also be called an indoctrinator, a conclusion which the original proponent of argument (b) would surely wish to deny. If the teacher inside the system *is* an indoctrinator, it is therefore inconceivable that his avowed intention is also his real intention.

(c) Let us now look at the argument, that while intention (iii) to implant unshakable beliefs, is a necessary feature of indoctrination, it is not sufficient, for the beliefs to be thus implanted must be of a certain sort, i.e. doctrinal beliefs. What is meant by 'doctrinal beliefs' are beliefs in e.g. the two propositions discussed in the previous section, which form part of a religious, scientific or political system of beliefs, or ideology.

But what grounds are there for restricting the content of indoctrination to such beliefs as these? One might argue that the very word 'indoctrination' indicates that one is concerned with doctrines.

But what turns on this? It is true that one meaning of 'doctrine' is 'a belief forming a part of a religious, scientific or political system'. But another meaning of the word, given in the *O.E.D.*, is simply 'What is taught': and we have already seen that once all teaching could be referred to as 'indoctrination'. So appealing to linguistic usage is not helpful.

One problem with this analysis is that it does not seem to cover all cases of what people have in mind when they worry about indoctrination. What of those schools where in a hundred and one different ways some teachers try to get their pupils to see themselves as future hewers of wood and drawers of water? Such indoctrination may use an ideology, as Plato's guardians used the Myth of the Earthborn for a similar purpose; but this is not always present. What, too, of teachers who try to fix in some of their pupils' minds the ineradicable belief that they are of limited intelligence? I see no reason why this should not be called 'indoctrination'. One reply might be that in both these cases the teachers in question have themselves been indoctrinated into, say, political ideologies, of which the beliefs they are inculcating form a part. But it is equally likely that the teachers' beliefs rest on widespread untested assumptions about human nature which are not tied together into a close-knit system, like the religious and political beliefs we have been discussing.

I may, of course, be open to defeat on empirical grounds here, so I shall introduce what I hope is a stronger argument. It is not logically impossible to conceive of a teacher who tries to get a pupil to have an unshakable belief, which is not connected to a doctrine, in the 'system' sense. A teacher may want to get a child to believe that Melbourne is the capital of Australia. He may try to fix this belief unshakably by associating it with his charismatic influence on the boy: for the boy, whatever the teacher says *must* be right. The teacher may, further, try to prevent the boy from revising his belief in the face of contrary evidence by, for instance, not allowing any atlases in his school, getting the boy to believe that it is wrong to look up things in atlases at home, persuading him to enter a Trappist monastery on leaving school, etc. If a teacher did this, would it not be indoctrination? The fact that we *generally use* the word 'indoctrination' only in connexion with the teaching of ideological beliefs cannot be used to prove that the *concept* of indoctrination covers only such cases.

There are two ways at least in which one may attempt to deny that this is a case of indoctrination. First, one might argue that the example *is* inconceivable unless the teacher has some ulterior purpose in mind—for why else would he teach as he does? The only conceivable ulterior purpose is that he wants the belief to be held as a part of some wider ideology. One might object to this that the teacher might be crazy; but this objection could be blocked by the argument that there must be some reason why he is trying to get the boy to hold *this* belief, and that this is unintelligible unless one assumes that it forms part of some private, crazy ideology that the teacher has himself. But what of the teacher who is not crazy, but wants to get the boy to hold the belief unshakably, just to show that it can be done? He has no reason for selecting this belief rather than another, beyond the convenience of this one for his purposes; it would be harder, for instance, to get him to believe that Melton Mowbray was the capital of England. In this case, the belief need not form part of an ideology.

The second argument is that in his attempts to prevent the boy from finding out the truth about the capital of Australia, the teacher has to get him to believe all sorts of other things, e.g. (in our own example) that it is wrong to look up things in atlases. If his intention is to be realized, he will also have to teach him that it is wrong to speak to Australians, to be interested in Test Matches, radio quiz games, etc. He may have to teach other beliefs to back up these demands if the child wants to know why listening to quiz pro- grammes, for instance, is wrong. In this way a whole network of beliefs will be created, all clustering round and supporting the original belief. Together they form a self-contained ideology of their own. So, if this is to be called 'indoctrination', this is because of the way the belief is enmeshed in an ideological system, not only be- cause of the teacher's intention.

There are two points to be made about this argument. First, if 'ideology' is to be taken to cover not only political and religious systems, as originally proposed, but to cover also such cases as these, then indoctrination has nothing to do with the *content* of beliefs, if one means by 'content' that they be political rather than religious, or scientific rather than metaphysical. If indoctrination has to do with content, then on the above argument, 'content' must refer to the fact that the beliefs to be indoctrinated must form part of an ideo- logical system, in the broader sense. But, secondly, it is not necessary to indoctrination that the belief be associated with an ideology. This is only important when a pupil is likely to question a belief: he has to be taught that he should avoid certain people and certain books, etc. which might start him thinking. But a case could be imagined where the pupil is not likely to find counter evidence. Beliefs about what is happening on distant planets are less likely to be contra- verted than false beliefs about Australia. A teacher on a tiny, remote island might want to see if he can get a pupil to believe unshakably that Uranus has seven moons. The boy trusts him utterly: he has no access to books on astronomy; he is never going to leave the island; and no one ever visits the island. Given such conditions, the teacher would be indoctrinating, but without an ideology.

If this argument is correct, then the claim that all indoctrination is ideological throws no light on the concept of 'indoctrination' but only on one instance of it. It is, of course, always possible to make indoctrination require an ideology *by definition*, as this is how the term is generally used. One might deny that the imaginary case described above was really a case of indoctrination, for this reason. But in this case, there is nothing to argue about. The supporter of a 'content' criterion wins his case by making it trivially true. It may be true that we usually use the word 'indoctrination' only in ideological cases, but that is no reason to let the matter rest there. The problem is to find what concepts are necessarily connected to 'indoctrination' and what are only contingently so. The hypothetical example given above gives grounds for saying that while intention (iii) is necessarily connected, 'doctrine' or 'ideology' are not. If one asked the teacher on the island what he was doing, and he replied, 'I am indoctrinating the boy', why should we disbelieve him? The case is sufficiently like the more usual cases of ideological indoctrination to justify him in so calling it.

The contingency of 'ideology' is even more apparent if 'ideology' is used to refer not to the *content* of one's beliefs—e.g. a religious or political system—but to the various beliefs which might be taught in order to prevent a person questioning the particular belief or beliefs to be indoctrinated, like the beliefs used above to prevent the child from questioning whether or not Melbourne was the capital of Australia. For to say that in *this* sense indoctrination is connected with ideologies is to make a point, not as much about the content of what is taught, but about the *method* of teaching it. Ideological indoctrination in this sense of 'ideology' attempts to get certain beliefs drummed home, by enmeshing them in other beliefs, not only beliefs that one should not look at certain books, etc. but also, especially if the pupil is of an enquiring nature, beliefs which apparently provide grounds for the original beliefs (e.g. 'There must be an afterlife, because otherwise life would have no purpose'). Here ideologies are useful methods of indoctrinating people. But they are not the only method. Threats and torture might be effective in some cases. So may critical discussion, to a point. A skilful religious indoctrinator may get his class intelligently to discuss the validity of some religious argument. But the subject chosen may be such (e.g. Is God one person or three?) that merely to have agreed to enter into the discussion commits one to a belief in God, a belief which is reinforced by taking part in the discussion itself. (A discussion about whether the invention of the radio telescope will increase our astrological knowledge can only go on when the participants all accept that the stars influence our destinies.) The indoctrinator may encourage people, therefore, to air their views in such a discussion, because this commits them to accepting another (presupposed) belief. The only belief that cannot be subjected to critical examination is the belief presupposed.

The conclusion of this section is, therefore, that to say that indoctrination requires an ideology in this wider sense of 'ideology' is to confuse the concept of indoctrination with a particular method in which instances of indoctrination may be carried out. Threats, tortures, critical discussion are other methods, on a par with ideologies.

(d) This brings us to 'brainwashing'. It is sometimes said and often believed that indoctrination is a sort of process. It is a matter of breaking down established patterns of neural activity in a man's brain and building up fresh patterns, so that the man's beliefs become fixed in a new mould. What marks out the indoctrinator, therefore, is the *method* he uses to reach his end, i.e. the 'brainwashing' method.

This view is put forward in William Sargant's 'Battle for the Mind'. Religious and political conversions are said to be based on the same techniques which Pavlov used to produce 'experimental neuroses' in dogs; and these 'neuroses' are said to have involved the deliberate creation of structural changes in the brain. There are all sorts of difficulties in this thesis, and I cannot go into them all here. But what is clear is that while the structure of the brain *may* change when a person comes to hold a new belief, the indoctrinator does not do anything directly to the brain to bring about a change in belief. The term 'brainwashing', as Schein points out in his study of the Chinese Indoctrination Program for Prisoners of War in Korea (Maccoby, Newcomb and Hartley: *Readings in Social Psychology*, Third Edition), does not refer to a new and awe-inspiring process of social control, but to a whole battery of techniques, many used since antiquity, to enforce belief: punishment, reward, group discussion, lectures, social isolation, interrogations, forced confessions, self-criticisms. As he says, 'the only novelty in the Chinese methods was the attempt *to use a combination of all these techniques and to apply them simultaneously* . . . ' (His italics). It is wrong, therefore, to identify indoctrination with a process; a polymorphous concept, like 'education' or 'gardening', the concept of 'indoctrination' may be used to describe all sorts of processes, as long as they are seen by the indoctrinator as effective ways of enforcing belief. But it is also wrong to identify indoctrination with brainwashing, taking this to mean the all-out assault on one's beliefs which has been described. This may be a particular form of indoctrination—and not apparently a very successful one—thought necessary in an age when, for one reason and another, *adults'* beliefs have sometimes to be remoulded; but this battering ram is not necessary for indoctrinating *children*, whose conceptual schemes are not yet formed, and therefore more susceptible to subtler methods. Once again, we might *choose* to define 'indoctrination' as brainwashing, but, as before, nothing turns on this.

## 4. Some educational implications of this analysis

I would like to conclude by touching on the problems of indoctrination in particular areas—political history, religion and morality—which were adumbrated at the beginning of this paper.

(a) *Political history.* The question I was here concerned with was: given that one has a free hand in choosing one's syllabus, how far can one teach recent political history without indoctrinating if one sympathizes with the views of a particular party? At first sight, it looks as if the answer depends on whether or not one intends to implant one's own political beliefs unshakably: if one is not doing this, one is not indoctrinating. But a difficulty arises. If several students of a particular political history teacher emerge with unshakable political beliefs similar to his own, we may well say, 'They have been indoctrinated.' Their teacher denies that he had any intention of indoctrinating. It is also clear that he is not deceiving us about this: independent observers report that he goes out of his way to show the many-sidedness of political issues and get the children to think critically about them. The difficulty is that even knowing all this, we might *still* want to say that students emerge from Mr Jones' class indoctrinated with the belief that Tory freedom works. If it is legitimate to talk in this way, this would seem to imply that one can talk of unintentional indoctrination. Just as one can offend people without meaning to, so too, perhaps, one can indoctrinate them without meaning to. But it does seem rather odd to say this, for if indoctrinating is a matter of getting people to believe things unshakably, does it make sense to talk of *getting* someone to do something without meaning to? 'Indoctrinating' goes perhaps with 'marrying', 'sending for', 'signing' as a member of a whole class of activities that, as Anscombe points out,[8] can *only* be intentional or voluntary. If so, then do we merely mean, when we say the students have been indoctrinated, that they have come to hold unshakable beliefs? It cannot be *merely* this. For a man may come to believe unshakably that he had once seen a flying saucer, but we would not say he was indoctrinated. We would deny this, because no one was getting him to learn anything. It is because the students have come to hold fixed beliefs as a result of being in a learning situation, that we would call them—if indeed we would call them—'indoctrinated'. Whether or not we accept this extended use of the term does not affect the practical issue that a teacher of political history who is committed to a particular political viewpoint does run the risk that his pupils may adopt his attitudes unshakably if they identify with him in other respects. If the teacher's main aim is to get his pupils to think about current political issues, he might be better advised not to do this through history but more directly, by openly discussing them with his pupils.

(b) *Religion.* In religious education, as in history, there is also a danger that a pupil who identifies with a teacher who is himself a believer will be indoctrinated—or, if the term is inapplicable, will come to have fixed beliefs—even though the teacher is not intending to fix these. For taking part in a religious discussion, or in hymn-singing, or saying 'Amen' at the end of a prayer have no point unless the participants accept certain implicit propositions, e.g. that God exists, or that there is a life hereafter; and participating in these ways may reinforce acceptance of these propositions, so that they become entrenched in one's view of the world.

There is also reason to be concerned about the possibility of indoctrination in religion, not only in the sense described, but also in the full-blooded intentional sense. For many religious teachers openly avow that they want their pupils to have faith, to believe in God, etc. This faith must moreover be held with intensity, with passion: the belief must be rock-like.

> 'Only believe and thou shalt see
> Thy joy and crown eternally.'

It looks as if such teachers are trying to get their pupils to hold unshakable beliefs. That this is indoctrination is only thinly disguised by the aura of mystery and positive emotion with which the notion of 'faith' is surrounded—an aura which effectively prevents one from analysing what it involves. The difficulty with religious education is that if the teacher denies having this intention, it is hard to see what other intention he might have which is compatible with there being such a subject as religious education. He might say that his intention is to get his pupils to think historically about the life of Jesus or the Prophets. But—apart from the difficulties about how far he could prevent his pupils getting fixed beliefs if he is a believer, which we examined just now—there is also the doubt whether, while he is certainly teaching history, he is still teaching religion. An alternative intention he might have might be to get his pupils to think for themselves about *all* religious questions, including the fundamental ones about the existence of God and immortality. But the only problem here would be—assuming that he can prevent his own beliefs from affecting his handling of the discussion—that he could never proceed beyond discussing the fundamental questions into more substantive issues unless everyone in the class was rationally convinced of the truth of the basic presuppositions. If rational conviction is here impossible, it is difficult to see how one could teach religion (*qua* religion) without indoctrinating.

(c) *Morality.* Whether teaching moral rules without rational backing to a young child who is incapable of understanding such reasons is indoctrination depends on one's definition of indoctrination. If this merely means teaching without giving reasons, as it does for Green, (above, p. 117) then obviously early moral education involves indoctrination in this sense. What of Atkinson's claim (loc. cit.) that such teaching is only indoctrination if the moral rules which are taught cannot be known to be true? But this definition of indoctrination in terms of the content of what is believed will not do. For suppose moral rules were rationally justifiable and a parent tries to fix in his child's mind the unshakable beliefs that he ought not to lie, to steal, etc.—is this man not an indoctrinator? The notion of indoctrination is independent of the notion of the justifiability or otherwise of the beliefs indoctrinated.

Hare's article (op. cit.) argues for a similar position. But it is important to notice that on the non-propositional account of moral judgments that Hare gives in *The Language of Morals*, his position could not be the *same* as this, because, on Hare's view to indoctrinate a child in the rule that he ought to do x cannot mean to get the child to *believe* unshakably that he ought to do x. If moral rules are not propositional, they are not the sort of thing that can be believed. Indeed, in his article on indoctrination, Hare never describes indoctrination in terms of belief. He says (p. 52), 'indoctrination only begins when we are trying to stop the growth in our children of the capacity to think for themselves about moral questions'. To decide whether Hare is justified in talking of indoctrination in terms of preventing thinking, but not in terms of getting people to believe things, would require an analysis of his non-propositional moral theory, which is here out of place. But it does seem, prima facie, odd to say that one could indoctrinate and not be interested in what one's pupils believed.

For the rest, the problems about indoctrination in morality concern the same issue as was raised when we discussed indoctrination
in history. The moral educator has to be careful that his pupils do
not grow up indoctrinated, in the sense that they have introjected
his moral attitudes unshakably without his having intended this.
The danger is more acute in moral education than in later learning,
because here our attitudes are implanted so early and are so con-
stantly reinforced in our behaviour that they may easily be held
unreflectingly for the rest of our lives.

## Notes

1  T. F. Green, 'The Topology of the Teaching Concept', *Studies in Philosophy and Education*, iii, No. 4, Winter 1964–5, p. 312. [p. 45 this volume—ed.]
2  My brackets.
3  R. F. Atkinson, 'Instruction and Indoctrination' in *Philosophical Analysis and Education*, ed. R. D. Archambault. [Paper 5 in this volume—ed.]
4  R. M. Hare 'Adolescents into Adults', *Aims in Education*, ed. T. H. B. Hollins.
5  'X indoctrinated Y' is ambiguous. X might have attempted to get Y to hold a belief unshakably, but not succeeded in doing so. In this case, we might say that 'X indoctrinated Y' is false because he did not succeed, or true because he attempted to do so. What we say depends on whether we take 'indoctrination' in the 'task' ('attempt') sense of the word, or in the 'achievement' ('success') sense. On the 'task-achievement' distinction as applied to education, see R. S. Peters' article in *The Concept of Education*.
6  J. Wilson, 'Education and Indoctrination' in Hollins, op. cit.
7  Not, of course, in the case of unintentional activities. But the criteria for identifying unintentional activities are parasitic on those for identifying intentional activities.
8  G. E. M. Anscombe, *Intention*, p. 84.

# Indoctrination as mis-education

## Brian S. Crittenden

The concept of indoctrination has been the subject of discussion in a number of recent articles by English philosophers.[1] Of course the term has been much used and examined by theorists of education in the U.S. for many years. Since about 1920 it has tended to be used increasingly in that country with a pejorative connotation and frequently set in contrast with 'education.' It is interesting to notice that the criteria for this negative evaluation have been drawn, for the most part, from political and social philosophy rather than from a direct examination of what is entailed by the educative process itself. For this reason the terms of reference have tended to be the pluralistic character of the American society, the problem of gaining commitment to the basic democratic values, and the specific question of State support for Church schools.

The recent articles to which I have referred are not written in this context; although they do take note of the use of 'indoctrination' in relation to political and religious beliefs. In general, they are inclined to approach the question more in the setting of the teaching-learning process itself. Of course, their interest is with 'indoctrination' as a term of censure and they seek to establish the crucial criterion or criteria by which the activity of indoctrination can be marked off from what is to be properly called 'teaching' or 'educating'. They are particularly concerned with the implications which the analyses have for the status of moral, and to a lesser extent religious, training.

In the articles the acid test of indoctrination is located in one or a combination of the following: the content which the teacher presents, the methods he uses, or his intent. I wish to examine the use of these, and possibly other, categories in making a distinction between teaching which is educative and other activities which, while they may be called 'teaching' and have superficial similarities to that which is educative, are really negations of it.

The articles I have mentioned approached their task by attempting to describe the logical features of 'indoctrination'. As I am even less confident than Flew[2] that this procedure can take one very far, I will try to approach through the concept of teaching itself.

## I. The concept of teaching

As a prelude to a more complete discussion of teaching in the context of education, I wish to examine the conditions that must be fulfilled if a person is to be correctly described as being engaged in the activity of teaching. I am not concerned with 'teaching' as it is used simply to refer to an occupation; at the same time, it is essential to attend to what people called teachers typically do when they are working at their trade.

Following on various recent analyses of 'teaching,'[3] I think these characteristics of the concept can be confidently claimed:

1. Teaching is an *intentional* activity;[4] it involves some psychological condition being satisfied on the part of the agent. To find out whether John has been teaching it is not enough to establish that someone else has been learning from what John has been doing. The fundamental psychological condition to be satisfied in this case is that the agent should recognize what he is doing as being for a certain purpose, namely, that of engaging and influencing the mental efforts of another person so that a relatively enduring change is effected in what or how the latter thinks or acts or in the attitudes he takes.[5]

The intention referred to here does not have to be explicitly formulated by the agent either before engaging in teaching activities or during them. It is directly concerned with the logical point that the verb 'to teach' cannot be adequately described without involving a mental or psychological verb.[6] The agent must be aware of what he is doing in such a way that he would acknowledge as correct a description of his activities in terms of trying to bring about enduring change of the kind mentioned above. Thus 'teaching' in this general respect is like 'imitating', 'helping' or 'pretending' and unlike 'sitting' or 'cutting'. Certainly one may be sitting or cutting with awareness (that is, intentionally), or form an intention in advance to do these activities, or do them for a purpose. The important difference is that a correct classification of these kinds of activities does not depend on the agent's awareness or purpose (contrast 'cutting with a knife' and 'murdering with a knife'). Of course, when a person is satisfying the intentional condition for teaching, he may still act from a variety of motives and for a wide range of other purposes.

Taking the concept of teaching in the strict sense, the intentional characteristic excludes all influences on behavior of which the agent is unaware. Students learn both more and less than the teacher intends. Of course, in common usage the term 'teaching' is frequently extended to this kind of influence or to a situation in which the agent knows someone is learning from what he is doing although this is not part of his intention. Giving an effective example, good or bad, in one's behavior does not necessarily constitute an act of teaching.

In terms of the intention, the concept of teaching also excludes *merely* giving information, or telling a person what to do on an occasion. When someone asks for directions, for example, we usually just *tell* him the way. I think we would be teaching him only if we adapted our performance in an attempt to ensure that he would accurately retain and recall the directions on other occasions.

When we say that inanimate objects teach us or that 'experience is the best teacher', either we are not recognizing that these are instruments being used by a human agent (whether we are teaching ourselves or being taught by another) or we may mean that learning has occurred without any teaching.

2. 'Teaching' does not refer to a 'unidimensional' activity as 'whistling' and 'walking' do. It belongs to the class of terms that embrace a wide range of component activities, terms like 'gardening', 'cooking', 'thinking', 'travelling'. Thus teaching involves such activities as telling, questioning, explaining, instructing, informing, giving examples, persuading, demonstrating, training, drilling, conditioning, gesturing, setting an example, structuring a situation, approving, reproving, correcting, grading, and so on. These kinds of activity constitute teaching when the agent performs them in order to bring about learning.

Although some segments of a teaching episode may be carried on without any use of language, in most teaching activity in which human beings are subjects language predominates. In fact, its role is so significant that an analysis of the use of language in teaching is probably the best way to clarify the nature of teaching. As the list above indicates, there is however no unique kind of didactic utterance which would form a distinct classification like questioning, describing, evaluating, commanding. Didactic speech involves all these and other uses of language.

It is evident that 'teaching' is not the only way by which a person may deliberately effect an enduring change in another's manner of thinking or acting. Broadly speaking, although there is no single form of behavior called 'teaching', if an activity is to be classed as such, it must involve some kind of instruction or training, or setting of example, or practice under guidance and so on. What the agent does must evoke and guide mental effort on the part of the person being taught, or at the least be capable of doing so. Precisely because the concept of teaching is 'multi-dimensional' it is difficult to specify the line of distinction between it and other deliberate activities which have a somewhat similar effect. It is clear enough that if someone produces a permanent change in another's thinking or behavior simply by a brain operation or the administration of drugs, he is not teaching. It would be less certain, however, if someone were using shock conditioning or hypnosis as one method among a group clearly recognizable as 'giving instruction, setting an example, guiding practice, etc.'

Since teaching is directed to learning, a clearer understanding of the procedures that count as teaching really depends on the kind of changes in a human being that can properly be called *learning*. Whatever the specific criteria may be, it is certainly the case that simply becoming able to do something is not necessarily to have learnt it. It seems that enduring changes in thought or behavior are not learnt unless some conscious (though not necessarily self-conscious) effort relating to the change is made by the subject. Machines do not learn to perform mathematical computations or recall information, and although many changes may be effected in the behavior of human beings or animals while they are asleep or drugged or hypnotized, in such circumstances they do not *learn* these changes any more than they learn to breathe or digest.

3. Following Gilbert Ryle's terminology,[7] 'to teach' logically has characteristics of both a 'task' and an 'achievement' word. If it is treated as a performance verb that signifies an achievement, it is clearly different in important respects from verbs of this kind like 'win', 'find', 'arrive'. (a) The presence of the criterion of achievement, i.e. learning, also depends on successful performances of a different kind and done by another agent. (b) In many cases—and these are probably most significant among the teacher's goals—the learning that is the criterion of successful effort on the teacher's part does not occur at a particular instant nor is it the kind of occurrence that excludes intelligible talk about degrees of success.

These factors are enough, I think, to suggest that 'teaching' should not be treated as simply referring to the successful outcome of certain activities. Perhaps, a better analogy can be drawn with 'curing'. Here, of course, we do have distinct words for describing the efforts of the doctor. We say, for example, that he treats the patient; and to the extent that it can be determined that the treatment has been successful, we say that he has cured the patient. But the success criterion does have complexity similar to that of learning. Moreover, a favorable judgment on the quality of treatment in any given case, although its criteria are determined in relation to curing, may be made even when a cure does not occur. This obviously has serious consequences for questions of competence and moral responsibility. I wish to argue for a similar relationship between teaching and learning.

The claim 'no teaching without learning' faces serious difficulties. (a) It is often the case that teaching episodes have to be repeated and reinforced many times before a satisfactory level of learning is accomplished. The criterion of success occurs only in the last of these episodes. Are we to say that this was the only occasion on which the teacher taught? It seems more reasonable to treat the learning achievement as due, along with other factors, to the cumulative effect of *teaching* activities. (b) In the acquisition of complex knowledge, skills or attitudes, it is difficult to see how we could determine the amount or kind of change in any particular learner on a given occasion of apparent teaching that would count as learning and thus show that the teacher had, in fact, taught. (c) Even when there is clear evidence that a student has achieved the teacher's learning objective, there may be good reasons for claiming that the teacher's performance was unsatisfactory. The student may have learnt despite the efforts of the teacher. In this connection, I think it is clear that the selling-buying analogy is not appropriate. Not only is the occurrence of the latter activity far more determinate than is typically the case with teaching; but if someone buys, then necessarily someone else sells, regardless of how the latter promotes his goods.

Since the performance which we call teaching necessarily involves the effort of the agent to bring about learning, he must adopt procedures which it is reasonable to assume are apt to contribute effectively to learning in the particular situation. Despite a person's intentions and his choice of language and methods, he could not be said to be teaching five-year-old children about ethical theories or ten-year-olds (say) about the theoretical components in the statements we make about ordinary physical objects. Perhaps the necessary achievement aspect of teaching is that the teacher should engage the learning efforts of his students with a reasonable expectation of a successful learning outcome. If he fails to do this, or because of the circumstances—such as noise or inattention—cannot, then we would say that, although he may be trying very hard, he is not teaching.[8]

In summary, the necessary conditions for an activity to be called 'teaching' (and these apply to both verbal and non-verbal activities) are: (1) that the agent intends what he does to effect an enduring change in the subject's way of thinking or acting; (2) that the procedures adopted fall within the range of activities that are broadly classified as 'instructing, training, exemplifying, guiding' and are consistent with the conditions required for learning (in particular, a conscious adaptation by the subject to the influence of the agent); (3) that the teacher succeeds to the extent that the efforts of the student to learn are engaged; and (4) that in the particular situation it is reasonable to assume that the content presented and the procedures adopted are apt to produce the learning objectives.

If the fulfillment of these conditions is sufficient for an activity to be called 'teaching', the following implications for the concept of teaching can be drawn:

(a) Not all teaching discourse (or other teaching activity) is appropriate to the school and much teaching that is indisputably appropriate (e.g. developing the skill to read or write) is also done outside it. There is also much teaching which, although suitable, is not on the school's agenda for other reasons. Thus, the earliest teaching of language in a child's life is usually done by his parents and other members of his family. Moreover, the traditions and style of life of particular families and many associations within a society are taught and learned apart from formal schooling.

(b) The concept of teaching does not have an evaluative component. Given the intention and the technical appropriateness of the procedure, it is logically correct to say that an adult teaches a child to believe what is false (whether the adult knows it is false or not is irrelevant) or that Fagin taught Oliver Twist and the others to be pickpockets. If we wish to attach any evaluation to a teaching performance we need to apply methodological, moral, aesthetic, or educational criteria. Of Fagin's teaching we might say: technically competent, morally bad. And, obviously, many successful pieces of teaching will be judged as educationally trivial. But provided the conditions that have been mentioned are satisfied, teaching as such cannot be distinguished from non-teaching in terms of the kinds of subject-matter or skill which the agent is trying to impart, nor in terms of the methods which he uses.

## II. Teaching in the context of education

In the foregoing, I accepted a distinction between teaching and teaching which is also appropriate to the school. It is obvious that the school as an institution engages in other functions besides teaching and learning (even when these activities are interpreted very broadly). It is equally obvious that many aspects of the educative process which go on both inside and outside the school cannot be translated into teaching-learning procedures. I use 'schooling' to select that teaching (and consequent learning) which is judged to be an essential or important part of becoming educated, and for whose proper conduct the institution of the school exists. 'Teaching that is schooling' is educative teaching normally conducted in the school. As I will be using the expression frequently, I will abbreviate it to 'teaching(S).'

I wish now to look more closely at the distinction between teaching and teaching(S). Obviously one cannot adopt the naive criterion that whatever the teacher says to students counts as teaching(S). A teacher certainly does not intend all that he says throughout a school day or even within a teaching episode to be in the didactic mode. Nor can one adopt the hardly less naive criterion that all discourse which fulfills the above mentioned three criteria is teaching(S) simply because it is happening in a school or is implementing a curriculum. Even when all the varieties of teaching discourse which are actually used in schools have been scrupulously described and classified,[9] and when consideration has been given to the level of maturity and comprehension of the students, it is still logically and philosophically in order to ask of any item whether it *ought* properly to belong there.

The reason for this is that the concepts of education and teaching(S) unlike that of teaching in general, do have an inbuilt element of evaluation. Although people may disagree on the criteria of what in fact constitutes schooling and being educated, their conferring of the terms 'schooling' and 'educated' on the objects which their criteria pick out invariably carries an expression of approval. In other words, in any society the teaching which is also schooling must meet criteria of what is significant, worthwhile, desirable and so on. All modern societies, of every political variety, treat schooling as profoundly important; in most it is even compulsory for ten or so years in a person's life.

Precisely because of this evaluative aspect in the concepts of schooling and education, we can meaningfully ask two questions when we know what teaching (including method, content, and objective) has in fact been admitted to the school. First, does this kind of teaching meet the criteria of what is worthwhile, significant, etc. that are commonly accepted by this society? Second, and even more important, are the criteria of schooling and education which our society, or any other, adopts really the *right* criteria? Do they, for example, contradict any general formal characteristics of the various realms of value, including moral and aesthetic as well as educational? If we cannot raise those questions (and particularly the second), I do not see how we can give a satisfactory justification of what teaching we include in our schools or reject, offer a reasoned criticism of the doctrine that the school should be the servant of the prevailing social and economic needs, or defend the claim that much of what happened in the schools of Germany during the Nazi regime was a very pernicious form of miseducation.

What in fact constitutes schooling and education for a group at any time is highly colored by socio-cultural, political, economic and historical factors. Thus, to speak of schooling as the process by which each new generation is initiated into the beliefs and practices of a society is to ignore all but the last hundred years in the history of education—and it is still not universally true. What seems to be essential to the concept of schooling throughout the long history of the institution is that it involves initiation into the best available body of theory for explaining and interpreting man and his world and for guiding human action, along with the various methods of inquiry through which the theory has been developed; and the acquisition of skills for applying, at least in part, this theory and the methods of inquiry.

Although the school is not the only agency through which people become educated, and although being an educated man involves more than can be achieved by schooling even under optimal conditions, those activities which form the essential work of schooling are also central to our understanding of what constitutes 'being educated.' The teaching-learning process which is judged to be distinctive of the school is both a fundamental means of becoming educated and an engagement in the life of the educated man. The substantive details of the formal requirements which have been stated depend, of course, on the stage which a society has reached in its understanding of the general nature of inquiry. But when these are made explicit at the most advanced level that we know, we possess the basic criteria for distinguishing between the teaching discourse (and other teaching activity) which is the essential business of the school, that which is clearly miseducative, and that which is educationally trivial.

In terms of the *content* which is taught these criteria would exclude from the school such matters as the following: the teaching of what is false or wrong as though it were true or right; what is probable as certain; what is metaphorical as literal; what is a policy as a theory; making claims without evidence or giving evidence which is inadequate or inappropriate; giving motivations in the guise of reasons. Of course, these tests would be applied significantly to whole teaching episodes, rather than to each minute step of which they are composed. Also, it should be stressed that, from the viewpoint of what teaching is admissible as schooling, it can make no difference whether the teacher is malicious or merely mistaken in failing to meet these criteria. Good faith might save the teacher from moral censure, but it does not prevent his teaching from being any less miseducative.

In terms of the *skills* which are taught the proposed criteria would exclude from the school the teaching of any skills without attending to the general principles or conceptual framework; or the teaching of skills—apart from component elements in a complete activity—which have only slight dependence on the mastery of theory.

The criteria would in general exclude from the school any *pedagogical methods*, however effective they might be in changing a student's way of thinking or acting, which violated the conditions for learning implicit in the general nature of inquiry. For example, the learner must be in a position to examine the evidence voluntarily, to raise questions and objections and so on. They would exclude any technique which, in a significant teaching-learning unit, promoted behavioral changes at the expense of understanding.[10] These criteria would also require the teacher to justify any claims he makes about when children are capable of appreciating reasons, the necessity of using certain techniques, and so on.

If a necessary condition for any teaching is that it be performed in such a way as might reasonably be expected to achieve its purpose and if teaching(S) must in addition meet the criteria for evidence, justification, etc., then a school teacher's efforts must obviously be measured against the present capacity of his students to understand the explanations and so on that are given. Since a child's capacities for understanding develop with maturation and learning, it is necessary to state more exactly the general criteria for teaching(S). It is clear that a teacher, even when he has mastered the most exhaustive explanation, cannot always present it to his students. To require this criterion would frequently be too severe even at University level. Moreover, students can often intelligently apply a procedure in an area they understand, although they are not capable of grasping the theory on which the procedure itself depends. There are at least two conditions which would make the criteria more explicit.

(i) There must be an adequate justification for whatever is taught—both what is taught and why it is part of schooling—although it might not be possible to present it fully because of the children's level of development.

(ii) In any situation the teacher should present the best reasons the children are capable of grasping.

With reference to this second condition it could be claimed that there are examples of teaching in the schools where the first condition is fulfilled but, because of the children's immaturity, no reasons or only very trivial ones can be given (e.g., teaching moral behavior to six-year-olds). I think such a case may be treated in one of two ways. It may be classed as not being a form of teaching(S), and then would be admitted to the school only if it was judged to be a necessary foundation for teaching(S) at a later stage in the child's development. Or, by taking a longer perspective, it may be seen as one phase of an extended teaching(S) episode.

In his analysis of 'teaching', Israel Scheffler claims that its standard use involves 'submissions of oneself to the understanding and independent judgment of the pupil, to his demands for reasons, to his sense of what constitutes an adequate explanation'.[11] In the light of the earlier discussion of the concept, I would argue that this is not a required characteristic of its general use. If this is what Scheffler intends, then he is prescribing rather than uncovering conditions for the proper application of the term. In the context, however, it seems that he is referring to teaching which is also schooling. Hence, the question is whether his criterion is substantially the same as those I have just set out. As his statement stands, I think there is some confusion in it between the logical entailment of the concept of teaching(S) and certain psychological features of the teaching-learning situation.

If his claim is understood as expressing a piece of methodological advice to the teacher it may be quite acceptable. However, it cannot be accepted as a way of stating a criterion for the concept of teaching(S) derived from the general nature of inquiry. The child's capacity to understand, his powers of independent judgment and 'his sense of what constitutes an adequate explanation' are imperfect, limited and in the process of being enlarged. They set the conditions for the teacher's pedagogical effort but not the criteria of what constitute good reasons or adequate explanations. We all know that children and adolescents (and even adults) can, in some circumstances, be more satisfied with inadequate or even wrong reasons than with those that are relevant. A teacher may meet the 'logical' expectations of his students and still be miseducating them.

The criteria of what constitutes intelligent, rational inquiry for the various spheres of knowledge and action are fundamentally logical and epistemological in character. In this respect they also include standards for the dimension of morality which apply to all teaching(S), to teaching in the specific area of morality, and to the general life of the school as an institution. However, because the evaluative component of the concept of education has always included moral worth, because teaching(S) has always taken the development of a morally good person as being one of its primary tasks, and because the bearing of moral principles on the conduct of teaching is of a different kind from that of an empirical generalization in, say, physics or economics, moral requirements may be considered as a further set of criteria for teaching(S).

It should be emphasized that persuasion is not excluded from the concept of teaching(S). If a teacher intends that his students learn

X, he must be prepared to persuade them, if necessary, that learning X is worthwhile. As we have seen, the whole educational enterprise expresses a preference for certain ways of proceeding (giving reasons, looking for sufficient evidence, etc.). Assuming it to be possible, the teacher is not required to adopt the strategy of uttering only descriptive statements in the presence of his students: giving sociological reports about what is held to be true, good, or beautiful, what reasons are given, how many hold the various positions, their qualifications, etc. Provided a teacher respects the appropriate methods of inquiry and the state of knowledge about the matter under discussion, it is a normal part of teaching for him to state and defend the theory, interpretation, procedure, judgment or whatever else it is that he adopts. And part of what we do when we say that X is 'true' or 'probable' or 'doubtful' or 'false' is to persuade our listeners to take a particular stand about the value of X as knowledge. Moreover, to engage seriously in teaching(S) requires that the teacher be committed to the values involved in the methods of inquiry (e.g., humility in the face of evidence, integrity, honesty, thoroughness, courage in defending what is true and criticizing what is false) and to the general principles of morality (e.g., treating his students as being essentially equal as moral agents), and that he encourage this commitment in his students.

The criteria of teaching(S) apply to the pedagogical methods as well as to the content which is taught and the intention of the teacher. It follows that he may not adopt any method of persuasion which does not meet these criteria.[12] In making a decision in a given case, the teacher has to take account of such contingent circumstances as the level of intellectual and emotional development of his students and the emotional quality of his relationship to them. It also follows that we may expect that when a teacher adopts one pedagogical method from several he might use he does so deliberately and has good reasons for his choice.

## III. Indoctrination

I have so far been discussing the grounds for distinguishing between any kind of teaching and that which is schooling; and between teaching which is educative and that which is miseducative. I wish now to examine the concept of indoctrination and relate it to this discussion. Before proceeding directly with this task, I will comment briefly on the attempt to connect indoctrination with political concepts.

## 3.1 *Indoctrination and political concepts*

In the period since World War I American writers have frequently identified 'education' as what happens in the schools of a democracy after the fashion of the U.S., and 'indoctrination' (meaning a perversion of education) as what happens in totalitarian societies like Nazi Germany, Russia, or Red China, and in schools controlled by an authoritarian institution like the Roman Catholic Church.[13] Apart from its gross oversimplification of the school situation in both kinds of social order, this approach, by translating the educational process into political concepts, leaves unanswered the question of what distinguishes 'education' from 'miseducation'. It obviously depends on what one means by 'democracy'.

If we limit the reference of this term to a particular form of political organization, it is relevant not to the meaning of education but to its conduct: for it leaves teachers and students more or less free to apply the various methods of inquiry and to be responsible to the evidence. Although both the Western and Communist groups freely invoke 'democracy', it is not difficult to distinguish important differences between them in their forms of political organization. And on this basis, I think that the schools in the Western democracies are in a better position to meet the criteria set by the methods of inquiry and to engage in genuine critical discussion.

Many of the American writers who have made 'democracy' the criterion of education, work within the context of Dewey's social philosophy (or at least some version of it). On the basis of his interpretation of the method of scientific inquiry, Dewey prescribed, in effect, that those conditions of social and political life which he claimed were required for the full application of this method should be the characteristic features of democracy. Only when both the educative process and democracy are fully interpreted within a single theory, as Dewey did, does it make sense to distinguish genuine education as 'democratic'. But this move raises some fundamental questions: (i) To what extent does the American social and political order reflect or confirm or show consistency with Dewey's theory? (ii) Is Dewey's interpretation of the method of inquiry adequate? (iii) Is the scientific method, however one interprets it, an entirely suitable model on which to base an interpretation of, or prescription for, the entire range of human life? (iv) Is there a logical transition from the model of scientific inquiry to the pattern of social life which Dewey proposes? On the first question, it is clear that Dewey's theory is not an attempt to explain the actual state of affairs, but to propose an ideal which should be realized if a society is to be properly called 'democratic'. On the other questions, it is enough to notice that Dewey's position (or any variation on it) is seriously disputed among those who are commonly recognized as experts. Thus, in light of our criteria of teaching(S), a school which accepted Dewey's theory as certain or highly probable and attempted to implement it in all its activities would be engaging in a form of mis-education.

To say, then, that some teaching practices are educative because they are democratic and that others are miseducative because they are totalitarian or authoritarian is not in itself very informative. In their ordinary meaning as political terms they seem to have no relevance for the content which is taught nor for the pedagogical techniques, but only for the way in which the teacher exercises the authority he has in relation to his students. Even on this point it seems that the teaching-learning situation and the teacher-pupil relationship (particularly when the pupil is a child) have distinctive characteristics which are not found in the general political order and the relationship between the political authority and the citizens. The attitude of the teacher might be thoroughly 'democratic' (that is, regarding the exercise of authority) and yet his teaching could be miseducative. Equally, it would be gratuitous simply to assert that teachers in totalitarian or authoritarian societies usually teach what is false and do it knowingly.

This, I think, gives the clue to the basic weakness in appealing to the political concepts as criteria of what is or is not education. For one can always ask the further question, 'But why are democratic schools educative and totalitarian schools miseducative?' Any effort at a satisfactory response will, I think, be forced to move to other ground, as Dewey did: ultimately it must involve an investigation of the criteria and conditions for knowledge and inquiry along with an appeal to some moral principles.

Hence, if it is asserted that the schools of Russia tend, as a whole, to be miseducative, it must be shown that the claims made for their comprehensive theory of dialectical materialism (which determines their criteria of truth and of moral and other values) are not warranted by the available evidence and/or that they act on principles which do not meet the criteria of morality. And this will have to be done without begging the question. There is a similar requirement of proof in the case of the assertion that the schools of a religious institution like the Roman Catholic Church are fundamentally mis-educative. The doctrines about God, revelation through a Divine-Human being, a Divinely-guided teaching authority in the world, history as the unfolding of a Divine plan presumably entail assumptions about the nature of reality and human knowledge. An adequate critique must be able to challenge this general theory. It is not sufficient to intone slogans about democracy and authoritarianism.

## 3.2 *Indoctrination as a form of miseducation*

The *Oxford English Dictionary* identifies the first and common meaning of 'indoctrinate' as being 'To imbue with learning, to teach' ('To instruct *in* a subject, principle, etc.'; 'To imbue *with* a doctrine, idea, or opinion'; 'To bring *into* a knowledge of something'). It is synonymous with 'teach' when the direct object of the activity is some*one*, rather than *what* is taught. The second, and rare meaning which the dictionary gives is 'To teach, inculcate (a subject, etc.)'. There is no reference to its use as a derogatory term. The only approximation to this meaning is in the two entries under 'To imbue *with* a doctrine, idea, or opinion' where the use is ironical (and this effect depends on the term having its normal meaning, 'to teach'). All the other dictionaries I have checked agree with the *O.E.D.* in giving terms like 'teaching' and 'instructing' as synonyms for 'indoctrinating' in its primary sense. Although the order of preference varies, all dictionaries seem to agree that 'indoctrinate' may mean either simply 'to teach' or 'to teach a doctrine, belief, principle . . . ' There is no reference, however, which applies 'indoctrinating' to an activity that involves only, or predominantly, the influencing of action. Finally, there was only one dictionary which explicitly referred to the use of 'indoctrination' as a pejorative term.[14]

Of course, as we saw at the beginning, the term is commonly used in a derogatory sense in the somewhat technical vocabulary of educational theorists. I think this use is also fairly widespread among political and social commentators. Perhaps it is much more common in popular usage than the dictionary entries would lead us to suppose. In any case, given that we accept the two senses, what useful comments can be made about the concept of indoctrination from the viewpoint of philosophy of education?

The first and obvious point to make is that the term can be used in reference to the activity of teaching either in a purely descriptive way, or to distinguish teaching which is educative and thus to express a positive evaluation of it, or to distinguish teaching which is miseducative and thus to express a negative evaluation of it. Depending on the use, the concept of indoctrination will broadly speaking exhibit the logical features of either 'teaching', 'teaching which is schooling' (i.e., educative), or 'miseducation', which we have been discussing.

The main question to be answered now is whether the job which 'indoctrination' does is exactly coextensive with 'teaching' in each of these employments. If we adopt the method of uncovering the logical entailments of the actual use of 'indoctrination', the answer may as well be 'yes' as 'no'. If one wishes to give a definite answer, I think it has to be in the form of a recommendation. I propose a negative answer, my justification being that such a position is based on certain tendencies in the actual use of 'indoctrination' and that it is an attempt to render an otherwise very blunt instrument a little sharper for making distinctions about education.

In its neutral use 'indoctrination' does not seem to apply to teaching a skill in the performance of a non-verbal activity where there is no reference to theory. We commonly speak of teaching someone a skill in performance (without implying that he has grasped any theory) e.g., to swim, to drive an automobile. But it would be unusual to say that we indoctrinated someone in the activity of swimming or the successful manipulation of an automobile. This distinction applies to more fundamental skills such as the acquisition of language and other approved patterns of behavior by young children. Although parents give no theoretical backing, it is correct to say that they teach their children these skills. I do not think we would want to say that they are indoctrinating their children in the use of language or in behaving with consideration for others.

If this distinction is accepted, 'indoctrination' will be restricted to teaching what is known or believed, the methods by which this content is reached, and the consequences (for attitudes and actions) of accepting such beliefs and methods of inquiry. However, on the basis of the use which educators and political theorists make of 'indoctrination', it seems that the concept should not be accepted as referring to this whole sub-class of 'teaching'. It is not that there are some beliefs or methods which *intrinsically* belong to, or are excluded from, the activity of indoctrinating. The crucial condition, I suggest, is that they should be part of a world-view or comprehensive 'philosophy' of life. Thus, in certain circumstances teaching science and the scientific method would properly be referred to as indoctrination (whether in praise or censure is not the point here). This would be the case, for example, if it were done in the context of Comte's positivism or Dewey's social philosophy, or if the theory of evolution were taught as part of Social Darwinism. The teaching of history to illustrate the Marxist interpretation of life or the Liberal belief in the inevitability of progress are both examples of indoctrination. When the world-view being presented in the school is, in fact, the official ideology of the social order to which both teacher and student belong I think we have the paradigm situation for the use of 'indoctrination'.

If the above condition of 'content-in-context' is observed, it is clear that the criteria for the use of 'indoctrination' in either its positive or negative connotation are in general those which have already been given for distinguishing between teaching which is educative and that which is miseducative.

It would be a gain in clarity and usefulness, however, if the concept of indoctrination were limited to picking out certain forms of *miseducative* teaching.[15] I will concentrate finally, therefore, on this sense of the term and recapitulate the conditions under which it applies. The content of teaching that might, under certain conditions, be referred to as indoctrination (M) are those bodies of belief and knowledge, their methods of acquisition and justification (and the consequences in attitude and action entailed by their acceptance) which constitute a general 'view' of life. This 'view' or 'philosophy' of life would be usually, though not necessarily, the official ideology of the society in which the school exists. Now whatever qualifies as 'miseducation' within this broad area, according to the criteria earlier discussed, will also properly be called indoctrination(M). Certainly it should not be assumed that any teaching of content in this area is *ipso facto* indoctrination(M).

As we have seen, the criteria for distinguishing miseducation (or indoctrination(M) given the limitation of content) are not restricted to a single dimension. However, I think that any teaching, within the specified area of content may be judged as 'indoctrination(M)' when either of the following conditions is fulfilled:

(i) If the teacher presents the specified content in such a way that he violates the criteria of inquiry—unwarranted claims, suppression of critical evaluation of reasons and evidence, etc.

(ii) If the teacher uses any pedagogical method in the presentation of the specified content which is inconsistent with the requirements of the general nature of inquiry and moral principles, assuming that intellectual and emotional development of his students is taken into account.

It makes no difference for the concept of indoctrination(M) whether the teacher is in good or bad faith. A teacher who is not personally convinced by valid arguments and yet presents them as though he were is not indoctrinating(M), while a teacher who thinks he has adequate evidence for certain beliefs and proposes it as such is indoctrinating(M), if in fact he is mistaken. Nor is it necessary for the concept of indoctrination(M) that the teacher's effort always be successful, just as it does not follow that because some students have accepted beliefs uncritically, their teacher must have been engaging in indoctrination(M).

At the beginning of this paper I mentioned a number of recent articles on indoctrination. I wish now to comment briefly on the criteria they suggest. Although R. M. Hare recognizes the criteria of method and content, he claims to give primacy to the teacher's aims. It seems to me that in applying this criterion Hare really moves into the area of method.[16] However, if we accept his claim as it stands I would argue that the teacher's intention is not a particularly useful criterion for indoctrination(M). Hare summarizes his position by saying that the educator is trying to turn children into adults; the indoctrinator to keep them perpetually children. Now, I think it extremely unlikely that any serious indoctrinator would state his intention either publicly or to himself as being to keep his pupils perpetually children. If, for example, he presents beliefs as certain, absolute, unquestionable, to be accepted without reserve and held without further inquiry for the rest of one's life, we must assume that he believes the nature of the world and knowledge are such that this kind of response is appropriate for a human being. Not to respond to the belief in this way is, he would no doubt claim, to be irresponsible, immature, childish. In other words, as we have already seen in another context, in order to justify our claim about the indoctrinator's intention we would have to shift to a discussion of the general nature of inquiry and the prescriptions it contains for methods of teaching and learning. Hare's argument to the effect that the criterion of content is useless because anyone can claim that his program does contain knowledge, would operate against his own appeal to aims. Of course, as Flew points out, the mere claim proves nothing.

It seems to me that the only situation in which the criterion of aim might apply usefully is that in which the teacher is the agent of a governing elite acting for its own self-interest in exploiting a country and using the schools to produce a loyal, docile, intellectually benumbed community who believe that the governing elite is equipped with charismatic qualities and is acting for the good of the whole society. Perhaps this form of teaching should be called *propaganda* rather than indoctrination, since it is probably much more concerned to have conforming behavior than belief. Moreover, it would hardly be effective unless the school was simply one unit in a massive and relentless campaign carried on through the mass media, public demonstrations, posters and the like. Still, even in this situation, it seems that the fundamental aspect under which the teacher's activity is to be judged as indoctrination(M) is its failure to meet the conditions for intelligent inquiry and moral action.

John Wilson argues in favor of a certain content as the crucial test of indoctrination(M). I have suggested that 'indoctrination' should be restricted to a certain content, but that the presentation of material falling within this area is not necessarily to be called indoctrination(M). Although there is no doubt, an intricate relationship between method and content, I would argue that the presentation of any of this content by a teacher is indoctrination(M) when it fails to meet the criteria of the methods of inquiry. This seems to be broadly the approach which Wilson does in fact take. From this point on, whether we agreed or differed would depend on how the details of the criteria were filled out.

I have already attempted to account for the difficulty that Wilson sees in using the criterion of method for indoctrination(M): It seems to him that on this criterion the moral training of young children must be counted as indoctrination(M).[17] All the articles to which I have referred give special attention to the problem of avoiding indoctrination(M) in moral training. Although there are obvious pitfalls and many methodological difficulties in this area, I see no difference in principle on the issue of 'indoctrination' (M) between the moral training of young children and their being taught a first language. In fact, there is some critical discussion of moral principles in our society, while very few people ever become aware of the theoretical assumptions built into the ordinary language they learnt from infancy. Naive realism is the unquestioned outlook of most people. A special problem does arise for moral education (and any other aspect of education, for that matter) if the criteria for justification, adequate reasons, relevant evidence and so on are imposed from another domain or inquiry: for example, to insist that there be 'ultimate' justification for moral principles (or for the principle of induction) on a deductive model. If the conduct of morality and science does not depend on such 'ultimate' justifications, it is an irrelevant issue when one is considering the circumstances in which the teaching of morality or science might be a form of indoctrination(M).[18] An adequate account of what constitutes intelligent inquiry should be sufficiently pluralistic to encompass the various modes of knowledge without giving primacy to any single model. For this reason it is a mistake to assume that by appealing to the criteria of inquiry one is committed to some kind of arid rationalism. The task of determining the characteristics of intelligent inquiry in any sphere includes an assessment of the appropriate role of feelings, emotions, desires, intentions, and it must provide a theory of the relationship between thought and action.

I conclude, therefore, that in prescribing for a useful application of indoctrination(M) one should first mark out from the general content of teaching those matters to which indoctrination(M) could properly be applied. Then it seems that the crucial criteria for determining when the teaching of this content is in fact indoctrination(M) are set by the methods of intelligent inquiry and the conditions of moral action. These criteria apply both to what is taught and to the pedagogical procedures employed.

## Notes

1 R. M. Hare, 'Adolescents into Adults'; John Wilson, 'Education and Indoctrination', *Aims in Education: The Philosophic Approach*, T. H. B. Hollins, ed., Manchester University Press, 1964.
   Antony Flew, 'What is Indoctrination', *Studies in Philosophy and Education*, iv, 3, Spring 1966. [Paper 6 in this volume—ed.]
   John Wilson, 'Comment on Flew's "What Is Indoctrination" ', *Studies in Philosophy and Education*, iv, 4, Summer 1966. [Paper 8 in this volume—ed.]
   R. F. Atkinson, 'Instruction and Indoctrination', *Philosophical Analysis and Education*, R. D. Archambault, ed., Routledge & Kegan Paul, 1965. [Paper 5 in this volume—ed.]
2 A. Flew, op. cit. [p. 72, this volume], 'Whereas its occasional running mate *conditioning* is, in the relevant sense, derived from a technical expression with a classical and standard definition, *indoctrination* is a word of an unspecialized vocabulary', also p. 87. However, Flew does seem to overlook the fairly technical use which educational theorists in the U.S. have made of the term 'indoctrination'. See, for example, Richard H. Gatchel, 'Evolution of Concepts of Indoctrination in American Education', *Educational Forum*, 23, March 1959, 303-9. [Paper 1 in this volume—ed.]
3 For example, Israel Scheffler, *The Language of Education*, Springfield, Illinois: Charles C. Thomas, 1960, Chapters 6 and 7, pp. 99-114, 115-36.
   B. Othanel Smith, 'A Concept of Teaching' in *Language and Concepts in Education*, B. O. Smith and R. H. Ennis eds., Chicago: Rand McNally, 1961.
   Thomas F. Green, 'A Topology of the Teaching Concept', *Studies in Philosophy and Education*, 111, Winter 1964.
   Gilbert Ryle, *The Concept of Mind*, New York: Barnes and Noble, Inc. 1949, Chapters II and IX.
4 For a discussion of psychological verbs and 'intensionality' see Antony Kenny, *Action, Emotion and Will*, Routledge & Kegan Paul, 1964, Chapter IX.
5 This account would need to be modified somewhat for reference to teaching ourselves and teaching animals.
6 Examples of such verbs: 'want', 'intend', 'think', 'believe', 'wish'.
7 Gilbert Ryle, op. cit., passim.
8 We do not say that a person has not been searching for something simply because he has failed to find it, but we will not accept *any* activity in a given case as searching. There must be some reason to

expect that what the person does could achieve the objective. Sometimes it may be necessary to say that one is trying to search, but, in
the circumstances, cannot.

9 In his preoccupation with describing the behavior of teachers in the
classrooms B. Othanel Smith seems to underplay the aspect of
evaluation involved in the concept of teaching that is schooling. See
'The Logic of Teaching in the Arts', *Teachers College Record*, 63, 3,
December 1961, pp. 176–83.

10 In general, 'understanding' involves some grasp of general principles
through which the individual is in a position to interpret, explain and
predict in relation to a whole system. It implies that in any activity
an individual is in conscious control of the techniques he uses.

11 Israel Scheffler, op. cit., p. 57.

12 In terms of teaching(S), the most crucial question is *how* the teacher
persuades his students. J. N. Garver in an article 'On the Rationality
of Persuasion', *Mind*, lxix, 1960, pp. 163–74, gives the criteria which
distinguish rational persuasion, and thus the kind which is admissible
as teaching(S): 'We call persuasion *rational* when it is the case both
(a) that reasons, facts, or arguments are the agent of persuasion
(either directly or as revealed when we probe behind the apparent
agent), and (b) that these reasons, arguments, etc., are to the point'
(p. 170). When a teacher persuades simply by the force of his
personality or by some technique which does not meet the above two
conditions, he is not engaging in teaching(S).

13 See Richard H. Gatchel, op. cit., also Ira S. Steinberg, 'A Brief Note
on Indoctrination and Ideals of Democracy', *Phi Delta Kappa*, 44, 2,
November 1962, pp. 66–8; Willis Moore, 'Indoctrination as a Normative Concept', *Studies in Philosophy and Education*, iv, 4, Summer, 1966,
pp. 396–403. [Paper 7 in this volume—ed.]

14 Webster (1959): '2. Sometimes, in a derogatory sense, to imbue with
an opinion or with a partisan or sectarian point of view.' As another
example of an entry under 'indoctrinate', the following is taken from
*World Book (Encyclopedia) Dictionary* (1963): '1. To teach a
doctrine, belief or principle. 2. To teach fundamentals, especially of
military customs and discipline: "The recruits were indoctrinated at
Camp Blanding". 3. To teach, inculcate'. In addition to the
three dictionaries mentioned, I also consulted those of Cassell (1949)
and Funk & Wagnall (1963).

15 I will subsequently use a shorthand form Indoctrination (M).

16 R. M. Hare, op. cit., pp. 52–4.

Since completing this paper I have read the chapter by J. P. White
on indoctrination in R. S. Peters, ed., *The Concept of Education*,
Routledge & Kegan Paul, 1967, pp. 177–91. [Paper 10 in this
volume—ed.] He claims that the necessary and sufficient condition
for indoctrination is the teacher's intention that 'the child should
believe that 'p' is true in such a way that nothing will shake this
belief'. This claim is subject, I believe, to the same criticism I have
made of Hare's position.

17 See above, p. 102.
18 R. F. Atkinson in 'Instruction and Indoctrination' (see note 1 above)
   tends, I think, to overstate the problem of ultimate justification for
   moral principles.

# Indoctrination and moral responsibility

## 12

## I. A. Snook

As has been indicated in the previous sections, there are three main candidates for the criterion of indoctrination. These are intention, method, content, or a combination of two or more of them. Without recounting the various arguments and counter-arguments, it can be said that any attempt to isolate the essence of indoctrination must take account of the following cases.

1. Cases which are clearly indoctrination:

   a. Teaching an ideology as if it were the only possible one with any claim to rationality.
   b. Teaching, as if they are certain, propositions the teacher knows are uncertain.
   c. Teaching propositions which are false and known by the teacher to be false.

2. Cases which may seem like indoctrination, but which are not since they are unavoidable:

   a. Teaching young children correct behavior.
   b. Teaching facts (e.g., the tables) by rote.
   c. Influencing the child unconsciously in certain directions.

3. Problematic cases:

   a. Inculcating doctrines believed by the teacher to be certain, but which are substantially disputed.
   b. Teaching any subject, e.g., chemistry, without due concern for understanding.

If method is taken as the criterion then all cases under 1 are accounted for, since each seems to require some degree of method control. It fails, however, to discriminate in 2a and 2b since a non-rational method is often used, and yet one would not want to call it indoctrination necessarily. Of the problem cases, method rules out some cases only of 3a, those in which this is done without adequate discussion or consideration of alternatives. However, because the teacher believes his doctrines to be certain he may have no fear of considering opposing doctrines since they, in his view, cannot stand the tests of reason as his can. Further, on this criterion it becomes impossible to indoctrinate if the teacher uses discussion or the problem-solving method. The second type of problematic case becomes a clear case of indoctrination. This led the Progressivists to eschew rote-learning. On this criterion, the harassed Latin teacher becomes an indoctrinator along with the political ideologist who is consciously forming the minds of children. Method is an inadequate criterion, since indoctrination loses its bad connotation and there is no further way of distinguishing 'good' indoctrination from 'bad'.

There are two senses in which content is taken by those who would use it as the distinguishing mark. Flew holds that for 'indoctrination' to be an appropriate term, the content must be an ideology or intimately connected to an ideology.[1] This rules out 1b and 1c as indoctrination unless some further condition is fulfilled. Cases under 2 are ruled out reasonably well unless the behavior reinforced is linked to some doctrine. The first type of problematic case becomes a clear case of indoctrination while the second is clearly not. If content is understood merely as beliefs which are either false or not known to be true, cases under 1 are taken care of. If any propositions are appealed to such as 'that makes God sad' or 'that leads to bad effects later', 2a becomes problematic, 3a is indoctrination, and 3b not. However, the notion of content is itself vague. If dealing with uncertain content is indoctrination, the philosopher of religion is indoctrinating as much as the teacher of religion. If one adds 'as if certain', method has been introduced.

If content and method are linked, the case becomes more tenable, but not completely; for it means that no matter how the teacher teaches nor how illiberal his aim, he cannot indoctrinate propositions which are certain. The argument then shifts to what is certainty: an epistemological question of great complexity. There is nothing to distinguish a science teacher deliberately making children rigid in their thinking from a busy teacher who cannot stop to discuss every scientific assumption.

If aim and content are joined, all cases of obvious indoctrination are accounted for, but again, the illiberal scientist is excused along with the harassed teacher. If aim is linked with method, the religious or political indoctrinator is excused provided he adopts a 'democratic' method. To hold that aim, content, and method are required would provide a sufficient condition but not a necessary one; for it rules out the illiberal scientist on grounds of content, and a clever political or religious indoctrinator on grounds of method.

As has been hinted from time to time, I believe that only intention can serve as an adequate criterion for distinguishing indoctrination from education, and attempts to link intention conceptually with another factor such as content or method will destroy the delicate balance. White came close to solving the problem. He defines indoctrination in terms of the intention that 'the child should believe that "p" is true, in such a way that nothing will shake this belief'.[2] Rightly understood, this formulation might be adequate. It is, however, open to misunderstanding.

1. As it reads, it seems to imply that a teacher of mathematics is an indoctrinator. White makes no provision for showing that normally we would not want to say that.

2. White's examples deal with beliefs that are either false (and known by the agent to be false) or doubtful. He makes no allowance for the application of 'indoctrination' to the teaching of knowledge that is certain, nor to the teaching of falsehoods not known by the agent to be false. These two criticisms seem to be in opposition, but it is in the tension between them that one of the main problems of indoctrination lies. For what has to be allowed for is the conceptual possibility of indoctrinating true and certain belief and the unwillingness we feel to brand as an indoctrinator one who teaches anything 'in such a way that nothing will shake this belief'.

I suggest that the following provides a necessary and sufficient condition for indoctrination: *A person indoctrinates P (a proposition or set of propositions) if he teaches with the intention that the pupil or pupils believe P regardless of the evidence.* Before demonstrating that this formula will distinguish education from indoctrination and take care of the doubtful cases in an intellectually satisfying manner, it is necessary to clarify the meaning of two terms contained in it: 'teaches' and 'intention'.

There is an ambiguity about 'teaching' which is important in the analysis of 'indoctrination'. This ambiguity can be best shown by a comparison of the two terms. We can say that a small child teaches his mother that the ancient Greeks worshiped Zeus; we would not say that the child indoctrinated his mother with this belief or any other, regardless of the manner in which the teaching was done. A college student might conceivably teach his professor some proposition the latter had not known; yet we are not inclined to say that the student indoctrinated his professor, no matter what sort of proposition was involved. Secondly, we can say that on Tuesday afternoon at 3:00 P.M. I taught the class the difference between 'uninterested' and 'disinterested'; 'indoctrination' seems to resist such close specification as to time.

These differences arise, I would suggest, from the fact that 'teach' can refer to any intentional handing on of information, but that its other use and indeed its main use is a narrower one. In this sense it implies that the person teaching has a position of some authority over the recipient. This authority may arise from any number of factors of which the following are most common: the agent is older than the pupil; he is possessed of wider general experience; he has some physical control over the pupil (e.g., a gaoler); he is possessed of some official status (e.g., a teacher in a school system); he has some prestige which inclines people to listen to him at least on certain matters (e.g., a doctor or lawyer).

Apart from this authority aspect, 'teach' in this sense suggests activities which are extended over a period of time rather than isolated instances. The noun 'teacher' captures this sense better than the verb: hence, we would not say that the child was his mother's teacher nor the student the professor's teacher simply because each taught something to the other. Of course, 'teacher' is not restricted to its institutional sense and applied only to those who are officially designated teachers in a school or university. They are included, of course, but the meaning is not restricted to them. 'Indoctrination' is related to this narrower sense of 'teaching'. As a task word it implies some degree of authority-control and performance extended over a period of time. In the formula given above, 'teaches' is to be understood in this sense.

'Intention' is a very difficult word to analyze. It is used in many different contexts, each of which has its own problems. As used here it is concerned with moral criticism: only if there is the intention to impart beliefs regardless of the evidence do we apply the term 'indoctrination'. This context helps to specify more closely the meaning of 'intention', or more accurately 'with the intention'. For 'teaching' itself suggests that the activities are intentional. 'Indoctrination' implies, I have argued, that this teaching is carried out with the particular intention that the pupil believe the propositions regardless of the evidence.

In the context of moral responsibility, 'intention' has three possible connotations: (1) What is desired; (2) What is foreseen as likely or inevitable; (3) What is foreseeable. My use is meant to include (1) and (2), but to exclude (3). Thus I argue that a person engaged in teaching can be accused of indoctrination if he:

1. Intends (desires) to indoctrinate.

Or

2. Intends (desires) his pupils to hold beliefs regardless of the evidence.

Or

3. Foresees that as a result of his teaching such a result is likely or inevitable (provided, of course, the results are within his control).

Since, in everyday usage, intention is sometimes restricted to what is desired, it is necessary to defend the view taken here.

*I. A. Snook*

The issue and its practical implications can be brought out by a consideration of two theories. Hart has pointed out that legal theory makes no distinction between the desired and the foreseen.[3] If a person intends (desires) to escape from prison by blasting the wall and knows that his action will kill a guard, he is guilty of murder of the guard. He killed him intentionally even though he did not desire his death. On the other hand, Roman Catholic moral theology makes a distinction. The best-known example concerns the mother-child issue. If the surgeon directly kills the child to save the mother's life, he is guilty of murder. If, however, he removes a cancer knowing that the child will die in the process, he is not guilty. Jonathan Bennett has argued that such a distinction is quite indefensible: each case is on exactly the same grounds, morally.[4] For the key factor, in the Catholic view, is the intention. If this is regarded as what is foreseen, the death of the child is foreseen equally in both cases; if defined as what is inevitable, death is equally inevitable in each case; if defined as what is desired the death of the child is desired in neither case. Any difference rests on the temporal distance between the events (expressed in terms of cause and effect); time should be morally irrelevant, for if it is not, the fisherman who poisons a reservoir serving a city is less guilty than the man who shoots his wife.

It may be true that if a person is typing and incidentally disturbing a neighbour, it is odd to say that he intends to disturb the neighbour. If asked what he is doing he will say he is typing, and the answer specifies his intention. Nevertheless, when the consequences are such that some harm is caused, and the person knew that the harm would be caused, it can be said that he intentionally caused the harm. True, any action has many consequences, and it is strange to suggest that the agent intended them all. As I write, I am using a typewriter and thereby helping the IBM company to make a profit; it seems odd to say I intend to help IBM or that I intentionally help IBM. However, when one of the consequences is one which is capable of moral appraisal, it is not so strange to speak of intentionally bringing it about. By comparison with the previous example, consider the case of a pacifist who realizes that his support of Company X helps the company to make money and produce more weapons for destruction. It has been the force of my argument that the results of indoctrination are such that they are a matter for moral concern and that to act with the knowledge that they will follow is to act intentionally and so render the agent liable to moral criticism.

It is also necessary to justify the exclusion of the foreseeable from the criteria of indoctrination. If what is foreseeable is often sufficient to ascribe responsibility, by what right do I exclude it here? In an earlier draft I was in fact inclined to include it: a teacher would thus be liable to the charge of indoctrination if it was foreseeable that his methods would lead to beliefs regardless of the evidence. It was pointed out, however, that the result of this was that no matter how liberal the aim of the teacher, nor how unforeseen the consequences, the teacher could be accused of indoctrination if a pupil came to hold beliefs regardless of the evidence and this was in some way foreseeable. It was easy to see that this result is absurd; not so easy to locate the error which led to it. It now seems to me that the reason is as follows. In ordinary circumstances we do hold people responsible for the foreseeable: if someone fires a gun in the city and injures another, the fact that he neither desired nor foresaw this outcome does not excuse. To reasonable men it is foreseeable. However, particular hazards are involved in some undertakings. A soldier on the front line runs the continual risk of killing a comrade rather than an enemy. In such circumstances he may be held responsible if he intended (desired) to do so or foresaw it as likely yet within his control. Apart from these circumstances any such killing might be foreseeable by some bystander, just as in the case of firing the gun in the city. But to hold the soldier liable for all such accidents would be to render him incapable of doing his job: killing the enemy.

Teachers are specifically concerned with ideas, beliefs, facts, propositions: their job is to impart knowledge. It is a hazard of such an occupation that some pupils will hold beliefs regardless of the evidence, and to an outsider such results will often be in some sense foreseeable. To hold the teacher guilty of indoctrination in these cases would stultify his whole work. It would be safer for him to impart no knowledge and so avoid any suspicion of indoctrination.

For this reason I have rejected the foreseeable as a criterion of indoctrination. For the term to be applied, the result (holding beliefs regardless of the evidence) must come from teaching in which this result was desired or clearly foreseen by the teacher.

Some writers on intention have stressed that the agent is *prima facie* the best qualified judge of what he is doing.[5] In ordinary cases this may be so. But it is not true in cases in which a moral criticism is written into the words being applied. 'Indoctrination' is one of a family of such words. Consider, for example: murdering, lying, stealing, wasting time, being unfaithful. In each of these cases the agent *might* apply the term to himself, but this is not typical. 'I killed her', says the broken hearted lover; 'you murdered her', says the police officer. 'I gave my excuse', says the school boy; 'you lied', says the teacher. 'I am resting', says the office girl; 'you are wasting time', says her employer. 'I'm having a fling', says the fickle husband; 'you are being unfaithful', says his frank friend. In each pair,

the observer statement is not a contradiction of the agent's statement. Each is a description of sorts, the observer merely adding a
moral criticism to the description of the act. It is similar with indoctrination. A person conceivably could claim 'I am indoctrinating
him', but normally he would not. Indoctrination must be intentional, then, but the intention need not be one to indoctrinate, in
the sense that the person would answer 'indoctrinating' when asked
what he was doing. However, he must intend something and normally that would be to teach. This brings out the connection between
teaching and indoctrination. It is pointless to talk of indoctrinating
unless the agent is doing something which could correctly be described as teaching, (normally teaching *that* rather than teaching *to*).
This rules out chance happenings and events over which the agent
has no control and limits the application of the term to events we
would describe as teaching.

This analysis of indoctrination must now be related to the cases
mentioned above. Those cases, it will be recalled, were:

1. Cases which are clearly indoctrination:

   a. Teaching an ideology as if it were the only possible one with
   any claim to rationality.
   b. Teaching, as if they are certain, propositions the teacher knows
   are uncertain.
   c. Teaching propositions which are false and known by the
   teacher to be false.

2. Cases which may seem like indoctrination but which are not
since they are necessary to education:

   a. Teaching young children correct behavior.
   b. Teaching facts (e.g., tables) by rote.
   c. Influencing the child unconsciously in certain directions.

3. Problematic cases:

   a. Inculcating beliefs believed by the teacher to be certain, but
   which are substantially disputed.
   b. Teaching any subject (e.g., chemistry) without due concern for
   understanding.

On the criterion outlined above all cases under 1 are covered: the
teacher intends fixed beliefs and intends them normally in the
strong sense of desiring such beliefs. If he denies such an intention he
need only be shown that it is an area of dispute and his method must
lead to fixed beliefs; once alerted, he can foresee this outcome. His
attitude to one who rejects these beliefs will be instructive too; if he
is not intending to fix beliefs he will be pleased, not sorry, when a

pupil for solid reasons (even solid reasons which the teacher does not accept) rejects his view. If such rejection is seen as a betrayal of all he has taught, he has been indoctrinating.

Case 2a is excluded if the teacher sincerely desires that the child exercise his critical faculties in disputed areas and provides the best reasons he can when these become acceptable to the child. Since there is little chance of the tables impairing the judgment of the child, 2b is excluded: there is no consequence liable to be reviewed morally and intention does not arise as an issue. Case 2c is ruled out since unconscious acts are not intentional in the first stage, and the consequences cannot therefore be intentional either.

Case 3a is a case of indoctrination provided the teacher knows that the beliefs are substantially disputed. Case 3b might be indoctrination if there were positive intent to make the child incapable of further appraisal of the subject or if irrational methods were so consistently used as to lead to a contempt for the evidence. The charge could always be defeated by showing, first, there was no positive intention, which may be done by showing the absence of any motive for doing this. If the critic can point to a motive (e.g., the theory of chemistry being taught was part of an ideology to which the teacher subscribes), further reference to method may be required to determine intent.[6] Secondly, in the main, rational methods were being used even though they were not in evidence all the time. The same line of defense would be open to the busy teacher drilling verbs or setting material for a test; the overall intention is the key. That is, the person accused can rebut the charge by showing that fixed beliefs were neither desired nor foreseen.

In this way there is provision both for a distinction of content on the grounds of whether fixed beliefs are more or less appropriate, and also for the realization, currently being stressed, that an unduly dogmatic view even of an exact science can warp thought: 'Let [a body of knowledge] be taught in such a way that the student learns what substantive structures gave rise to the chosen body of knowledge, what the strengths and limitations of these structures are, and what some of the alternatives are which give rise to alternative bodies of knowledge.'[7]

The positing of intention as the key to indoctrination has been attacked by Crittenden on the grounds that 'in order to justify our claim about the indoctrinator's intention we would have to shift to a discussion of the general nature of inquiry and the prescriptions it contains for methods of teaching and learning.'[8] Indeed we would, to *justify* our claim, but I am not concerned about how we would in practice make the charge of indoctrination stick but about what is meant by the charge. It is one thing to determine what constitutes murder, another to show that a certain person committed it. I believe that the notion of intention I have outlined is involved in the *concept* of indoctrination in a way that content and method, important as they are, are not.

In another place Crittenden says that in applying the criterion of aims, Hare moves into method.[9] He does, too, but again this is done in *applying* the criterion to cases. It seems to me inevitable that as soon as we try to apply the criterion we will be involved in a discussion of content, method, and what Crittenden calls 'the criteria of the methods of inquiry'. But this is a different matter from the analysis of the concept of indoctrination—it is with this that the various writers have been mainly concerned.

In summarizing, it can be said that 'indoctrination' is a term used to condemn some teaching; it is dependent on the intentional bringing about of undesirable states of mind of a specified sort. An active desire to bring this about is a sufficient condition for its application to a style of teaching even if the agent should fail in his task: 'indoctrination' is both a task and an achievement word. Such a desire is not necessary, however, if it is foreseen that such states of mind are likely as a result of what is being done. Even in the latter case, some action must be intentional in the first sense of desired or willed: a person cannot be accused of indoctrinating if he is not doing anything intentional at all. One cannot indoctrinate simply by omission or default. A person's silence in the face of a child's misbehavior cannot be termed indoctrination simply because it leads the child to think that such behavior is acceptable. Similarly, a parent cannot be accused of indoctrination because he neglects to give some information a child should have. One can be held responsible for such omissions, but 'indoctrination' is not an appropriate term for them.

Intentions, then, are paramount, but method and content are important. For it is from a consideration of method that an observer can often detect the intention to indoctrinate. He can point out the likely results and argue that since method is under the teacher's control such results are intentional. Content is important, for not all content is equally susceptible of indoctrination since not all is equally liable to disproof or doubt. Hence, drill in French verbs is less likely to arouse the charge of indoctrination than drill in patriotic sentiments or catechetical responses. The first is much less likely to result in 'belief regardless of evidence', than the latter two. Ideologies, stressed by Flew, are not essential to the term. Nor are they to be regarded as methods, as White suggested. Indoctrination as a process requires explanation; ideologies often explain by furnishing the motive. They do not excuse but explain the action.

As White showed, other motives are possible, e.g., a bet, a psychological or pedagogical experiment. It is because we can rarely find a motive for indoctrinating mathematics that we tend to exclude such activities from indoctrination. I have argued that the concept can include them, but a motive is needed to explain them.

## Notes

1 [Paper 6 in this volume—ed.]
2 White, p. 120. [this volume].
3 This comparison was made by Professor H. L. A. Hart in a lecture at the University of Illinois in 1966.
4 Jonathan Bennett, 'Whatever the Consequences', *Analysis*, 26, January 1966, pp. 83–102.
5 'If intentions identify the actions, the reverse is also true. For example, if someone asks me what I am doing, the *description* I give of my act identifies the *intention*'. T. F. Daveney, 'Intention and Cause', *Analysis*, 27, October 1966, p. 24.
6 An interesting example of these criteria in operation is furnished by a recent case. The administration of Adelphi University hired a sociology professor, knowing that he had strong Marxist sympathies. He was later dismissed when it found that Marx was the only reading prescribed for any of his courses, his examinations covered only polemical questions. and he announced his intention of continuing to teach in this manner. Compare this case with two hypothetical cases: (1) A Marxist professor who gave fair consideration to other theorists. (2) A professor, with no Marxist leanings, who also restricted his readings to Marx. See 'Academic Freedom and Tenure: Adelphi University', *AAUP Bulletin*, 53, September 1967, pp. 278–91.
7 J. J. Schwab, 'Structures of the Disciplines: Meanings and Slogans', in J. M. Rich, ed., *Readings in the Philosophy of Education*, Belmont, Calif.: Wadsworth, 1966, p. 258.
8 Brian S. Crittenden, p. 147 [this volume].
9 *ibid.*, p. 147.

# Indoctrination: inculcating doctrines

13

## I. M. M. Gregory and R. G. Woods

The presentation of yet another paper on indoctrination seems to call for some kind of justification. There is already a voluminous literature on the topic and the chances of saying anything new or original are slight. We do not pretend that anything we have to say is new; we can offer no fresh insights. In addition, the paper being offered furthers and encourages a tendency that there are grounds for thinking undesirable, namely, a tendency among philosophers of education to devote their attention to a certain limited number of concepts to the exclusion of batteries of concepts cognate to the concepts around which so much activity centres. In the same way that until relatively recently philosophers were obsessed with goodness or rightness in the sphere of ethics and with beauty in aesthetics, so philosophers of education are, perhaps, concentrating too much on notions such as education, indoctrination, learning and teaching. The interestingness of some recent work in Ethics and Aesthetics stems partly from the realisation that there is a whole mass of concepts in those areas other than goodness, rightness and beauty. In like manner, it might be argued that what is required in the philosophy of education is detailed work on a whole range of concepts related to those concepts referred to above. Thus, it seems to us of some importance to concentrate attention upon notions such as urbane, sophisticated, cultured, stylish, wise, adaptable, informed, perceptive, and the like, predicates which if ascribed to a person give one some inkling of his or her merit in a way that 'educated' does not. Similarly, in connection with the concept of indoctrination, what would be very useful if one wants to be clear as to the logic of the whole area would be a detailed examination of terms such as 'doctrinaire', 'bigoted', 'prejudiced', 'obsessed', 'rigid', 'inflexible', 'dogmatic', 'fixated', and so on.

But if this is so, why this paper rather than the detailed analysis of the kind referred to? It is simply that we had occasion to consider with a group of students John White's article entitled 'Indoctrination' in *The Concept of Education*,[1] and in the course of doing so we developed views of our own that stand in fairly sharp contrast to those of White. Further, in the course of our critical scrutiny we came to see that (a) White, unlike some earlier writers

162

who have confined themselves almost wholly to the connection between indoctrination and moral education, has cast his net wide in his analysis and has sought to develop a general account not tied to one particular area, (b) his arguments are detailed and forceful, and merit equally detailed attention, (c) en passant, he raises one or two interesting methodological points worth debating. Added to these considerations there is the fact that White's article appears in a volume which enjoys a wide circulation in University Departments and Colleges of Education and that no one, as far as we know, has subjected it to close analysis. For these reasons we came to the conclusion that perhaps there was some justification for a retreading of familiar, well-worn ground. This paper, then, is divided roughly into two parts. In the first part we develop our own analysis of the concept of indoctrination, and in the second part we refine our analysis as we consider White's arguments.

'Up to a point', says P. F. Strawson, 'the reliance upon a close examination of the actual use of words is the best, and indeed the only sure way in philosophy.'[2] With this remark of Strawson's we, in general, agree. How, in the course of the clarification of concepts, which we take to be a large part of the philosophic enterprise, can one, at least initially, go about the job without reference to the ways in which words are used? We concur with Geach when he says, 'The central and typical applications of the term "having a concept" are those in which a man is master of a bit of linguistic usage'.[3] But, just as Strawson found reference to linguistic usage inadequate to his desire 'to meet the full metaphysical demand for understanding',[4] so we, for a different, more modest, reason, find reference to usage not very helpful in exploring the concept of indoctrination; at any rate, not very helpful to start with. The 'ordinary man', whose philosophically uncorrupted habit of using language unselfconsciously in order to achieve his day to day purposes is so eminently worthy of study, does not seem to use the word much, if at all. On the other hand, it would not do to infer from the fact that the word 'indoctrinate' does not have a rich and varied ordinary usage that it therefore has no meaning at all. This is manifestly not the case. In the absence of such a rich ordinary usage, one has to have resort to the use of the term by what we can only call rather more educated sections of the population. In doing so, however, one must guard against the possibility that such uses may be far from unselfconscious, and that, instead of throwing light on the meaning of 'indoctrination', they obscure this central issue by serving the limited purpose of denigrating, for instance, a particular educational practice of which the user strongly disapproves. John White writes:

The word 'indoctrination' was often used in the past to refer
to teaching generally: to indoctrinate a person was merely
to get him to learn something. In this century the word has
taken on more precise meanings. It now usually refers to
particular *types* of teaching, distinguished by different intentions
that some teachers have in mind, e.g. to get children to learn
by rote, or without reasons, or in an unshakable way—intentions that were not clearly distinguished in the past when the
word was used more widely.[5]

Now, we were not aware that, say, getting children to learn things
by rote constituted indoctrinating those children. No doubt, even in
this enlightened age, some teachers insist upon their pupils being
able to say their tables without worrying overmuch about whether
the youngsters have got the concept of number, whatever this is
taken to mean, to start with. As we say, we were not aware of the
fact, if fact it be, that such teachers are 'usually' called 'indoctrinators'. It may be that a group of educational theorists refer to such
teachers as 'indoctrinators', but, then, it could be that this is an
instance of a deliberate attempt to denigrate a particular style of
teaching—a very self-conscious, calculated use of the word 'indoctrinator'. As White remarks, in this country, at any rate, the
word has come to be used pejoratively in most cases. An examination
of 'name-calling' uses is hardly likely to throw much light on the
descriptive meaning of the term. Far better, at the outset, to look
at more neutral, less impassioned uses of the term by those who seem
to have no particular axe to grind. Nigel Grant, for example. Grant
writes:

> As for the claims of other systems (i.e. those other than the
> Soviet system) to be non-political in aim, they are dismissed,
> in Lenin's words, as 'hypocrisy and lies'. Most non-communist
> countries teach religion in their schools, that is, they in-
> doctrinate the pupils with a particular world outlook; also,
> they might add, national tradition and patriotic attitudes are
> taught everywhere, openly and covertly. In the Soviet view,
> their own kind of indoctrination is franker, more thorough, and
> embraces a wider field of teaching than that of other systems,
> but they would deny that the process of indoctrination itself
> is a monopoly of the communist approach to education.[6]

In this passage 'indoctrination' is used to refer to the inculcation
of religious and political doctrines, among other things; further, the
tone of the passage is far removed from any kind of sophisticated
name-calling. There is the suggestion that the Soviet authorities

would accept that they indulge in indoctrination, but there is also the 'tu quoque' as far as religion is concerned. One seems to be on safe ground if one takes it that, in whatever other spheres it *may* go on, indoctrination certainly does go on in the spheres of religion and politics, preeminently, perhaps, in communist countries and in the Roman Catholic church. This narrowing of the field of application of the concept agrees with that passage in White's article where he says:

> Teachers who are worried about indoctrination in schools today are not on the whole worried because they are teaching children to learn by rote, neither do they mean by 'indoctrination' any sort of 'formal' teaching. Like myself, in my history teaching days, they have in mind, as paradigm cases of indoctrination, communist systems of 'political education' or, perhaps, the teaching of religion in Roman Catholic schools.[7]

The problem, then, is to unfold what is involved in the paradigm cases the better to be able to judge whether other cases are really cases of indoctrination at all.

At first glance one would guess that any adequate account of the paradigmatic cases of indoctrination would need to take into consideration why it is indulged in, how it is carried on, and what content is transmitted, the guess being prompted by the fact that any kind of teaching or transmission—and indoctrination seems to be a kind of process of transmission—involves content, methods and aims. We shall consider each of these components in turn in an attempt to specify the defining characteristics of each as far as the paradigm cases of indoctrination are concerned. We would stress that, as far as we can see, the components are inextricably interwoven one with another and that our considering them separately is a purely expository device. We begin with content.

On the face of it it seems reasonable to say that 'indoctrinate' means 'to inculcate doctrine'. Certainly a number of writers have seen fit to associate 'doctrine' with 'indoctrination'. Thus, for example, R. S. Peters writes: ' . . . whatever else "indoctrination" may mean it obviously has something to do with doctrines, which are a species of beliefs',[8] and Passmore writes: 'Indoctrination is a special form of drilling in which the pupil is drilled—e.g. by way of a catechism—in doctrines and in stock replies to stock objections to doctrine'.[9] So there seem to be fairly good grounds for saying that for indoctrination to take place it is necessary that the content should consist of doctrines. Two questions arise: (a) Do the paradigm cases involve doctrines? (b) is there anything distinctive about the doctrinal beliefs involved that marks them off from other sorts of

I. M. M. *Gregory and* R. G. *Woods*

beliefs? The second question is the more important of the two. If the term 'doctrine' does not delimit a particular range of content, then clearly indoctrination will be marked off from, say, teaching, by reference to the intention and method components. Content will be, as it were, a rather formal feature in the sense that any transmission process demands content. Now, the answer to the first question is simply 'Yes'. It is correct usage to speak of Catholic doctrine, Marxist doctrine or Communist doctrine, and if this simple-minded appeal to usage fails to carry conviction ('Just because we *say* that it's doctrine doesn't *mean* that it is') then perhaps the authoritative backing of the Pope will help our case. *The Times* reports that in Rome, on January 6th 1969

> The Pope today took the occasion of a ceremony in St. Peter's, at which he consecrated twelve new bishops, to appeal to episcopal solidarity in teaching orthodox doctrine 'clearly and strongly', and at the same time he sought to reinforce the authority of bishops as 'heirs to the treasure of revealed truths' . . .
> The Pope was talking quite explicitly about the worries of the Roman Church in general when he regretted that 'today, as everyone sees, orthodoxy, that is the purity of doctrine, does not seem to have first place in the minds of Christians' . . .
> . . . his principal intention was to recall episcopal authority as a supernatural power, in his reminder that the bishops were custodians of the deposit of the faith.[10]

This quotation does more than reinforce our claim that it is correct to speak of Catholic doctrine; more importantly it casts light, as we shall see, on the question of the epistemological status of Catholic (and for that matter, Communist) doctrine. Initially, with respect to this question, it is eminently worth observing that religious and political matters are matters of great moment to mankind involving as they do considerations relating to man's place in the universe and the ways in which societies may best be organised. Further, because this is so, acceptance of the doctrinal system or ideology is no mere academic matter—there is commitment to act in particular ways, to profess and act out a particular value and way of life. The committed Catholic or Communist does not simply subscribe to a set of doctrines that in no way impinge upon the way he lives his life. To see this one need only reflect for a moment on the manifold ways in which Marxist-Leninism dictates what men shall do—how they are to educate their children, what sorts of works the musicians, painters, sculptors, film-makers, dramatists, novelists, and poets among them shall produce, how their industry and

166

agriculture is to be organised, and so on. Similarly the Catholic is expected to live his life in the sight of God and to strive at all times to see that the quality of that life measures up to the Divine Law as interpreted by the theologians. It is interesting to compare these kinds of belief with belief, say, in Berkeley's metaphysical doctrine to the effect that 'esse est percipi'. It is difficult to see what difference to one's daily life acceptance or rejection of this thesis would make. Again, one of the stock criticisms of scholastic philosophy consists in urging that the rarefied problem debated and the wiredrawn arguments displayed have nothing at all to do with the fundamental question of how men ought to live. Certainly one cannot say the same of the Catholic and Communist systems of belief; with respect to these systems there is an intimate tie-up of doctrine and action, and this seems to us to be of the very first importance. More germane, perhaps, to the question of epistemological status is the fact that over-riding claims are made for the doctrines we are considering. Thus, in the case of Catholicism one marks the sort of phrases used in the extract from *The Times*, quoted above—'heirs to the treasure of revealed truths', 'custodians of the deposit of faith'. The very meaning of 'doctrine' seems here to have become something like 'that which is put forward as revealed truth'. From the Catholic or Communist standpoint the doctrinal statements making up the particular ideology are absolutely and incorrigibly true. There is no question about them, and against this background of unshakable doctrinal belief the phrase 'false doctrine' appears to have little or nothing to do with the notion of satisfying the demands of a simple correspondence theory of truth. 'X is the repository of false doctrine' stresses less the lack of correspondence of X's doctrine with a state of affairs in the world than the fact that he has run counter to the official line and is hence a heretic. As far as Marxism is concerned, Galbraith brings out well the characteristic of unfalsifiability:

> Had Marx been mostly wrong, his influence would have quickly
> evaporated. The thousands who have devoted their attention
> to demonstrating his errors would have turned their attention
> elsewhere. But on much he was notably right, especially in
> relation to his time. The latter point is worth emphasising.
> Most economic philosophers needed only to be right as regards
> their own time. No one defends Adam Smith in his conviction
> that corporations—joint stock companies—had no future.
> But the Marxists require that Marx be right not only for his
> own time but for all time. This is a truly formidable test.[11]

In other words, to put it mildly, there seems to be something in what

Marx said. But this something is seized upon by the ideologist and elevated to the status of a universal truth against which nothing can count. The doctrines become unfalsifiable as far as the ideologist is concerned, and he who accepts them is required to commit himself in a way that may be characterised in terms of passionate belief or conviction. Galbraith quotes Schumpeter:

> The religious quality of Marxism . . . explains a characteristic attitude of the orthodox Marxist towards opponents. To him, as to any believer in a faith, the opponent is not merely in error but in sin. Dissent is disapproved of not only intellectually but also morally.[12]

And Galbraith goes on to comment, 'The man who argues with a Marxist has always been assaulting a rock fortress with a rubber flail'.[13]

This account of the nature of the beliefs associated with Catholicism and Communism is necessarily brief and sketchy, but we would hope that enough has been said to justify the conclusion that we now draw, namely that these beliefs can be distinguished as a separate class. They are intimately related to action and purposive activity in a way in which many other beliefs are not; they have a scope and generality that others do not. Thus our believing that the milkman will come in the morning might well bring about action (we put out the milk bottles tonight), but the limited 'field of force' of this belief stands in sharp contrast to our belief in God, or our belief that economic considerations are at the root of man's behaviour. From the standpoint of the believer they have the status of universal, unfalsifiable truths, and this fact, plus the fact that the beliefs in question are of momentous concern to mankind, leads to a strong urge to convince others, the waverers, the unbelievers, of their essential truth. It becomes important to persuade others to believe. There may be other defining characteristics, but these seem to us to be the salient ones.

Our reference to the 'natural' desire on the part of the devout Catholic or Communist to spread the glad tidings among their fellow men leads directly to a consideration of the place of intention within the concept of indoctrination. That, as a matter of fact, intention is involved seems fairly obvious. As we suggest, those who take up distinctive positions vis-à-vis religious and political questions, positions characterised in general by reference to a theoretical superstructure constituting an ideology, are usually intent on winning adherents to their views. If one follows Wittgenstein's advice to 'look and see', one sees clearly this intentional element in the paradigm cases. The Pope, it will be remembered from the passage we quoted above, referred to teaching orthodox doctrine 'clearly and strongly', and *Izvestia*, on February 19th, 1969, stated the Soviet view concerning 'samizdat', the practice of publishing and distributing banned manuscripts, novels, and poetry:

> Marxism-Leninism does not recognise 'classless' freedom of speech. In conditions of socialism, the spoken and printed word must serve the interests of the people as the propaganda of advanced progressive views that contribute to the success of socialist and communist construction.[14]

Considerations of method are involved here, but at the same time intention to promote the right kind of belief is manifestly present. However, intention is not only a contingent feature. It is logically necessary to the concept of indoctrination. Simply to present Catholic or Marxist teaching to a group of students with the injunction to have a look at it and take it or leave it would (logically) certainly not constitute indoctrinating those students. We said above that it seems reasonable to say that 'indoctrinate' means 'to inculcate doctrine'; intention is logically necessary in that it is bound up with the notion of inculcation.

Intention is a very difficult, elusive concept, and it is by no means a simple matter to bring out what *sort* of intention is necessarily involved. Perhaps one has to allow for different manifestations of it. Thus, (a) quite specific, as when the indoctrinator admits that he intends to get his charges to believe; his motives might be quite diverse, ranging from a desire to retain, say, a position of power, to an altruistic desire to show his fellow men the paths of truth, but, whatever his motives, his intentions will be quite clear because admitted. (b) The indoctrinator refuses to admit—quite honestly— that he has any intention to get particular beliefs over. He claims that he is simply presenting the truth or that the various issues involved are fairly presented and the students invited to come to a conclusion as a result of critical analysis. In cases like this talk of indoctrination is apposite, for the intention to get something across may fairly be inferred on general contextual grounds in spite of protestations on the part of the teacher that he did not consciously intend to get his students to embrace a particular belief or set of beliefs. There is no mysterious process at work by which a group of students emerges from a class holding the same beliefs and yet at no stage has the teacher given any sort of clue as to what *he* believes, or at no stage has 'led' the class along the path that leads to the conclusions that he happens to embrace. (c) As an illustration of a third possible manifestation of intention consider the man who claims that with respect to, say, religious issues, he has no opinions and does not care one way or the other whether other people take sides or not. Such a man might well find himself, if he is a teacher, furtively concealing his real beliefs and passing on to young children a set of beliefs—Christian doctrine—to which he does not subscribe, or he may find himself conducting a daily act of worship in the form of a school assembly although he concedes no real meaning to the act of prayer. Here there seems to be no intention to do anything other than to hold on to a job. To this extent our teacher is like an indoctrinator who employs low cunning—conning people into believing in order that he may retain a position of power—but he is unlike him in that he has not got to ensure that his charges *believe* the things he puts over, it being sufficient that he should be seen to be going through the motions. Intention in this context begins to take on a much more generalised aspect to the extent that one needs to begin to distinguish between the general point of an activity and the particular purposes of individuals engaged in it. It is here that sociological observations concerning the nature of institutions, rôle-playing, and so on, are relevant. The uncommitted teacher may have no intention of bringing about certain beliefs, but his position of authority within the institutional set-up, his rôle as teacher, lends powerful backing to his words; the system within which he operates endows his actions with a sense of purpose of which he, as an individual, may be quite unaware. We are loath to talk about things like, 'The intentions of society', but, in this context, such talk begins to look as if it makes sense.

Finally method. It might be urged that method is in no sense a necessary condition in that several different methods could be employed in carrying out the process of indoctrination and that no one of these is essential. Thus, for example, deliberate falsification or suppression of evidence is not a sine qua non. The particular techniques used may well, in fact, vary with the nature of the audience—wiredrawn theoretical argument is not likely to cut much ice with a class of young children; the revolutionary Marxist at the factory gates may seek to inflame passion by the use of crude terminology ('exploitation' and 'bloated capitalists'); with intellectuals, on the other hand, what better than a forceful presentation of the doctrine? After all, the doctrinal structure, worked over by men of undoubted ability, is sufficiently intellectually coherent and sufficiently flexible to take care of any theoretical objections, or so the would-be indoctrinator will think. In sum, *how* one goes about the job will be dictated by circumstance. But while no one particular method is necessary to the concept of indoctrination, method is nevertheless logically involved in so far as the indoctrinatory transaction necessarily involves lack of regard for the rationality of the person being subjected to indoctrination. It is at this point that reference to the kinds of beliefs being transmitted cannot be avoided, and reminds one of the fact that the three components we are considering are bound up together. For, we might well say to someone who has undertaken a course in, say, Marxism (run by a Marxist), and who emerges a firm believer in it, 'Look, can't you see that you've been indoctrinated? You can't *really* believe all that stuff'. The clear implication here is that no rational man could, logically, by rational processes, have come to believe in these particular doctrines. Somewhere along the line non-rational methods must, logically, have been employed, even though they cannot be specified. It is in this sense that we hold that method is logically necessary to the concept of indoctrination.

This completes our brief account of the paradigm cases in which we have argued that the components of content, method, and aim are necessary and conjointly sufficient conditions for indoctrination. We wish next to consider in rather more detail the logical characteristics of doctrines in general, for it is by no means clear that the concept of indoctrination is tied specifically to the sorts of doctrines that one encounters in Catholicism and Communism.

Doctrines must be distinguished from facts and from manifest untruths (we prefer the term 'manifest untruths' to the term 'false facts'). As we shall argue later when we consider John White's arguments, linguistic usage runs counter to the description of statements like 'That man is wearing a hat', or 'London is the capital of Sweden' as doctrines. Unlike facts and manifest untruths, the salient characteristic of doctrines is the fact that they are not known to be true or false. We have already observed that it is correct usage to speak of 'Catholic doctrine', 'Marxist doctrine', 'religious doctrine', and so on, and certainly to the unprejudiced bystander it is by no means evident that religious and political doctrine is simply true, or for that matter, simply false. This not-known-to-be-true-or-false property seems, as we say, to apply to all uses of the word 'doctrine'. Thus, consider the following three examples:

(i) Mr McNair Wilson said, that contrary to popular doctrine, he had found neither disillusionment nor apathy among voters. [It is noised abroad, *as fact*, that voters are disillusioned or apathetic. This *may* be true, but it is not *known* to be true. Indeed, McNair Wilson denies that it is true. He, of course, is not an unprejudiced bystander, which perhaps explains his comment on the doctrine.]

(ii) The Master of King's College, Cambridge was recently accused

. M. M. *Gregory and R. G. Woods*

in a letter to *The Times* of promulgating the 'Leach doctrine', to the effect that if students express a desire to study X, then X ought to be provided for them at a university. Two points about this example. Doctrines provide, as it were, room for manoeuvre in debate. There is something to be said in support, and something to be said against. Secondly, doctrines may be cast in the form of statements, as in (i), or in the form of injunctions—'One *ought* to lay on courses for which there is student demand'. When they appear in the form of injunctions it is not so much a matter of their not being known to be true or false as a matter of it not being known whether they ought to be followed or not. But not all injunctions are doctrines. 'You ought not to feed that child to the lions' is not a doctrine.

(iii) Rusk called one of his books, *The Doctrines of the Great Educators*.

As far as this example is concerned it might with justice be contended that Rusk could equally well have called his book, *The Theories of the Great Educators*, and in so doing would not have violated normal usage; in other words, the contention might be made that the words 'theory' and 'doctrine' function roughly in the same sorts of ways. But this is not generally so. In the well developed physical sciences—Physics, for example—the tendency is not to talk about doctrines. We don't talk about the molecular doctrine of gases, or of the wave and quantum doctrines of radiation; we talk of the molecular *theory*, or of the wave and quantum *theories* of radiation. The logical status of such theories is not on a par with that of facts, for they are not simply seen to be the case. But nor are they simply not known to be true in the way in which doctrines are not known to be true. For they function as part of a very complex theoretical system designed to explain facts of a certain kind and their success to this end gives them a kind of guarantee that is something more than a grudgingly conceded, 'There may be something in this'. But while it is absurd to talk of doctrines as far as the physical sciences are concerned, there are, nevertheless, uses of the word 'theory' in which theories amount to no more than doctrines. Loose interpretations placed upon facts, speculations, conjectures—all of these are referred to as 'theories'. It was this fact to which Hirst was appealing when he took O'Connor to task for suggesting that educational theory wasn't really theory at all, when he charged O'Connor with failing to understand the nature of educational theory.[15] It is the same fact that makes it linguistically correct to speak of Marxist 'theory' as an alternative to Marxist 'doctrine', for Marx was operating in the sociological sphere where, to some extent, loose interpretation, speculation and conjecture obtain. At the other end of the scale, running from the bona-fide theories (not doctrines) of the physical sciences through the quasi-theories or doctrines of the human sciences, lies the pure doctrine of religion. We say 'pure' doctrine to bring out the fact that one does not talk of religious theory—one does not talk of Catholic theory or the theory of Apostolic Succession. And one does not talk in this way because religious truths are not arrived at by the use of scientific method—it is a logical nonsense to talk, in the sphere of religion, of the setting up of hypotheses and of the subsequent attempt to confirm or disconfirm them experimentally. Something akin to the Kierkegaardian leap of faith seems to take place as far as religious truths are concerned.

The concept of doctrine may be fuzzy round the edges but it is not so fuzzy as to render impossible the demarcation of a limited content with respect to which the notion of indoctrination alone makes sense. If a given subject-matter is presented as a candidate for serving as indoctrinatory material the first question to ask is 'What are the doctrines?' And if there are no doctrines then there is no question of indoctrination arising. Thus there is no question of indoctrinating in the sphere of science, if the canons of scientific inquiry that have emerged over the years in the course of scientific practice are adhered to. Only if science is made the creature of doctrine as it appears, say, in the paradigm cases of Catholic and Communist ideology, does the question of indoctrination arise, but then it is not so much a case of scientific indoctrination as a case of science no longer being practised. One thinks in this context of Lysenko:

> In the face of such complete lack of supporting evidence for the
> inheritance of acquired somatic modifications, and the
> difficulty of conceiving of a mechanism for such inheritance, it
> may well be asked how it came about that the doctrines of
> T. D. Lysenko, a Russian biologist well known for his work on
> vernalisation, gained so much favour for many years in Soviet
> Russia—so much so that Lysenko became President of the Lenin
> Academy of Agricultural Sciences, and many 'orthodox'
> geneticists disappeared from the Soviet scene.[16]

And the answer comes:

> Suffice it to say that Marxism ascribes to the environment an
> over-riding significance in determining the course of history.
> It is a short, if not necessary, step to extend this idea to cover

173

the whole living kingdom, and see in external conditions not merely an agency which directs evolution by weeding out the unfit and preserving the fit, but an active force which moulds animals and plants directly in each generation, the modifications so acquired being passed on at any rate in part to the progeny. For this view there seems to be no factual basis.[17]

Scientific activity cannot be carried on if its would-be practitioners are compelled to work within a specified ideological framework; the whole 'modus operandi' is inconsistent with the idea of scientific findings being dictated by some kind of revelation or authority.

On the other hand, if one considers that middle area in which we have claimed that it is correct to talk of theories or doctrines then one finds a great many more or less systematic doctrinal structures of which one might say that they could well serve as indoctrinatory material. For example, if one looks at the teachings of F. R. Leavis, one finds a great many doctrines ranging from assertions as to the importance of English to claims concerning the place of universities in the world. Again, in the sphere of education, Professor Perry has compiled a list of doctrines associated with the name of 'child-centred theorists'.[18] On the other side of the coin, if one glances at the 'Black Paper' one will find no dearth of doctrines there. The classification of these various 'systems' could be made in a number of different ways. Thus to take two examples:

(i) What is the scope of them? We have already suggested that the scope and range of Marxist doctrine is very great, involving as it does basic questions relating to the organisation of societies and the rôles of individuals within these societies. Compared with Marxism how does Leavisite doctrine or child centred educational doctrine compare with respect to scope and range? We would hazard the opinion that the scope of these two doctrinal systems is great—they are concerned with the ways in which individuals should be educated and this is intimately connected with what sort of people they are to become, how they are to relate to other people, what sort of lives they are to lead, and so on. But then consider something like a Teetotal organisation concerned to promote belief that alcohol in no matter how small quantities is bad for people. Here it would seem that the scope is more limited; and the same would apply to the doctrines promulgated by a hundred and one pressure groups. Even when scope is limited, however, it would seem that the relevant doctrines are meant to be of over-riding importance; they are meant to dominate people's outlook in the areas with which they are concerned.

(ii) To what extent are the particular doctrines linked with action? That the paradigm cases are concerned to promote purposive activity has already been argued, and it would seem that the same is true of the examples considered in (i) above, If a teacher accepts, or is got to accept, as true the salient teachings of child-centred theorists, then presumably he will act in certain well-defined ways in the class-room situation, either positively or negatively. He may, for example, do little direct teaching but let the child discover things for himself, or he may refuse to have anything to do with reading schemes. Again, the Leavisite doctrine has implications for what shall go on in universities in, at least, the English department and it will also have implications as to what sort of students are to be allowed to enter universities. It will certainly stand in sharp opposition to the 'Leach doctrine', and this opposition will be manifested in different recommendations related to action, to what shall be done. But while it is easy to see close links with action of the kinds referred to as far as some doctrines are concerned, in other cases it is not so easy. We have already mentioned the Berkeleyan doctrine of 'esse est percipi' as appearing to have little or nothing to do with the way one lives one's life, and the same might with justice be said about a number of metaphysical or philosophical doctrines. Men of action seem to recognise this; the Russian leaders sometimes appear to take the view that intellectuals can be left to their harmless pursuits provided that they do not meddle in politics, and, of course, there is the Marxist dictum to the effect that philosophers seek only to understand the world whereas the Marxists seek to change it. No generalisations are really of much assistance here; the really fruitful thing to do is to examine each case on its merits, and when one does so one will no doubt find that some philosophical doctrines are more related to action than others. G. E. Moore's brand of ethics with its emphasis on states of mind is more likely to be related to ways of living than is, say, the acceptance or non-acceptance of Monism, although even here it might be said that one ought not to commit oneself to such remarks until one has taken the trouble to investigate in detail the practical consequences of being a Monist. And then there is the more general question as to whether the activity of philosophising itself does not have wide ramifications as far as a style of living is concerned. The neutrality with respect to doctrines engendered by the modern analytic school of philosophy might itself be characterised in terms of action, negative in the sense that no self-respecting philosopher of this school of thought will take up the cudgels on behalf of any particular doctrine but will content himself with trying to understand what it is all about and indicating the degree to which there seems to be truth in it and the degree to which there does not seem to be truth in it.

The upshot of all this is that indeed there is a plethora of doctrines of a more or less systematic kind and more or less related to the notion of purposive activity, and many of these will certainly have little or nothing to do with Communist or Catholic ideology. And in so far as there are doctrines, in so far is there a danger of indoctrination being carried on with respect to them. Of course, the presence of doctrine serves only as a warning light, and in itself does not automatically signal that indoctrination is taking place. Just as in the paradigm cases, so in these other possible cases intention and method will be necessary conditions for indoctrination. Our remarks about intention and method, indeed, made in connexion with the paradigm cases, apply directly to these other possible cases.

We take it that an important part of the educational philosopher's job is to examine candidates for the title of 'indoctrinatory' with a view to establishing to what extent they measure up to the criteria established in the course of the analysis of the concept of indoctrination. We stress the importance of this particular activity. In view of the strong unfavourable emotive meaning carried by the term 'indoctrination' (in this country at any rate), to characterise a particular teaching transaction as 'indoctrinatory' might well have as a consequence the abandonment on the part of teachers of that particular way of going about things. Certainly, there seems to be some evidence to suggest that people's attitudes to things are often coloured by the language used to describe those things. We are not suggesting that the philosopher ought consciously to apply or withhold a particular name to or from some activity so as to bring about conformity to his beliefs; indeed, this would not constitute doing philosophy. We are simply advocating great care in examining cases other than the paradigm ones before one decides to what extent they involve, or run the danger of involving, indoctrination. It does seem that not everyone is prepared to exercise such care, and often one suspects that this is because they are concerned not with the pursuit of truth but with making out a case, by fair means or foul, for a particular way of proceeding. This one suspects is sometimes true of those who too readily accept a crude analysis of indoctrination as being no more than one way of teaching. We have in mind an often quoted passage from McGucken's *The Catholic Way in Education:*

Every educational institution makes use of indoctrination. Child-ren are indoctrinated with the multiplication table; they are indoctrinated with love of country; they are indoctrinated with the principles of chemistry and physics and mathematics and biology and nobody finds fault with indoctrination in these fields. Yet these are of small concern in the great business of life by contrast with ideas concerning God and man's relation to God, his duties to God, his neighbour and himself, man's nature and his supernatural destiny. The Catholic educator makes no apology for indoctrinating his students in these essential matters. To instruction in the arts and sciences, the Catholic university adds the notion of an unchanging standard of morality, the ideas of duty and responsibility to a personal and omnipotent God . . . [19]

We may be unkind, but we find it difficult not to see in this passage a desire on the part of the author to blur the distinctions between the teaching of religion and the teaching of mathematics, physics, and so on, not because analysis has convinced him that the dis-tinctions are blurred, or even non-existent, but because it suits his book so to argue.

Having identified an area in which indoctrination occurs, or is in danger of occurring, it is a further question as to whether it should be allowed to go on, and this further question is not a philosophical question and hence no part of the philosopher's concern. His con-cern is one of identification, of looking closely and carefully at particular activities with an eye to describing as best he can what is involved in them. Thus he will mark the fact that there appear to be more or less specific doctrines associated with the child-centred educational movement, that there are a number of people in Colleges of Education and University Departments who elevate these doc-trines to the status of incorrigible truths, who passionately believe in their essential truth, who clearly seem intent on getting others to believe wholeheartedly in them and to gear their practices to them, and so on. And in so far as these sorts of things are the hallmarks of indoctrinatory activity in so far will the philosopher judge that in-doctrination does occur in this area. Again, as far as the Leavisite doctrine is concerned, the philosopher will be occupied in following in detail the arguments as to how the Leavisites proceed. Thus Mr Guido Almansi wrote a letter to *The Times Literary Supplement*[20] in which he made some interesting observations about an article by Leavis in a previous issue of that journal.[21] We quote part of the letter:

Dr Leavis writes:

'Immediately it can be said, with regard to the student considered
as someone undergoing Higher Education, that the problem
of acquiring something coherent, meaningful and organic, a
living reality that he can carry away with him (or *in* him),
will obviously be affected radically, and in a very desirable
way, by his collaborative membership.' This seems to me a very
pernicious view, and fundamentally anti-educational. I believe
that the task of the educator in the humanities is not to
offer a coherent, meaningful and organic view of the world,
or of his discipline, but to leave the students in a state of alert
perplexity about the complexities of the problems involved.
The alternative is cultural Maoism, even if Lawrence or
the Great Tradition replace the red book.

Mr Almansi clearly regards Leavis as an indoctrinator. But is he
justified in his belief? If one turns to the Leavis article one finds the
following statement:

The form of a judgment being 'This is so, isn't it?', the question
is a request for corroboration; but it is prepared for an
answer in the form 'Yes, but—', the 'but' standing for qualifications, reservations, additions, corrections.

Is this consonant with the idea of someone trying to force home
a particular way of looking at literary works? On the face of it, it
doesn't seem to justify Mr Almansi's use of terms like 'cultural
Maoism'. We say 'on the face of it' to bring out the fact that we
have not scrutinised carefully the Leavisite doctrines nor have we
detailed knowledge of the ways in which Leavis and his supporters
would try to get them over, but this sort of work the philosopher
would certainly have to undertake in some detail before he could
arrive at a balanced judgment as to whether or not indoctrination
was taking place.

Consider, again, as a final illustration, the teaching of morality.
There are moral doctrines—'Do unto others . . . ', 'Turn the other
cheek', 'Don't cause unnecessary pain to animals'—clearly linked
to action, for many, if not all, moral doctrines are injunctions to
act in certain ways. If some person were to regard these doctrines
as unfalsifiable truths and sought to get others so to regard them,
never question them, always act in accordance with them, used his
position of authority—if he were in a position of authority—to get
these beliefs over, and so on, then, in line with our suggested
criteria, he would be an indoctrinator. But suppose someone were to
say, 'Some moral propositions aren't doctrines at all. They are *facts*.

Hence they can't be indoctrinated'. Here it would be necessary to examine the contention that some moral propositions are facts.[22] To what extent is 'Don't cause unnecessary pain to animals' like 'The sun rises in the East'? It seems to us that if moral propositions were facts, that if they could be seen to be true in the way in which facts are seen to be true, this would have interesting consequences as far as the possibility of indoctrinating in the sphere of morality is concerned. For then just pointing to the moral fact would be sufficient to command acceptance of its truth though not acceptance of it as a guide to action. There would be no logical possibility on our view of indoctrinating taking place under these circumstances, for no doctrine needs to be inculcated. And if conformity to pre-scribed action is what is wanted, then this has nothing to do with indoctrination. Making someone do something is not to indoc-trinate him. These observations bring out quite forcibly that the nature of the beliefs to be transmitted is a vital consideration in deciding whether or not indoctrination can logically occur, perhaps of more importance than questions of intention and method. It is at this point that we can fruitfully turn to John White's arguments, for ranking high among them is one to the effect that content in the form of doctrines has got nothing to do with the concept of indoctrination. Pari passu with a close critical scrutiny of his argu-ments we shall refine the positive comments we have already made.

White makes his general position clear:

> I want to argue that 'indoctrination' in this sense (i.e. as applied to the paradigm cases) is definable solely in terms of intention (iii) [viz.]. Indoctrinating someone is trying to get him to believe that a proposition 'p' is true, in such a way that nothing will shake that belief. Definitions in terms of the sort of proposition which is taught (content) or in terms of the methods of teaching 'p' will not do.[23]

And on the particular question of content, consider the following passage in which he queries the truth of the assertion that for there to be an indoctrinatory transaction the beliefs transmitted 'must be of a certain sort, i.e. doctrinal beliefs', where doctrinal beliefs are those forming 'part of a religious, scientific or political system of beliefs or ideology'.[24]

He writes:

> But what grounds are there for restricting the content of indoc-trination to such beliefs as these? One might argue that the very word 'indoctrination' indicates that one is concerned with doctrines. But what turns on this? It is true that one meaning

N

of 'doctrine' is 'a belief, forming part of a religious, scientific or political system'. But another meaning of the word, given in the *O.E.D.*, is simply 'What is taught' and we have already seen that once all teaching could be referred to as 'indoctrination'. So appealing to linguistic usage is not helpful.[25]

White, then, is more or less prepared to accept that indoctrination has to do with doctrines, but sees nothing following from such acceptance. Linguistic usage, he claims, does not enable one to demarcate a special set of beliefs under the heading of 'doctrine', and hence the essential meaning of 'indoctrinate' will reside in the notion of inculcation. Now, it is here that methodological considerations loom large. Has White, in fact, appealed to linguistic usage? He has appealed to a dictionary and he has appealed to a no longer current usage of 'indoctrination'. Now, as far as dictionaries are concerned, they are sometimes helpful when they list usages that we recognise, in virtue of our possession of what might be called a feeling for language or a language sense, as current and correct. Thus, a dictionary reminds us that people do say things like, 'He doesn't know a hawk from a handsaw', or 'I don't know him from Adam', and hence provides us with evidence for claiming that there is a sense of the word 'know' that has to do with the ability to distinguish one thing or person from another thing or person. Dictionaries are also useful when we come up against words that we have not met with before, words, say, like 'hetman' or 'picaroon'; the dictionary then presents us with the meaning of such words in that sense of 'meaning' that has to do with verbal equivalence—the meaning of the unfamiliar word is given in terms of other words with which we are familiar. But dictionaries are not very helpful when they give meanings, of the verbal equivalence type, of words with which we are already familiar as evidenced by our ability to use these words correctly. For, in the absence of supporting examples of usage, such meanings may be simply incorrect, or, at best, too vague and general to be of assistance. They are incorrect when, in fact, no supporting examples of usage can be adduced for the simple reason that usage conflicts with the given definition or meaning. To say, in such a case, that an appeal to the dictionary constitutes an appeal to linguistic usage is, we suggest, simply false. In the particular case under discussion it is clear that usage does not sanction the blanket definition of 'doctrine' as 'what is taught'. Suppose, for example, that we teach a child how to do up his shoe laces, and suppose we are subsequently asked, 'What did you teach that child?', and we reply, 'We taught him how to do up his shoe laces'. Then is it seriously contended that there is a use of the word 'doctrine' such that how to do up shoe laces can be correctly described as a matter of doctrine? Or if it is thought that a 'teaching how to do' example is, in this context, not to the point, what about a 'teaching that' example? If we teach someone that eight pints equal one gallon, then is it seriously contended that, since 'Eight pints equal one gallon' is what is, in this instance, taught, it follows that 'Eight pints equal one gallon' is a doctrine? Whatever the dictionary may say, people do not, as a matter of fact, go around talking about the doctrine that eight pints equal one gallon, or the doctrine that two twos are four, or the doctrine that Harold Pinter wrote *The Caretaker*, and in so far as they do not, in so far is it simply false to assert that these sorts of statements constitute doctrines. It is perhaps worth observing that there *is* a conceptual link between doctrine and teaching. We talk of 'the teachings' of a particular person, as we might, for example, talk of 'the teachings of Christ' or 'the teachings of Herbert Marcuse', but the use of 'teachings' in such contexts involves a relatively specialised sense of 'teaching'. 'Teachings' are here equivalent to 'doctrines' and, as we have argued, form a distinctive sub-set of the set of things that are taught. Just as linguistic usage does not entitle us to claim that 'doctrine' means 'what is taught', so usage does not entitle us to claim that 'indoctrinate' means 'teach'. In so far as teachers of, say, Mathematics and Biology, do not go off to their classrooms saying (quite seriously), 'Well, I'm off to indoctrinate 3B', in so far is it untrue to say that 'indoctrinate' means 'teach'. There is the general point involved here, relating to White's second appeal, that when one talks of referring to linguistic usage one means current usage, not outmoded or defunct usage.

These considerations relating to linguistic usage are of the very first importance for a proper understanding of White's position, when he writes:

The fact that we *generally use* the word 'indoctrination' only in connexion with the teaching of ideological beliefs cannot be used to prove that the *concept* of indoctrination covers only such cases.[26] Or:
It may be true that we actually use the word 'indoctrination' only in ideological cases, but that is no reason to let the matter rest there. The problem is to find what concepts are necessarily connected to 'indoctrination' and what are only contingently so.[27]

When he makes statements like these he is not enunciating some crude metaphysical thesis to do with concepts as entities of some kind, nor is he, as far as we can see, presupposing some thesis to do with thought being independent of language. He is saying, in effect, 'I know that "indoctrination" is usually used only in ideological cases—the paradigm cases—but it can justifiably be used in other cases'. And he gives examples of such cases, two actual and two imaginable:

  (i) Teachers who 'try to get their pupils to see themselves as future hewers of wood and drawers of water'.[28]

 (ii) Teachers 'who try to fix in some of their pupils' minds the ineradicable belief that they are of limited intelligence'.[29]

(iii) The teacher who goes to great lengths to get a child to believe that Melbourne is the capital of Australia.

(iv) The teacher on a tiny, remote island who attempts to get a pupil to believe unshakably that Uranus has seven moons.

Now, it is clear from these examples that, for White 'doctrine' means, in one sense, just what the dictionary says, namely, 'what is taught'. Linguistic usage as a philosophical technique is not here at issue. White simply maintains that usage, as far as the word 'doctrine' is concerned, is of no assistance, but, as we were at pains to point out, he maintains this as a result of consulting a dictionary and not as a result of consulting linguistic usage. Then, having 'established' that no significance attaches to the fact that indoctrination has to do with doctrines, he returns to the paradigm cases and asserts that the fact that doctrinal systems of belief (another sense of 'doctrine') are involved in these cases is a purely contingent matter; their presence is not what makes, or helps to make, the paradigm cases cases of indoctrination; they just happen to be what is transmitted in these instances. The whole argument really turns on this simple point about the meanings of 'doctrine'. Accept that it means no more than 'what is taught' and one will thereby concede White's case. His other arguments for that case are not so much arguments as bald assertions or rhetorical questions. Thus, referring to case (ii), he says, 'I see no reason why this should not be called "indoctrination".'[30] Referring to case (iii), where the teacher who is trying to implant the Melbourne belief has recourse to banning the use of atlases, persuading the boy to enter a Trappist monastery when he leaves school, and so on, he asks, 'If a teacher did this would it not be indoctrination?'[31]; referring to case (iv) ('A teacher on a tiny remote island might want to see if he can get a pupil to believe unshakably that Uranus has seven moons. The boy trusts him utterly: he has no access to books on astronomy; he is never going to leave the island; and no one ever visits the island')[32] he asserts, 'Given such conditions, the teacher would be indoctrinating, but without an ideology',[33] and, again, this example, he claims, gives grounds for saying that while intention to produce unshakable belief is necessarily connected with indoctrination, doctrine or ideology are not. 'If one asked the teacher on the island what he was doing, and he replied, "I am indoctrinating the boy", why should we disbelieve him? The case is sufficiently like the more usual cases of ideological indoctrination to justify him in so calling it.'[34] But, of course, if one has removed the doctrinal element from the notion of indoctrination, all of these will be cases of indoctrination, either because they satisfy White's single condition, or because they satisfy our other conditions of intention and method.

However one might seek correctly to characterise the notion of a doctrine, one will not do so by assimilating it to the notion of what is taught, for this latter notion is altogether too wide and all embracing. It includes teaching how to do any number of comparatively simple things and teaching that a large number of things are the case (facts), and these things simply do not rank as doctrines. It follows that if indoctrination has to do with doctrines then there is a delimitation of subject-matter with respect to indoctrination and hence part of the meaning of the term will be explicated by as detailed as possible a characterisation of the nature of that subject-matter. In confirmation of this general statement it is of interest to note that with respect to, say, facts, the other suggested ingredients of indoctrination—intention to produce unshakable belief and the use of devious methods that essentially over-ride a person's rationality—seem to be by the by. No violation of a person's rational nature by the employment of doubtful methods is needed to get him to believe that Big Ben is in London, and it is virtually impossible even to make sense of someone who says that he intends to get a boy to believe unshakably that Big Ben is in London. To go along with the idea that anything can serve as indoctrinatory material is so to widen the field of application of the term 'indoctrination' as to render difficult the distinction between teaching (it may be bad teaching, but bad teaching is teaching) and indoctrination and thereby to render the task of those who would seek to justify the paradigmatic variety—cf. the passage from McGucken quoted above—more easy.

It is rather difficult to decide if White accepts the idea that facts are candidates for serving as indoctrinatory material. He nowhere states that his proposition 'p' is such that p is always false, so one might conclude that, on his account, true propositions as well as false propositions are capable of being used as indoctrinatory material. His logically conceivable examples are examples of the transmission of false propositions, but, on the other hand, his example of the teacher who tries to get his pupils to believe that they are of limited intelligence might be an example of the transmission of a true proposition—the pupils might, in fact, be of limited intelligence. If they were, then we would argue that a teacher who made it clear to them that they were might be being unkind, but would not, indeed could not, be indoctrinating them. Intelligence is not a simple, clear concept, but it is not (yet) so complex and vague as to render impossible the judgment that a boy who consistently scores zero in a series of simple intelligence tests is unintelligent. Further, the presentation of this evidence to the boy would be sufficient to demonstrate to him—provided he has the requisite intelligence!—that he is unintelligent, and talk of unshakable or ineradicable beliefs being inculcated is quite beside the mark.

It seems likely, in fact, that White is concerned with untruths rather than with facts; 'p' is such that p is always false. This raises the general question, 'Is it logically possible to indoctrinate someone with manifest untruths?' Certainly, manifest untruths do not rank as doctrines. It is every bit as incorrect to refer to statements like 'Two twos are five' or 'Harold Wilson is the leader of the Conservative Party' as doctrines as it is to refer to facts as doctrines. But, whereas in the case of facts the intentional and methodological elements inherent in the notion of indoctrination were seen to be by the by, in the case of untruths the parallel seems not to hold. It makes sense of a sort to assert that one intends to get someone to believe unshakably that birds do not have wings, and, certainly, one would have to employ some devious manoeuvres to bring this about. So is not doing this kind of thing getting close to indoctrination? Indeed, says White, isn't it indoctrination? For here we meet with his logically conceivable cases once more, or the 'What would we say if . . . ?' philosophical gambit. Well, yes, it is like indoctrination, and it is like practical joking, and it is like the act of a con man. But it isn't *exactly* like indoctrination; it has only got features in common. Perhaps the unshakability of the beliefs being got over is the element that brings it closer to indoctrination than to playing pranks or conning people. But then this notion of unshakability is not made very clear by White. In the example of the boy on the island who is got to 'believe unshakably' that Uranus has seven moons, how do we know that the boy believes this unshakably? What are the tests for unshakability? In this case, presumably the only test is whether the boy answers 'Seven' when the teacher asks, 'How many moons has Uranus got?' But, if this is so, how do we tell when the teacher is indoctrinating him? If the teacher simply tells the boy 'That's a palm tree', and has no intention other than to give the boy a bit of information, how do we distinguish this bit of telling from the bit of indoctrination that takes place when the teacher tells the boy that Uranus has seven moons? Does the boy believe unshakably that 'That's a palm tree'? Presumably, we tell the difference by ascertaining that in the one case the teacher intended to indoctrinate the lad whereas in the other case he intended to tell the truth, but, then, whatever the intention in either case, all that is involved is a bit of telling. Not the same kind of telling, however. For in the case of the palm tree the teacher is telling the truth, whereas in the case of Uranus he is lying, and 'lying' is an accurate description of what the teacher is doing. We do not need to have recourse to the term 'indoctrinate' to describe what he is doing, and to this extent the example throws no light on the concept of indoctrination.

One would have thought that the real test for unshakability consists in going forth into the world and coming up against evidence and arguments that run counter to one's beliefs, and that one demonstrates the unshakable nature of those beliefs by simply refusing to countenance the opposing evidence and arguments. And, if this is so, then going forth into the world nursing simple untruths as unshakable beliefs is hardly likely to result in any confidence on the part of the 'indoctrinator' that these beliefs will remain unshakable. Indeed, given the certainty that such beliefs will collapse in the face of the appropriate evidence, one might raise significant doubts as to whether it makes sense even to talk of intending to produce unshakable belief in this context. The acid test of whether or not indoctrination is successful seems to lie precisely in the being able to withstand the counter-arguments and counter-claims of one's ideological—ideological at least in the paradigm cases—opponents. We certainly would not like to lay odds that a Russian coming to this country nursing the unshakable belief that there are no trees in Great Britain would return to Russia still holding that belief. We wouldn't mind laying odds that a Russian coming to this country nursing the unshakable belief that the course of history is determined by economic forces would return to Russia still holding that belief. The history/economic doctrine possesses a feature lacking in the untruth about the trees, namely a wide-ranging generality that allows considerable freedom of manoeuvre in the sense that one can take up a distinctive position and not be easily dislodged, or even not be dislodged at all.

Of course, it may well be the case that straightforward lying, the purveying of manifest untruths, has a part to play in the total indoctrinatory process. The 'rewriting' of history involving deliberate falsification of records is a case in point. But in such a case indoctrination is involved in that the falsification is tied to the service of the central doctrines, is used, as it were, to bolster up those doctrines.

Some might argue that it is a nice point as to whether the manifest untruths themselves, as opposed to the doctrines they support, are to be described as serving as indoctrinatory material. We ourselves take the view that wholesale lying and misrepresentation is more closely linked with the notion of propaganda than with the notion of indoctrination. Convinced of the essential truth of the relevant doctrines the indoctrinator regards any means whereby these doctrines can be got over to others as fair, and this being so, lying is eminently justifiable; it's all in a good cause.

We have argued in some detail that John White is wrong in dismissing 'content' as an integral part of the concept of indoctrination. We would certainly not accept that our arguments constitute a definition of 'indoctrination' if by 'definition' is meant an arbitrary or stipulative definition, and to this extent we would jib at his remarks to the effect that:

> It is, of course, always possible to make indoctrination require an ideology *by definition* as this is how the term is generally used . . . The supporter of a 'content' criterion wins his case by making it trivially true.[35]

Seeing why it is that in the paradigm cases ideological content is of such importance, and seeing why it is that in the other cases content in the form of doctrine—not necessarily so tightly structured and systematic as to merit the description of 'ideological'—is of such importance, ought not, we feel, to be dismissed as a matter of definition. Nor does it seem to us quite just to employ a phrase like 'trivially true' of someone who argues for the 'content' criterion, when the arguments deployed might well rest upon a fairly close analysis of linguistic usage. After all, the philosophical implications of our ordinary use of language are not exactly all there on the surface, and those philosophers, like J. L. Austin for example, who have laboured long and hard to bring home the implications hardly merit the title of 'trivial'. But perhaps we are being too sensitive on this point!

As far as intention and method are concerned our views are not too far removed from White's. On intention he writes:

> Now we normally distinguish one activity from another in terms of the agent's intention. We can say that a person raising his arm is engaged in one activity rather than another, say signalling rather than doing P.T., not from observing his bodily movements (which may be the same in both cases), or from looking at the results of what he is doing (in both cases a taxi may draw up), but only when we know what intention he has in

mind. Since indoctrination is an activity, it can only be distinguished from other activities in terms of the particular intention the indoctrinator has in mind.[36]

Here we would object to such a precise specification of intention and would, in the case of indoctrination, see this specification as one possible manifestation of intention along the lines we have argued above, just as we would object to the more general thesis that one must know what intention is in the mind of the agent before one can say what activity he is engaged in. And on method, while agreeing with his general observation to the effect that indoctrination is a polymorphous concept and may be used to describe all sorts of processes as long as they serve the fundamental aim of enforcing belief, we enter the reservation that nevertheless method is conceptually and therefore logically related to the concept of indoctrination in that only partial regard is had to an individual's rationality.

Finally we raise two specific problems that have caused us a lot of trouble in the course of thinking about our subject:

(i) How is one to distinguish the indoctrinator from the man who seeks to persuade others by rational means of the truth of his beliefs? On this question collaborative authorship has proved difficult, one of us arguing that the devout Catholic, say, who sets about trying to convince another person of the truth of Catholic doctrine by the use of rational argument and with no suggestion of browbeating, that such a Catholic is no indoctrinator, the other arguing that the very nature of the beliefs involved is such that no rational person could logically ever be rationally persuaded of their truth. John White has clearly had to face the same problem:

> If rational conviction is here impossible, it is difficult to see how one could teach religion (qua religion) without indoctrinating.[37]

This problem, which we find difficult to resolve, certainly seems to highlight the significance of the method component in cases of indoctrination.

(ii) The second problem concerns the vexed question of standpoint, although in a sense this problem is a variant of the first problem. What we mean by the question of standpoint has been put neatly by Flew in terms of connotation and denotation:

> People will agree about the connotation but dispute over the denotation. The typical challenge is then to ask why it is

supposed to be indoctrination when they do it, but not apparently, when you do it.[38]

Thus, the protagonists of the American way of life accuse the Communists of indoctrinating, but then it is not hard to see the possibility of this accusation being applied to those Americans themselves. And, bringing the matter nearer home, is it not possible to unearth a number of doctrinal propositions that provide the rationale for our own paper? Thus, 'It is impossible to reach true conclusions as far as doctrines are concerned', or, 'The rational way is the only way to get at the truth'. We could twist and turn, arguing, perhaps, that it isn't a doctrine that it is impossible to reach true conclusions as far as doctrines are concerned, but a fact, a linguistic fact. Nevertheless there remains unease on our part that we may be half-way towards being characterised as indoctrinators ourselves, on our own criteria at any rate.

## Notes

1 J. P. White, 'Indoctrination' in R. S. Peters ed., *The Concept of Education*, Routledge & Kegan Paul, 1967. [Paper 10 in this volume; all page references to White are to this volume. ed.]
2 P. F. Strawson, *Individuals*, Methuen, 1964, p. 9.
3 P. Geach, *Mental Acts*, Routledge & Kegan Paul, London, 1967, p. 13.
4 P. Strawson, (1964), op. cit., p. 10.
5 J. P. White, (1967), op. cit., p. 120.
6 N. Grant, *Soviet Education*, Penguin Books. Harmondsworth. Revised Edition 1968, p. 24.
7 J. P. White, op. cit., p. 120.
8 R. S. Peters, *Ethics and Education*, Allen & Unwin, 1966, p. 41.
9 J. Passmore, 'On Teaching to be Critical' in R. S. Peters ed., op. cit., note 1, p. 194.
10 *The Times*, 7 January 1969.
11 J. K. Galbraith, *The Affluent Society*, Penguin Books, 1962, p. 68.
12 *ibid.*, p. 69.
13 *ibid.*, p. 69.
14 *The Times*, 20 February 1969.
15 P. H. Hirst, 'Philosophy and Educational Theory', *British Journal of Educational Studies*, xii, No. 1, November 1963.
16 C. M. M. Begg, *Introduction to Genetics*, E.U.P., 1959, p. 229.
17 *ibid.*, p. 231.
18 L. R. Perry, 'What is an Educational Situation?' in R. D. Archambault ed., *Philosophical Analysis and Education*, Routledge & Kegan Paul, 1967.
19 Quoted in J. S. Brubacher, ed., *Eclectic Philosophy of Education*, 2nd Edition, Prentice Hall, New Jersey, 1962, pp. 335–6.
20 *The Times Literary Supplement*, 12 June 1969.

21 *The Times Literary Supplement*, 29 May 1969.

22 cf. G. Warnock, *Contemporary Moral Philosophy*, Macmillan, 1967,
pp. 60–61:

> That it is a bad thing to be tortured or starved, humiliated or hurt,
> is not an opinion: it is a fact. That it is better for people to be
> loved or attended to, rather than hated or neglected, is again a
> plain fact, not a matter of opinion. We find here no doubt a very
> wide penumbra or indeterminacy in which judgments must be
> made and may diverge, in which opinions and attitudes may differ
> irreducibly: but who believes, except for bad theoretical reasons,
> that there are no facts at all?

23 J. P. White, op. cit., p. 120.

24 *ibid.*, p. 122.

25 *ibid.*, p. 122.

26 *ibid.*, p. 123.

27 *ibid.*, p. 125.

28 *ibid.*, p. 123.

29 *ibid.*, p. 123.

30 *ibid.*, p. 123.

31 *ibid.*, p. 123.

32 *ibid.*, p. 124.

33 *ibid.*, p. 125.

34 *ibid.*, p. 125.

35 *ibid.*, p. 125. [White's italics].

36 *ibid.*, p. 121.

37 *ibid.*, p. 129.

38 A. G. N. Flew, 'What is Indoctrination?', *Studies in Philosophy and
Education*, 4, 1966, pp. 281–306, [p. 78 in this volume—ed.].

# Indoctrination without doctrines?

## J. P. White

## 14

### 1. Introduction

I first must make sure just what is at issue between Gregory and Woods on the one hand, who claim that indoctrinated beliefs are necessarily of a restricted kind, and myself, who deny this. What is the 'content' for which they argue?

To step back a bit. My original article was conceived as a reply to a lecture by Antony Flew. Flew maintained that indoctrination was analysable in terms of both intention and content: 'indoctrination must presuppose the aim of implanting beliefs, and the beliefs to be thus implanted must be of a certain sort'.[1] These beliefs must be 'doctrines'. About what doctrines are Flew is, as he admits, none too clear. He holds that, as a necessary condition, a doctrine is a belief which, if not false, is at least not known to be true. But this is not sufficient, because, he says, there are many such beliefs which are not doctrinal. To be so, he implies, they must be connected with 'something wider and more ideological'.[2] Indoctrination, therefore, seems necessarily to involve an ideology. Further problems arise here, of course, about what Flew understands by 'ideology'. He says nothing directly about this; but his examples are of political ideologies like Marxist-Leninism and religious ones, like Roman Catholicism. Perhaps J. P. Corbett's view, quoted by C. P. Ormell in his paper at last year's Conference—that an ideology embraces 'a set of beliefs about the conduct of life and the organisation of society; a set of beliefs about man's nature and the world in which he lives; a claim that the two sets are interdependent; and a demand that these beliefs be professed, and the claim conceded, by anyone who is to be considered a full member of a certain social group'[3]— would therefore meet with Flew's approval. Or perhaps, like Ormell, he would prefer an account which would include such things as the doctrine of Logical Sequence in mathematics teaching—perhaps something on the lines of Ormell's 'militant beliefs based on obsession with a theory (usually grossly over-simplified) of what is wrong with society, or a sub-system of society.' But in whichever sense the word 'ideology' is being used, one thing is clear: that ideologies are (at least) *systems* of beliefs, of different degrees of coherence and of rationality. I take it that Flew would agree with this. My original claim about indoctrination was that indoctrinated beliefs need not form such systems.

This, at least, was my weaker claim, deployed specifically, though not by name, against Flew. Gregory and Woods' paper makes it clear to me that this weaker claim must be distinguished, in a way I did not do, from the stronger claim I made, that indoctrinated beliefs could be *of any kind whatever*. I am still confident about the weaker claim, which I shall try to substantiate more fully; and I am *fairly* confident about the stronger, about which I shall also say something.

I said at the beginning that I was not sure quite what was at issue between Gregory and Woods and myself. I am pretty sure that they would deny the stronger claim; but I am less sure how far they would deny the weaker. While I am clear, that is, that they wish to restrict indoctrinated beliefs to those of a certain sort, I am less clear what that sort is.

Let me review their position. Indoctrination, they agree with Flew, is into doctrines. What are doctrines? They first give Catholicism and Communism as examples; then, to rule out features peculiar to these doctrines alone, they examine the 'logical characteristics of doctrines in general'.[4] Doctrines, we are told, 'must be distinguished from facts and from manifest untruths'. The statements 'That man is wearing a hat' or 'London is the capital of Sweden' are not doctrines. 'Unlike facts and manifest untruths, the salient characteristic of doctrines is the fact that they are not known to be true or false.'

There are several points here. First, it seems to be implied that *single propositions*, as long as they are not known to be true or false, can be doctrines—perhaps 'Every event has a cause', for example. If this is so, then—so far—their concept of indoctrination is compatible with my weaker claim, that indoctrination does not necessarily involve putting across a *system* of propositions. This would seem to be borne out further by their later reference to the ' "Leach doctrine" to the effect that if students express a desire to study X, then X ought to be provided for them at a university.'[5] Here the term 'doctrine', as in the expression 'the Monroe Doctrine', does not carry the implication of a connected system, which it has when it implies, in some sense or other, ideology. Neither does it carry this implication in another of their examples: 'moral doctrines—"Do unto others ... ", "Turn the other cheek", "Don't cause unnecessary pain to animals".'[6]

So far, then, there is no necessary difference of opinion between the two authors and myself, at least over the weaker claim. For clearly no ideology is necessarily required to stamp in such moral precepts as those just mentioned: one *might* be used, but other methods are also possible. On the other hand, other parts of their paper do *appear*—it is not 100% clear—to challenge this weaker claim. (i) With the exceptions of the 'Leach doctrine' and of moral propositions, all their other examples of doctrines—and certainly the ones on which they lay most stress—are, to a greater or lesser extent, systems of belief. (ii) In their discussion of my paper, they criticise my attempts to deny a connexion between ideology—i.e. doctrinal system—and indoctrination.[7] (iii) They say that the crucial test of whether a person has been successfully indoctrinated is his ability to withstand the counter-arguments of opponents.[8] In these places, it is not clear, therefore, whether or not they accept my weaker claim; while in other places what they say is consistent with it. The difficulty may arise from their use of 'doctrine' in different senses, (i) as implying the notion of 'not known to be true or false' and (ii) as implying this plus the notion of 'system of beliefs'.

If they *are* challenging my weaker claim, their position comes close to that of Flew. I shall try to substantiate the weaker claim in a moment. But before I do so, there is another difficulty which must be cleared away in their claim that whatever else doctrines are, at least they are not known to be true or false.

This claim comes in tandem with another, from which it is not distinguished, although it is plainly distinct. This is that doctrines 'must be distinguished from facts and from manifest untruths.'[9] (Here, I take it, 'fact' is to be understood as 'true proposition'.)[10] Clearly, a proposition not known to be true (e.g. that Gladstone sneezed ten times on 10th August, 1886) may *be* true; and the same goes for false ones. So, if Gregory and Woods are right in claiming that indoctrinated propositions are not known to be true or false, this does not preclude them from being true or false. 'God exists' may well be an indoctrinator's proposition par excellence: and it may be a true one, even though this is not known, or even knowable. In response to Gregory and Woods' query about whether I would accept the possibility of indoctrinating true propositions,[11] my answer is that this is perfectly possible.

Having distinguished between 'not known to be true or false' and 'not true or false', I am not sure which of these Gregory and Woods wish to write into their analysis of 'doctrine'. There seem to be difficulties both ways. If a doctrinal proposition is neither true nor false, this offends against the law of excluded middle. (Or is the implication that a doctrinal proposition is only a 'pseudo'-proposition, i.e. not really a proposition at all? Relations, metaphysical and moral statements—of the sort which Gregory and Woods often refer to as doctrinal—have been held by positivists like Ayer to be just such pseudo-propositions; but I do not know how far they would wish to follow him in this).

The other alternative—that doctrines are propositions not known to be true or false—is also troublesome. Nobody knows, I suppose, whether or not it is true that Mr Gladstone sneezed ten times on 10th August, 1886; but it is hard to see what is especially doctrinal, on any account, about this proposition. Perhaps the point is rather that doctrinal propositions are unverifiable and unfalsifiable. There may well be something in this, if it is not pushed too far. J. W. M. Watkins has argued that unverifiable and unfalsifiable, doubly-general ('all and some') statements are often at the basis of scientific, political or religious systems of belief.[12] One has only to think of the belief that for every historical event there is some predestinating cause; or the mechanist's belief, that for every human action there is some mechanical explanation. One might add to these an important educational example, one which has been at the root of the doctrines of the Intelligence Testing movement since that movement began: that for every man there is an intelligence-ceiling. Such doubly-general statements may well find themselves supporting ideologies: not only these, but other unverifiable and unfalsifiable propositions as well, like 'God exists', for example. But not every ideology need rest on an unverifiable and unfalsifiable proposition. Plato's 'noble lie', that men are made of different metals, is not: it can be shown to be false.

## 2. Indoctrination without doctrine?

There are these difficulties, then, in analysing 'doctrine', at least in the ideological sense, via the notion of 'not known to be true or false'. It is time now to try to defend the weaker claim, that indoctrination need not be into doctrine (ideology), where 'doctrine', whatever else it implies, at least implies a system of interconnected propositions.

I first want to distinguish three different situations, in each of which one person (A) is trying to get another (B) to believe something unshakably. (i) A is a 'true believer' in some doctrinal faith and wishes to proselytise that faith. He teaches B the doctrine and the official answers to all the stock objections to the doctrine. It matters very much to him that B remembers all this correctly, for it is the Truth. If he forgets it, or gets it wrong, A will consider that he has failed. (ii) A is a member of a rich minority ruling over a poor majority of another colour. The minority has devised an ideology— in which it does not believe—designed to keep the majority in subjection. A teaches the ideology to B, a member of the majority.

As long as it serves its purpose of keeping B meek and uncritical, A will consider himself successful—even though B later forgets the ideology or gets it all wrong. (iii) A is a schoolteacher in a working class district, deeply concerned, for the sake of the country's economic growth and political stability, with the old problem of producing a docile labour-force. He tries in various ways to stamp into his pupils (including pupil B) the belief that they are fitted only to become manual workers—*not* by getting them to accept any system of beliefs, but by, for instance, engaging them in all sorts of in- and out-of-school projects—visits to factories, bus-garages, etc. —designed to make them feel that manual work is for them. He invites policemen, clergymen and magistrates to give talks at the school so as to reinforce respect for authority figures. He gives B vocational guidance, giving him all sorts of career information (but all about manual jobs), encouraging him if he expresses an interest in manual work, discouraging him from any professional career for which he shows a preference by showing him the results of psychological tests of his abilities and aptitudes which 'prove' that he is not fitted for it.

An opponent of my weaker claim will hold that (iii), unlike (i) and (ii), is not an example of indoctrination, since it involves no doctrine. But, provided that he agrees that (ii) is a case of indoctrination, I would draw his attention to the fact that in one respect (ii) is more like (iii) than it is like (i): in (ii) the doctrine is not seen as important for its own sake—for it can be forgotten—but only as a *method* of implanting the belief that one ought to accept one's lot. As a method, it is on a par with the various non-doctrinal devices used for very much the same purpose in (iii). We may, indeed, even go so far as to say that it is the *same* activity which is being exemplified in (ii) and (iii): in each case A is trying to get B to believe that he should be a placid 'hewer of wood': only the means are different. Gregory and Woods might say of case (iii)—I am not sure —what they said about a similar case in their paper: 'Well, yes, it is like indoctrination . . . and it is like the act of a con man. But it is not *exactly* like indoctrination; it only has features in common.'[13] But my point is that (iii) in one sense *is* exactly like (ii): in each, A is trying to do the same thing. If (ii) is indoctrination, then so is (iii)—because in each case the indoctrinator is trying to implant a belief of some sort or another in such a way that this is never questioned.

But here I may well be accused of *stipulating* a meaning for 'indoctrination', rather than seeing how the term is actually used in ordinary language. Gregory and Woods make much of this appeal to ordinary language, claiming that 'indoctrination', as ordinarily

used, implies the implanting of doctrines. They argue that the cases
I cited in my paper of alleged non-doctrinal indoctrination offend
against the normal use of the term. But what is their evidence?
I admit that I tended to assume that people *would* call these cases
of indoctrination. I did not present evidence, e.g. from a public
opinion poll, to show that the word is used in this wider sense.
But then neither do Gregory and Woods produce such evidence.
Part of the trouble with my earlier examples was that some of them
were rather outlandish—the one about teaching the boy on the
desert island that Uranus has seven moons, for instance—too far
removed from more obvious cases of indoctrination for one clearly
to see analogies with them. But my case (iii) above is much closer
home; and it is not clear that I am *obviously* wrong in saying that
people would call this indoctrination—as I would be if I argued,
for instance, that to indoctrinate was to steal apples. Neither am I
sure just what sort of result of an opinion poll would be decisive
either way. If 25% were willing to accept my view, would this show
that it conformed with ordinary language? Or would it have to be
a majority? Is ordinary language itself precise enough to claim a
single answer?

Finally, of course, it is an empirical question what people would
actually say on this issue, and one which it is not philosophically
interesting to pursue. And perhaps at this point in this sort of
discussion, where one side says 'X' means so-and-so, and the other
says it means something else, where there seems no obvious way
of resolving this, one should take the claims not merely as analyses
but also partly as *recommendations* that the word be used in such-
and-such a way.

What can I say in favour of my recommendation? First of all,
it is at least not an arbitrary one—as it would be if I wanted 'indoctrination' to mean 'stealing apples': and it has the virtue that all the
cases which Gregory and Woods and Flew wish to label 'indoctrination' are included within it. Secondly, it helps to draw attention to
the fact that there may be other ways, besides doctrinal ones, of
implanting beliefs unshakably: it is a complacency-puncturing
recommendation, which may encourage us to be on the qui vive for
examples of attempts to implant beliefs unshakably in our own
society, outside the Catholic Church and other ideological movements. And notice how awkwardly the phrase 'implant beliefs unshakably' sounded in that last sentence. For if we do not use the
word 'indoctrination' to label this practice, then we are left without
a word to describe it. Without a word to label this concept, the
concept itself may not find a place in the conceptual schemes of
historians, sociologists and political theorists, to whom it may be

O

of value. Of course, 'indoctrination' need not be used: we could keep this for the practice of implanting doctrines, and introduce another word for the more general practice. I have no very strong feelings about this, as long as the more general activity is not over-looked—although I am inclined to think it better to use a word we already have, which is not obviously unintelligible when used in this wider sense, than to make up a new one.

I would like to illustrate this wider concept of indoctrination by pointing to what may be an actual example of it; otherwise the discussion might seem too academic. My case (iii) above, of the schoolteacher trying to get his pupils to accept themselves as manual workers, was not an actual one: I doubt, in fact, whether many *teachers* are guilty of indoctrination of this sort. For one thing, teachers generally teach only one or two subjects, at least at the secondary level with which this example was concerned. To fix unshakably in children the belief that they can be nothing other than manual workers means that one must try to prevent them from criticising this belief. If the teacher in case (iii) were working in a school in which other teachers were busily teaching his pupils to be critical in just this way, he would be wasting his time as an indoc-trinator. But imagine now a different situation. Imagine a man equally concerned, for the sake of social and economic well-being, with the problem of ensuring a docile manual labour force. Unlike the man in (iii), however, he is not a teacher, but a highly influential official in the Board of Education, about the year 1900. I am, of course, thinking of Robert Morant. Morant had been worried for some years about the way in which the post-1870 system of ele-mentary education was producing—partly through the growing number of 'higher-grade' schools—too many aspirants to white-collar jobs. He was impressed, as his Special Report on higher ele-mentary schools in France shows, by the way in which these schools —through their 'practical' curriculum and through the direct in-fluence of the headmaster as vocational counsellor, running a school which was in effect, as Morant observed, a 'bureau de placement'— were 'a potent instrument in the hands of far-sighted statesmen, for shaping the thoughts as well as the aptitudes of the cleverer children of the working class towards a particular end—the increase and improvement of the *manual workers* of the community.'[14] After 1900 Morant destroyed the higher-grade schools in England and restricted the curriculum of all children except the very few who went to the new secondary schools, to elementary subjects which did not allow them to develop a critical attitude to their station in life.[15]

Morant, I feel inclined to say, on the evidence I have seen, was something of an indoctrinator in the wider sense; and an indoctrinator on a large scale. He wanted to 'shape the thoughts of' working class children towards a particular end: 'the deep, inner meaning of the true function of popular education', he wrote, was that the primary school was 'a means of giving every child a liking and taste for (his) inevitable occupation.'[16] The means he adopted were not doctrinal, but the tailoring of the elementary curriculum to suit his purpose: just as the beliefs of a person indoctrinated with a doctrine are unshakable because he has a stock of arguments to withstand any objection, so the belief of Morant's elementary school products that they were fitted only for manual labour was to be made unshakable by making them intellectually unable even to come across any objection to it. Whether the intention always succeeded is another matter; but, then, indoctrination may exist in the 'attempt' as well as in the 'success' sense.

## 3. Indoctrination without intention?

This concludes my defence and illustrations of the 'weaker claim'. But the reference to Morant not only helps to illustrate this claim: it also throws light on another issue: whether or not the concept of indoctrination implies that of intention. Since it is part of Gregory and Woods' argument that it does, it would be useful to go into this a little, before looking, finally at the 'stronger' claim. A problem arises, on the 'intention' view, that there seems to be room, in some cases, for talking of children being indoctrinated even when their teachers have no intention of doing so. It is not difficult to imagine, the argument might run, a group of teachers ruefully surveying the attitudes of their school-leavers and agreeing with each other that they had only succeeded in indoctrinating them with a belief in the inevitability of their humble lot—even though they did not mean to do this (and even though there is no room for speaking here, as there might be room in other cases, of 'unconscious' intentions, of which the teachers later became aware).

What are we to say of such an 'admission'? Does it indeed show that intention is not a necessary feature of the concept? At this point I find myself drawn in two different directions. (i) On the one hand, I feel inclined to say that the 'admission' might well be unjustified. For if, for instance, the teachers are all working within the framework of a curriculum imposed by a 'Morant', the better they teach—the more diligently they try new methods of engaging children's interest in the pleasures of handicraft or whatever—the more effectively they realise the intentions of the curriculum planner. The teachers may be engaged in work of an indoctrinatory kind; but *they* are not indoctrinators, I half wish to say, but rather unwitting tools in the real indoctrinator's hands. For each teacher there is nothing necessarily indoctrinatory about his work; but piece what they each do together into a whole, and the indoctrinatory purpose becomes clear.

(ii) But suppose these teachers somehow found time—goodness knows how, if it were an English school—to reflect together on the larger purposes of their activities and became aware of the 'Morant' behind the scenes. And suppose, further, what is quite imaginable, that they *still* wanted to say that they had been indoctrinating the children. The 'Morant', they might say, had been responsible for setting up an indoctrinatory system; but it was *they* who were doing the indoctrinating within this system. Here the force of their remark would be that they were admitting *responsibility* for the indoctrination that had been going on. They did not want to see themselves as merely puppets and thereby absolve themselves: they felt they ought to have reflected before on what they were 'really' doing to the children.

Here the concept of indoctrination is coming adrift from that of intention: a person is indoctrinating not only if he intends to implant beliefs unshakably, but also if he is merely responsible for such implanting, even without intending this. In the same way, one might argue, someone may *teach* something without intending to. The teacher who says, 'I thought I was teaching Jones mathematics, but I now see I have only taught him to hate the subject',[17] is a case in point: again, it is responsibility which is being stressed here.

And yet . . . there *does* seem to be an important difference between teaching and indoctrinating, which tips the seesaw back to the 'intention' view. The teacher in the example just above is accepting, his responsibility for Jones' having acquired a hatred of mathematics. What are the self-confessed indoctrinators in the earlier example accepting responsibility for? For their pupils' having come to believe unshakably that they are to become manual workers? But if it is *just* this, something is lacking which is quite crucial to the activity of indoctrinating: the adoption of all sorts of means to prevent reflection on such a belief. This, it seems to me, must be something *deliberate*. 'Indoctrination without intention' only makes sense, I am finally disposed to believe, in so far as it is a truncated concept of this sort: the teachers in the 'Morant' example may have admitted responsibility for their pupils' emerging with fixed beliefs; but not for having looked for ways of stopping them thinking. The responsibility for *this* goes back to the 'Morant'. (And it will not do to say that the 'Morant' could not have been indoctrinating, because he was not teaching, or in a face-to-face situation with the pupils. Why should this always be necessary? We have no hesitation in talking, for instance, of the Party's indoctrination of the Soviet people.) If there has been indoctrination, then it is to the first of our two explanations, (i), that we must turn.

(I am doubtful, incidentally, how far explanation (i) could be given for alleged cases of 'indoctrination without intention' in the present, post-1944, period of unregulated curricula. There is no master curriculum-planner in the background, like the 'Morant' in the above story. And yet, in some cases, there may be thought to be room for saying of a teacher, to use a sentence taken out of context from Gregory and Woods, that the 'system within which he operates endows his actions with a sense of purpose of which he, as an individual, may be quite unaware'.[18] I would be equally as loath as Gregory and Woods to speak of 'the intentions of society' in such cases, for this would be to treat 'Society' as a kind of person. All I would say is this: that in so far as the word 'indoctrination' is correctly being applied, and not being used merely as an expression of disapproval, then there must be a person, or persons, to whom responsibility may be attached for attempting to implant beliefs.)

## 4. Indoctrination without any restriction on content?

Finally I would like to look briefly at the 'stronger claim': that *any* proposition, let alone merely non-doctrinal ones, can be indoctrinated. As I said, I am rather less confident about this one, especially after reading Gregory and Woods' paper. But before looking at the stronger claim directly, let me quickly neutralize a related argument—not that any non-doctrinal proposition can be indoctrinated, but that at least some non-doctrinal propositions, if they are taught at all, *must* be indoctrinated—at least according to my earlier definition of indoctrination, in terms of having the intention to put over *unshakable beliefs*. For it might be argued that if a teacher, either explicitly, in a lesson on Clear Thinking or Philosophy, or implicitly in other lessons, is reinforcing his students' belief in the Laws of Thought, he is indoctrinating them, since the Laws of Thought are in fact unshakable—they cannot but be true if assertive discourse is to exist. He is indoctrinating them, it is claimed, even though he welcomes any attempt they make to deny the Laws. Now there is clearly something wrong in calling this 'indoctrination'. The argument shows up the inadequacy of the earlier definition as it stands: the phrase 'unshakable beliefs' had better be removed. The crucial thing in indoctrination is that the indoctrinator tries to implant beliefs unshak*ably*, i.e. in such a way that they will never be questioned. Indeed, I am not sure now that *implanting* beliefs is a necessary feature of the concept. For the pupil may already possess the beliefs which the indoctrinator wants him to have. But I would still want to talk of indoctrination if the teacher began to employ all sorts of methods to *reinforce* these beliefs and prevent him reflecting on them. Hare, after all, was right, I think, in putting the emphasis on suppressing thinking, in his discussion of the concept.[19] (This shows incidentally, a second important way in which the concepts of indoctrination and teaching differ. Indoctrination is sometimes thought to be a *form* of teaching, at least in the broad sense of an activity intended to bring about learning. But teaching X p implies that X has not learnt p. In indoctrination p can be *already* learnt. So indoctrinating is not necessarily teaching). And while in this self-lacerating mood I might add that defining the concept in terms of 'intention to . . . ' may also be misleading. For a person could intend to implant or reinforce beliefs—and then not do it, because he forgot or changed his mind. It would be odd to call him an indoctrinator. The indoctrinator's intention is not an intention to do something in the future, but an intention-in-action:[20] he must at least be *trying* to implant or reinforce beliefs.

To return to the stronger claim. Is there any kind of proposition that cannot be indoctrinated? Non-doctrinal propositions can be. True ones can be. False ones can be. What about propositions known by the indoctrinator to be false? Let us take Gregory and Woods' case of the Russian 'coming to this country nursing the unshakable belief that there are no trees in Great Britain'?[21] He could not be indoctrinated in this belief, they suggest, because 'the acid test of whether or not indoctrination is successful seems to lie precisely in the being able to withstand the counter-arguments and counter-claims of one's ideological opponents': yet here his 'unshakable' belief would be shaken immediately. But providing counter-counter-arguments is only one way of fixing a belief: another is preventing one's victim from coming into contact with counter-arguments, either through lack of intellectual equipment, as in the 'Morant' case; or by making such contact *physically* impossible. (And, after all, it is not only the foreign exchange problem that prevents actual Russian citizens from freely visiting the West). Granted this, I see no reason in principle why even simple, true—and known to be true—ostensive statements, like, 'That is a palm tree', cannot be indoctrinated. The indoctrinator might have his reasons for getting his pupil to believe that that is what such trees are called, and for preventing him from coming into contact with anyone else who could confirm or invalidate this. One might object to this that he could not possibly have any reasons for implanting such a belief, so such a case could not arise. But until this is *shown*, it still seems to me a possibility—though, admittedly not one of any great *educational* concern. A kind of proposition I am mildly uneasy about is a higher-order one, like 'You ought to critically examine all your beliefs'. (Call this 'p'). It may seem that p cannot be indoctrinated because the pupil would apply the maxim in p to p itself. But would he necessarily? Could not the indoctrinator, in principle, get him both to assimilate p—and this not as a string of words, but with at least a minimum of understanding *and* devise methods to prevent him from questioning p? (After all, people do not always see the implications of all their beliefs.) If so, at least this objection to the 'stronger' claim is eliminated. But perhaps there are others which are not.

## Notes

1  A. Flew, 'What Is Indoctrination?', *Studies in Philosophy and Education*, iv, Number 3, Spring 1966. [Paper 6 in this volume—ed.]
2  [p. 71 in this volume—ed.]
3  C. P. Ormell, 'Ideology and the Reform of School Mathematics', *Proceedings of the Philosophy of Education Society of Great Britain*, 1969, p. 38.
4  I. M. M. Gregory and R. G. Woods, p. 171. [All page references to the paper by Gregory and Woods refer to this volume—ed.]
5  *ibid.*, p. 172.  6 *ibid.*, p. 178.  7 *ibid.*, p. 184.  8 *ibid.*, p. 185.
9  *ibid.*, p. 171.  10 See *ibid.*, p. 184.  11 *ibid.*, p. 184.
12  J. W. M. Watkins, 'Confirmable and Influential Metaphysics', *Mind*, 1958.
13  Gregory and Woods, op. cit., p. 184.
14  R. Morant, 'Higher Elementary Schools in France', in M. Sadler, ed., *Special Reports on Educational Subjects*, Vol. 1., H.M.S.O., 1897, p. 329 (Morant's italics).
15  cf. E. J. R. Eaglesham, *The Foundations of 20th Century Education in England*, Routledge & Kegan Paul, 1967. Cf. also Eaglesham's 'Morant on the March (1895–1901)', *Year Book of Education*, 1957; and the change in the elementary curriculum between the *1903 Code* (pp. 10–11) and the *1905 Code* (pp. 15–18), N.U.T. editions.
16  Morant, op. cit., p. 335.
17  I owe this example to Mr R. K. Elliott.
18  Gregory and Woods, op. cit., p. 170.
19  R. M. Hare, 'Adolescents into Adults' in T. H. B. Hollins, ed., *Aims in Education: The Philosophic Approach*, Manchester U.P., 1964, p. 69.
20  For this distinction, see G. E. M. Anscombe, *Intention*, Basil Blackwell & Mott, Oxford, 1957, p. 1.
21  Gregory and Woods, op. cit., p. 185.

# Index

Daveney, F. T., 161n
debatable issues, 108; *see also* controversial issues
deduction, 61
democracy, 10, 12, 13, 14, 15, 47, 50, 51, 52, 93, 94, 95, 97, 109, 142, 144
Demos, Raphael, 48
desires and morality, 60, 156
Dewey, John, 10, 12, 13, 14, 63, 66n, 89n, 93, 94, 95, 96, 106, 107, 109, 142, 143, 145
dialectical materialism, 143
discovery learning, 120
discussion, 59
  critical, 125
  rational, 121
dissent, 168
doctrine(s), 47, 50, 79, 81, 123, 173, 181, 183, 188, 191, 193
  as criterion of indoctrination, 11, 47, 70, 76, 80, 85, 86–7, 93, 96, 99, 102, 114, 122–3, 145, 152, 164, 165, 166, 171
  *see also* criteria; content
  Berkeleyan, 167, 175
  Christian, 11, 47, 77
  Communist, 79, 166, 172
  distinguished from theories, 172
  inculcation of, 7, 76 164–9 *passim*
  Leach, 172, 192
  Leavisite, 177
  Monroe, the, 191
  moral, 191
  orthodox, 166
  related to action, 167, 175
  religious, 75, 79, 93, 109, 114
  Roman Catholic, 106, 109, 166
  *see also* ideologies
drill, 56, 57, 165
Dryden, J., 48

Eaglesham, E. J. R., 201n
education, 9, 41, 98
  aims of, 15, 57, 63, 80, 178
  academic, 55
  authoritarian, 11, 86, 99; *see also* authoritarianism
  child-centred, 118, 120
  Christian, 40, 79
  coercive, 12
  concept of, 126, 137, 140
  contrasted with indoctrination, 6, 55, 81, 94, 95, 100n, 108, 117, 131
  democratic, 12, 13, 14, 47, 142; *see also* democracy
  natural, 1
  non-rational, 86
  political, 1, 95, 120, 165
  practice of, 57, 75
  prescriptive, 15
  problems of, 1
  traditional, 118
  vocational, 55, 56
educational theorists, 88, 117, 131, 144, 149n, 164
Edwards, P., 66n
Eglash, Albert, 46n
Elliott, R. K., 201n
emotion, 103, 128
emotive theory of ethics, 61
empiricist philosophers, 59
'enabling beliefs', 41–4
enculturation, 10, 11, 15, 16
ends
  and means, 13, 62, 94, 109
  and reasons, 90n
  use of persons as, 4, 13, 51, 57, 101
Ennis, R. H., 149n
epistemological status of beliefs or propositions, 84, 87, 107, 112, 114, 140, 166; *see also* beliefs; propositions
'esse est percipi', 167, 175
essentialism, 113
etymology, 96, 122
evidence, 25, 33, 34, 35, 38, 56, 68, 69, 99, 109, 112, 117, 123, 139, 143, 146, 185
  falsification of, 170
  and religious beliefs, 40
  suppression of, 170
evolution
  of the concept of indoctrination, 9, 11, 12, 16, 120, 142, 164

philosophical analysis, 101; *see also* language analysis; linguistic analysis

Pinter, Harold, 181

Pittenger, B. F., 14, 16n

Pius XII, Pope, 90n

Plato, 1, 123, 193

pluralism, 9, 15, 16, 94, 131
 limited, 9, 15, 16

political history, teaching of, 6, 127–8

'polymorphous concepts', 126, 133, 187

postulate, 30

pragmatism, 94, 95; *see also* experimentalism; instrumentalism

prejudice
 racial, 74
 in teaching, 50; *see also* bias in teaching

prescription, use of in analysis, 72, 87, 95, 105, 140, 194

primary and secondary senses of indoctrination, 86–7, 96

principles
 moral, 60, 143
 of procedure, 63
 scientific, 98

problem-solving, 152–3

Progressive education, 10, 11, 12, 13, 96

Progressive Education Association, 13, 14

propaganda, 2, 9, 24, 28, 29, 48, 61, 93, 147

propositions, 129
 false, 183
 moral, 178
 pseudo, 192, 193
 true, 184
 *see also* beliefs

Protestantism, 77

psychological
 contrasted with logical, 63, 103, 104
 mechanisms, 23
 structure of beliefs, 3, 5, 31, 32, 33, 103

verbs, 149n

racial superiority, 74

rationality
 of beliefs, 18, 68, 104, 111
 as characteristic of human beings, 83, 93
 in children, 17, 96–9
 conditions of, 62
 of desires, 60
 and indoctrination, 19, 20, 21, 22, 56, 183
 in teaching, 56, 97, 121, 150n

rationalization, 19

Raup, R. Bruce, 15

Reagan, Gerald, 45n

reason(s)
 for acting, 90n
 beliefs and, 18, 19, 25, 33, 34, 36, 45, 110–12
 in indoctrination, 24n, 34, 41, 80, 99, 102, 120, 152
 in teaching, 25, 36, 45, 56, 98, 118, 139, 146
 use of in an ideology, 38, 43

religion, 5, 33, 58, 65, 103, 104, 113–14, 125, 128–9, 165, 177
 and morality, 82
 *see also* Christianity; Islam; Protestantism; Roman Catholicism

Religious Instruction, 75

respect for persons, 13, 47, 48, 50, 51

Rich, J. M., 16n

rights
 of children, 1
 over children, 17
 constitutional, 12

Rokeach, M., 41, 45n, 46n

Roman Catholicism, 6, 11, 18, 76, 77, 79, 81, 83, 84, 89n, 90n, 106, 109, 120, 121, 142, 143, 156, 165, 168, 177, 187, 190, 191, 195

rote-learning, 86, 119, 120, 152, 158, 164

rule(s), 20, 117
 following, 64
 of procedure, 63